The Voice Within...

Social messages through Judgments

The Voice Within...

Social messages through Judgments

Justice Kailash Gambhir
Judge, Delhi High Court

Foreword by
Justice T.S. Thakur
Judge, Supreme Court of India

Special Message by
Justice Madan B. Lokur
Justice A.K. Sikri
Judges of the Supreme Court of India

Universal
Law Publishing
an imprint of LexisNexis

LexisNexis®

This book is a publication of **LexisNexis®**
(A Division of Reed Elsevier India (Pvt) Ltd)
14th floor, Building No 10, Tower–B, DLF Cyber City, Phase-II,
Gurgaon–122002, Haryana, India.
Tel : + 91 124 4774444 Fax: + 91 124 4774100

Website : www.lexisnexis.co.in / E-mail : help.in@lexisnexis.com

---

Justice Kailash Gambhir, *The Voice Within... Social messages through Judgments,* First Edition, 2015
ISBN: 978-93-5035-612-8

Printed by: Nice Printing Press, Delhi

Printed and bound in India.

Justice T. S. Thakur
Judge
Supreme Court of India

6, Moti Lal Nehru Place,
New Delhi-110011
Ph: 23018989
23018082

FOREWORD

> *Judges ought to be more leaned than witty, more reverent than plausible, and more advised than confident. Above all things, integrity is their portion and proper virtue.*
>
> —Francis Bacon

Justice Kailash Gambhir was a leading member of the Delhi Bar when he was called to the Bench in the year 2006. As a lawyer his helpful approach towards fellow lawyers and litigants alike had endeared him to everyone and paved way for his election to the Bar Association first as its Hony. Secretary and later as its President. As a Judge of the High Court of Delhi, Justice Gambhir practiced aloofness typical of judges but never lost touch with the realities of life and the social milieu in which we live. He not only bandaged the wounds of the victims but tried wherever possible to prevent injustice by adopting a people-friendly reformative forward looking and at times radical approach in interpreting and enforcing the laws. Justice Gambhir's pronouncements often reflected a certain amount of juristic innovation aimed at humanizing the law without departing from the salutary principles sanctified by judicial pronouncements of superior courts in this country. He championed the cause of anguished wives in several pronouncements concerning matrimonial disputes, while taking care not to be unduly harsh to the husbands and the parents-in-law even when the legal process was at times heavily loaded against them and used as a tool of harassment and oppression. He displayed anguish and dismay over offences of rape and sexual exploitation especially when such acts were committed against minors. He infused life and vigor in to the rights of employees and labourers by giving primacy to them. He adopted a positive approach in dealing with cases of motor vehicle accident victims and emphasized that human life was invaluable and the need to compensate the victims not only a legal obligation but an ethical precept. Justice Gambhir's bold and multifaceted personality is reflected in his articles, speeches and judgments which bear testimony to his scholarship and capacity for hard work as also his ability to connect to people.

This compilation, encompasses in a small measure the work done by Justice Gambhir and would in my opinion remain a storehouse of information for Judges, lawyers and the students alike. More importantly, the work done by Justice Gambhir would inspire teachers and lawyers not only in their quest for justice but also in their crusade against injustice wherever the same exists. I compliment the publishers for compiling the work and offering it to a wider readership. Nothing could have been a better tribute to Justice Gambhir than a recognition of his contribution to the development of law and services he has rendered to the cause of justice.

August 19, 2015

T.S. THAKUR

Madan B. Lokur
Judge
Supreme Court of India

4, Akbar Road
New Delhi-110011
Phone: 23014102
Fax: 23014107
E-mail: madanlokur@nic.in

August 17, 2015

MESSAGE

I have had occasion to go through the collection of the views expressed by Justice Kailash Gambhir through his judgments, articles and speeches. The subjects are varied and the overall impression gathered from the views expressed clearly indicate the compassion that he has for the people from all walks of life, particularly the disadvantaged. The writings of Justice Gambhir have this common thread all through, whether the judgments pertain to aspects of criminal law or aspects of civil law, whether the articles and speeches pertain to the environment or child rights or ADR.

In today's age, when almost everything has to be done in a rush, it is difficult to find time to pause and think but Justice Kailash Gambhir has been able to find the time and pen down thoughts of compassion. This is what makes the present collection worth reading and I am sure that it will be an excellent guide for the legal fraternity and those of us seeking justice with compassion.

My best wishes to Justice Kailash Gambhir and I hope he continues the good work for the benefit of society.

Madan Lokur

MADAN B. LOKUR

Justice A.K. Sikri
Judge
Supreme Court of India

Tel.: 23016022
23016044

MESSAGE

I am delighted to find that three Law Researchers of Justice Kailash Gambhir have undertaken this praiseworthy, and at the same time stupendous, task of writing this book on the judgments, essays, writings and speeches of Justice Kailash Gambhir. Let me first congratulate these youngsters, Ms. Aanchal Choudhary, Ms. Urvashi Malhotra Uppal and Ms. Vimija V. Nair who got the idea of writing this book.

A Judge of a superior court, particularly an Indian Judge, renders decisions on variety of legal subjects. Some Judges decide those cases simplicitor. But there are many other Judges who depict their legal philosophy as well, while rendering their judgments and thereby contribute to the growth of law. However, by very nature of things this kind of contribution would be sporadic and would even seem random, as that is reflected in bits in the different cases decided. Of course, if the entire work of that Judge is collated, studied, analysed and critiqued, his contribution to the legal system can be deciphered and explained. Precisely for this reason, I say that the authors need to be congratulated for their commendable idea indeed. And they need to be lauded for converting their thought into reality which was more challenging as it is not easy to sift through various judgments of a Judge on variety of subjects and decipher the underlying philosophy of the Judge as well as jurisprudence contained therein. It is more arduous task to arrange the random thoughts in different judgments in a systematic fashion. The style with which these are collated is worth appreciating. In fact, very apt to the title, they have found and presented 'THE VOICE WITHIN' the Judge. The depiction of Justice Gambhir's personality gets completed by including his speeches as well in this compendium.

2, Moti Lal Nehru Marg, New Delhi-110011

This was really a very painstaking, challenging, time consuming and arduous task which required lots of commitment, determination and passion. This commendable effort on the part of these youngsters is a testimony to the reality that today's breed of budding lawyers are intellectually stimulating, interested in varied work and have deep interest in the nuances of law. An important poser at this juncture is: what is the inspirational force behind the three law clerks? Obvious answer: their mentor who is none other than Justice Gambhir under whom they have been working. It goes without saying that they had the opportunity to observe and watch Justice Gambhir very closely. They must have been impressed by the judicial approach of the Judge in rendering justice in the matters coming before him. They would have admired the upholder of Rule of Law coupled with sensitive approach in social causes depicting robust sense of justice in the Judge. Therefore, Justice Gambhir also deserves accolades in equal measure who could inspire the authors to undertake this arduous journey. There could not have been a better gift to Justice Gambhir at his retirement and on the eve of his birthday by the three Learners to their Guru. Incidentally it happens when "Teachers Day" is also round the corner. Thus, it becomes an unprecedented and unique kind of *Guru Dakshina*. This book shall demonstrate contribution of Justice Gambhir to the judicial and legal system. At the same time, I'm confident that the book is going to be very useful for students, lawyers and the judges. My best wishes to Justice Gambhir for whom retirement from active life is still far far away. I wish that this book proves to be the "Opening Chapter" of his equally significant next phase of his life.

GOOD LUCK!

17 August, 2015 **A.K. SIKRI**

ACKNOWLEDGEMENT

One fine morning, I reached my chamber and was startled to see my old and new researchers at sharp 10 a.m. They zealously gave me an idea to come up with a book throwing light on my various judgments that I pronounced during my tenure wherein I gave social messages with an endeavour to sensitize the masses on a plethora of social issues we as a society are confronted with. Not even in my dreams had I thought of this, but since the cause was noble, I promptly agreed to the same.

It is well known in the public domain that Judiciary is the watchdog of the Constitution and Justice its first promise. In every case coming before the Court of law, every Judge is expected to do complete justice between the parties. But besides administering justice, in many cases a Judge comes across many issues faced by the society, and at times pens down his views to address such issues arising in a case keeping in mind the larger interest and good of the society. In his judicial philosophy, Justice P.N. Bhagwati, the architect of Public Interest Litigation and a great humanist Judge assigned an active role to the Judges, active in the sense that Judges not only interpret and apply the law, they also have the power to create and originate and that they shall and they must put this power into practice to serve the cause of "social justice".

In my journey of being a Judge, I came across many such cases where I saw societal evils perpetuating and felt the pain of the society; I ardently contributed a few lines to the judgments. I did this with a fervent hope that perhaps the concerns I expressed in my judgments might have a positive impact on some, if not many, and that would bring a great deal of satisfaction to me.

I am greatly touched and happy with the innovative idea that has taken shape in the form of this book and congratulate all the people behind it. Snigdha, currently a Judicial Officer, was the first to assist me as a Law Researcher and I thank her for her invaluable contribution in my day to day work and research.

I would like to acknowledge the hard work put in by my valued researchers, Anchal, Urvashi and Vimija, who not only came up with the idea but executed the same into a reality.

I would also like to express my thanks to the two interns Namisha and Brian who also assisted in this project.

Pankaj, who was entrusted with the task of sorting and compiling the voluminous database of judgments, Thank you.

Finally I would like to express my gratitude to M/s Universal Law Publishing for their encouragement and spontaneity in publishing this work within a very short span of time.

JUSTICE KAILASH GAMBHIR

INTRODUCTION

16 November, 2009, 10 a.m, nervous, anxious yet determined at the door of chamber no. 36 of the Delhi High Court, ready to start my first job, I entered an intimidating room, not knowing that this day would change the future course of my life in more ways than one.

I had the privilege to clerk for Hon'ble Mr. Justice Gambhir, an odyssey that gave me the rare opportunity to not only know the working of the Bench and an erudite Judge, but also to know a man of unmatched grit, gumption and compassion. Judges are often an enigma to an outsider or so I thought that they need to be, until I met Sir, who was to my utter amazement, simple, humble, down to earth, warm and straightforward.

Watching the court proceedings one day, I observed that in an application for grant of stay, he heard the counsel for almost thirty five minutes, ultimately resulting in its dismissal. With curiosity to be satisfied, I gathered the courage and asked him that I am sure that within less than five minutes, Your Lordships knew that the case had no legs to stand on, so why did he still hear the counsel for so long? He looked at me instantly and with his inimitable rhetoric and replied that does everyone not have a right to be heard fairly? Stunned, I realised that the principles I read about in Law School are the principles a distinguished and noble man as him, lived by everyday and I learnt more about law in that one epiphanic moment than I did in all those years in Law School.

This book is an endeavour to immortalise Justice Gambhir's insurmountable judicial conscience and a documentation of his remarkable humanism and quest for justice. His judgements not only expound the law but are a reflection of the current state of our society, mirroring the myriad forms of troubles plaguing it, giving them profound treatment. A maverick Judge, he combined the potency of law with the fearlessness of his soul, responding innovatively to the malaise penetrating and thus perpetuating in our society. An exemplar of reducing issues to their pith and lucidly enunciating the law, his judgements are neither embellished with unnecessary legal jargon nor confounded in a sea of mass verbiage.

Having authored landmark judgments, positively impacting the society as a whole, Sir is far too modest for a man of his stature. On the slightest hint of praise, he would often quip, *"I am no stalwart"*. A judge par excellence bestowed with charismatic persona, those who know him would concur with me that his humane qualities cannot be pigeonholed and no words, fancy, complex or simple can do justice to his accomplishments.

This book epitomises his ability to transcend the legal formalism to give greater meaning to the written word from his voice within. The voice of an unconquerable, indomitable spirit resonated when it mattered the most and will continue to reverberate through his judgments for times to come.

The macrocosm of justice has been enriched by him and the lives of those, like me, who he has touched by his presence. His prodigious vision to see a legal horizon far beyond the quotidian view of others and belief that law is a powerful instrument of social change has left an indelible mark on me and others alike. He is an inspiration and it has been nothing but an absolute honour to be able to contribute whatever I could in his stride for Social Justice.

ANCHAL CHAUDHRY
(Law Researcher)

INTRODUCTION

"The just man is not the product of a day, but of a long brooding and a painful birth. To become a power for peace, a man must first pass through experiences which lead him to see things in their different aspects: it is necessary that he have a wide horizon, and breathe various atmospheres – in a word, from crossing, one after another, paths and points of view the most diverse, and sometimes the most contradictory, he must acquire the faculty of putting himself in the place of others and appreciating them."–Charles Wagner

Enriched by his years of practice as a lawyer, Justice Kailash Gambhir is a living embodiment of the above-mentioned words. An illustrious man that he is; he was the youngest President that the Bar Association of Delhi ever saw. In addition to this, Justice Gambhir showed fondness for social and academic activities, in pursuance of which, he served as the Executive Council at the University of Delhi. It is laudable how within a very short span of time he became one of the pre-eminent Judges of his era.

His judgments appositely paint an image of a righteous and a compassionate Judge. It is also well accepted in the public domain that he has been the torchbearer of Social Justice. Time and again, he has given a plethora of social messages in a wide spectrum of matters ranging from; the atrocities inflicted upon women such as Rape, Dowry Deaths, Acid Attacks etc. to the heinous crimes of Murder and Dacoity. He fervently touched upon the subject of how old parents are being ill treated by their kin these days and denounced such practices. His efforts in issuing guidelines for cases under section 498A are estimable. Justice Kailash Gambhir vehemently opposed the act of drunken driving, in the celebrated BMW hit and run case. Well known for his repartee, he drew an analogy between 'drunk person' and a *'human bomb'* while issuing unprecedented directions in the said case.

He incorporated social messages in his pronouncements, in a bid to sensitize the masses on tectonic issues that we as a society are confronted with. Hence, through the medium of this book an endeavor has been made to spread the social messages he set out during his reign.

A facet of his personality that not many know about is the fact that apart from being a man who gave judgments a human face, he is also a terrific poet, who obviously does not parade his poetry abilities and may in fact never know that he has it in him. I'd like to give the readers an insight into his poetry which will give them an understanding of this man and the brain-child behind his perceptive judgments. A few stanzas from one of my favourite poems of his are:

"Mat aanko kisi ko uske pad se,
Mat aanko kisi ko uski daulat se,
Aur mat hi aanko uski shauhrat se,
Aanko toh aanko ek hi paimane se,
Kitni woh karta hai mohabbat zamaane se".

URVASHI UPPAL
(Law Researcher)

INTRODUCTION

Sobriquets like Legal luminary, embodiment of fairness and equitableness don't do unto him, what he did unto others; *Justice.*

In a profession flocked by many, he's managed to leave an enduring impression with his unimpeachable work ethics, proclivity for hard work and an unyielding quest for truth. Judges are often also referred to as officers of social change; HMJ Gambhir with his career has proved this right. Having authored approximately 1345 judgments, he's shown us that a humanistic approach is quintessential and is a pillar on which Courts these days thrive.

In Court, his refreshing candour translated into being both, soft and harsh on parties depending on the situations. A few questions are all he took to look beyond the courtroom, counsel and their submissions, adjudicating and establishing the truth. '*Satyamev Jayate*' just merely as words, seem noble but to work towards it, is a daunting task, which he handled with such finesse. This book aims towards sensitizing people towards certain social issues that our society is confronted with time and again. It enshrines judgments, wherein justice Gambhir issued unprecedented guidelines on issues which hold prime importance in today's social milieu. Through the medium of this book, we are trying to bring to the fore subjects such as dowry deaths, bride burning, rape, other forms of atrocities inflicted on women and children, drunken driving etc. His judgments are symbolic of the fact that he ardently took up the cause of women and children. They remarkably stand out, because of his penchant for writing judgments which traverse beyond legalese; they invariably have a societal message that manages to strike a chord with the masses and forces them to ponder upon them.

This book is not exhaustive apropos the judgments that Sir has authored, but is only expository and gives a peek into the judgments which come with social messages. It will give readers a chance to hear his voice; which resonates from within. And not only will they be able to appreciate Sir's work but also the great human that he is.

VIMIJA V. NAIR
(Law Researcher)

CONTENTS

SPEECHES AND ARTICLES

TABLE OF CASES

F

G

H

I

J

K

L

M

CHAPTER 1

CRIME AGAINST WOMEN

I. RAPE AND SEXUAL OFFENCES

Rape on a Minor Child: A Crime against Humanity

"Rape is an offence not just against a woman's body but also against her very existence."

It gives a chill in the spine and shuns away the faith of the society at large; it is one of such crimes that definitely should not be tolerated. Dreadful gang-rape and cold-blooded murder sparked raging protests in December 2012. Amendments in law were brought about owing to the ordeal that this brave lady a.k.a. as Nirbhaya went through and it all happened when the travesty of December 16, 2012 consumed the nation. The new law with an aim of providing a strong deterrent against crimes like rapes was formulated. The Criminal Law (Amendment) Act, 2013, on paper is although a welcome change but it has not been triumphant in deterring the desperate men who do not fear breaking the law. Despite this amendment numerous instances of rape have been recorded and are known in the public domain.

To add to the ghastly act of rape, it is sinful to commit it against a minor child. The children who are the future of the nation, for whom the world is beautiful and perfect, are made the targets of such horrifying acts. In the case of *Gurvinder Singh* v. *State of NCT of Delhi,* Crl. A. 659/2011 Justice Gambhir was faced with a wretched situation where a poverty stricken family was further crushed by the rape of their minor daughter where he held:

> *"In a case involving rape of a minor child, the consistent view of the Apex Court has been that crime of rape is a very heinous crime and it becomes more heinous when it is committed with a child of tender years of age. Rape is a crime not only against the human dignity but it is against the society as a whole. It has also been held that physical scar on a rape victim might heel up with time but the mental scar will always remain alive, as when a woman is ravished then what is inflicted on her is not merely a physical injury but a deep sense of deathless shame. It has also been held that the measure of punishment in a case of rape cannot just depend upon social status*

of the victim or the accused, it must depend upon the conduct of the accused, state and age of the sexually assaulted female and the gravity of the criminal act. It needs no reiteration that with the unexpected rise in the rape cases there appears to be no deterrence of law or fear in the minds of the perpetrators of the crime and had it been so the ratio of such crimes would have definitely come down instead of the same being increased. No doubt after the recent mass protest and awakening in the society there can visibly be seen a difference in the approach and tendency of the women, feeling comparatively stronger to come forward to raise their voice and take cudgel against such onslaughts for sexual assaults, thereby sending a clear message to the society that they will no more tolerate or forbear any such act of treating women as mere sex objects, however there is still a long way to go to curb this menace from the society.

In the series of many rapes being committed by the sex starves, sex depraved and sex maniacs not even sparing the minor children below the age of 12 years, the case in hand is an example of another horrifying incident of rape committed by this appellant on a prosecutrix who had not even seen ten summers of her life. It is an irony of fate that a family who is already a victim of poverty having no shelter over their head to save themselves from the heat of summers and chill of winters either sleep on the public pavements, sub-ways, buildings and houses under construction in different weather met their ultimate devastation when during the night one of their family member being a girl of ten years was take away by some sex starved person, hunting to take some such girl child to satisfy his beastly lust for sex".

He was confronted with a similar issue in *Umed Singh* v. *State (NCT of Delhi)*, 2013 (3) JCC 2001 and opined that to not be able to protect the children especially the girl child is a shame. This came to light when the minor girl child was raped shocking the conscience of this court. Justice Gambhir while sitting in a Division Bench expressed his dismay and held as follows:

In the immortal words of Dag Hammarskjöld: "Forgiveness is the answer to the child's dream of a miracle by which what is broken is made whole again, what is soiled is made clean again.

But there are certain devastating moments in one's life, which cannot be repaired, the loss that cannot be forgotten or forgiven. Each time we hear of a rape case, or any sort of assault against women, it gives a chill in the spine, daunts the faith overshadowing the entire system and shuns away the faith of the society at large, it is one of such crimes that definitely do not deserve to be assuaged.

Rape, is one of the most barbaric and heinous crimes. The cases of rape, gang rape and digital rape are on increase and perpetrators of this inhuman and brutal crime are worse than even the beasts and deserve to be dealt with a heavy hand. They need to be dealt with sternly and severely. Its a gruesome and ghastly act of rape wherein a man acts as a slave of his martinet and lowers himself to a baffling extent for the sole purpose of achieving gratification of his carnal desire. The case at hand very peculiarly exposes the inferior bequests of nature in the appellant who is a man of about 35 years of age and made an attempt to commit rape on a 2 year old female child.

For a second, oscillating from the case at hand, in the midst of triggered national outcry over the treatment of women, there are several females suffering at the hands of certain psychotic males. The Asian Human Rights Commission reported that child rape cases jumped from 2,113 cases in 2001 to 7,112 in 2011 in India. The unflinching reality but also deplorable, that not just one but many female children in their tender age, just bloomed into a flower on mother earth, having no clue of the demeaning crime, are made to face such cruel realities of life. The country where a female child is kept on the same pedestal as goddess "laxmi" or "durga", is the same place where some pervert members of the same society dehumanize the women by attacking her body and ruining her chastity. Rape is an aberrant, atrocious, horrendous and monstrous burial of her dignity in darkness. It is a crime against the entire society. With the advent of Justice Verma Committee, better, stringent procedures have been adopted, still a lack of deterrence is felt. Despite there being a social awakening, there is no decrease rather the cases are increasing manifolds and in order to deal with them, one can only be harsh but benignant. The viciousness and brutality of crime in such like cases is immeasurable. A child who in the initial years of her birth, away from the shackles of life, in her sweet symphony and beautiful innocent world cannot even echo the outrage that a female would go through, the torment, the wrath that would put her life to a standstill, and will not even remember when from an infant would reach the age of an adolescent that such a satanic moment was ever a part of her life when a man, aged like his father misused her physically for his personal desires, although it would leave a scar on her and her family members forever.

Before parting with the judgment, with deep concern, we may point out that leniency in such like cases would accord a wrong message to the society. Rather by deft modulation, sentencing process should be stern where it is called for, especially in the cases, where one tends to lark with human body and soul. The factors to be considered while adjudging a crime like the one in the present case are its atrocities, the conduct of the criminal and the defenceless and unprotected state of the victim. All sexual assaults on female children are not reported and do not come to light yet there is an alarming and shocking increase of sexual offences committed on children. It is majorly because children of such a tender age are ignorant of the gruesome act and are not able to battle against them. They become an easy prey for the lusty fiends who display an insidious art of luring female children and young girls. Therefore, such offenders who are peril to the urbane society should be mercilessly and relentlessly punished especially wherein a rape of a minor child is involved, it should be done in the severest terms. The country saw an increase of 336% of child rape cases in comparison to the last decade as per the statistic report of National Crimes Record Bureau. It has been noticed that out of the entire female population, 30% of the rape cases involve minor girl child between 1-7 years of age, and these are frequently noticed in the most downtrodden and backward classes/villages, where there exist no whiff or knowledge of any law prevailing in the society but the entire concept is based on male chauvinism. It would be important in this regard that certain steps imparting knowledge of law to all the classes, explaining people about the consequences of any sort of harm being caused to the women can make them suffer drastically should be adopted. The need of the hour is to sensitize the functioning at each front, the State shall also necessitate much quicker resort to the problems of each and every aggrieved female child or her family. For the very purpose, the State with the help of the Bar Council of India, various NGO's, RWA's and Bar Associations can arrange such campaigns or education programmes and find a reach to every nook and corner of the society. There has to be deterrence in the mind-set of any person having any such obnoxious and dissuading thoughts. A man before even developing that beastly thought, should feel that eke in his nerves, that a moment of pleasure, or a mere fulfilment of a few minutes desire with such horrendous intentions can cost him his entire life. A man has to understand that a female has a sacred place in our society which she can never be deprived of and anyone who even thinks to make such an attempt would never be spared at the hands of justice."

It is also pertinent to note that in the case of *Ramher* v. *State (Govt. of NCT) of Delhi*, 2014 (207) DLT 245 dismayed by the mirthless situation of a child abused sexually by her own father, who she looks up as her protector, Justice Gambhir, presiding over a Division Bench condemned the barbaric act, and held as under:

> *"In ancient times an individual's acts were driven by self-righteousness based on morals and values he imbibed. Treading on the path of precedents these morals and values took the form of laws. Sadly over the years these very morals started deteriorating and need arose for more and more stringent laws in order to maintain law and order and to govern the human behaviour. Shockingly in recent years the crime growth of rape cases has increased to an alarming proportion giving an impression that there is no deterrence, despite rape laws have been made stringent through the recent amendment Act, 2013. Every act of rape and sexual assault on a woman deserves severe condemnation and award of requisite punishment in accordance with law but even out of such cases the most barbaric act and unsavory is rape of a minor child which leaves one trembling. An act as that of rape of a minor child by her own father further shakes the very existence of a social fabric. The purity that a father-daughter relation carries, when shattered in such a manner, obliterates the sanctity and belief in any existing relation. A daughter looks to her father to protect her from outside evils and when the very same protector rips her apart, the trauma one suffers as a consequence of such an act cannot even be described in simple terms. "*

Further questioning the plight of a child who does not even know the seriousness of the offence committed upon her, he said that:

> *"The trauma attached to it destroys and shatters not only the normal growth of a child but her whole existence comes tumbling down. The beastly act of ravishing a child for exerting his position of a male dominance and violating her physical and mental well-being, is attitude of a savage tribe and not of a civilized society. To fathom the aftermath of the sentience of the happening of such tormenting act on the person is to add yet another monumental blow to her dignity. Taking note of such an extremely odious and debased offence, the Legislature recently by way of Criminal Law Amendment Act, 2013, incorporated a new clause under section 376(2) IPC as clause (f) to cover cases where rape is committed in a fiduciary relationship. The sole object of this provision is to visit with a more severe penalty to the persons in near relation and position of trust and authority who more often than not commit sexual assault on the members of the family or unsuspecting and trusting young persons.*

While committing an act as unsavoury as that of rape of his own minor child one not only forgets that it will destroy not only the life of the victim but his own life. The trauma attached as an aftermath of such acts not only victimizes the immediate sufferer but also the offender. An act done in the moment of rage mutilates the whole family and every existing relation with the offender. The remorse that sets upon the offender subsequently cannot free the offender of the virulent act he committed. The question that perturbs us or rather desolates us by the recent alarming increase in number of rape cases how can an individual, even after the introduction of such stringent laws be ignorant of the consequences of his act. The moral obligation of repentance and self-condemnation seems to be diminishing in this era. It's high time when men folk need to be gender sensitized from the very beginning from school to colleges to treat women not as sex objects but as an equal human being. The emboldening of the law should act as a deterrent to the prevalence of flouting the law with impunity. This can only be done through mass awareness and the media has a big role to play in this movement of great change in society."

As always with an aim to bring a change in the society, he asked for the better implementation of these laws. He also said that:

"We feel that a joint endeavour is required to be made on the part of the society at large to create an awareness of the legal ramifications of their vicious acts. The most potent tool to create awareness is to educate the public of the new law and create awareness about the rights of the victims and at the same time the severity of the punishment of the offence committed. In this regard, we also gave directions in the matter of Beeru *v.* State, *Criminal Appeal No. 1079/2010. While emphasizing and reiterating the same, we advise the appropriate Government Authorities, Non Governmental Organisations, Bar council of India, various State Bar Councils, Bar Assemblies, Delhi Legal Services Authority and law colleges and institutes to take effective steps in this direction to sensitize people and create awareness amongst them about the latest amendments and other laws dealing with the various sexual offences and the punishments provided for such offences."*

Sensitization and Awareness – Need of the Hour

Justice Gambhir impressed upon the Central Government and Government of NCT of Delhi to undertake some effective measures to sensitize, educate and create awareness amongst the people, with regard to the existing laws including the recent amendments dealing with various sexual offences and punishment provided for such offences.

While dealing with the case of *Lokesh Mishra* v. *State NCT of Delhi,* Crl. A. 768/2010, he succinctly held:

> *"It is appalling to see that rape rears its ugly facade almost every day. 'Rape' is one such dark reality in the Indian Society that devastates a women's soul, shatters her self-respect and for a few, purges their hope to live. It shakes the insight of a woman who once was a 'happy person', and had no clue of being a victim of the said horrifying and nightmarish encounters where the daughter had been raped by none else but her own progenitor. A daughter always looks upto her father as a shield of her dignity and honour which is an intrinsic facet of a family especially of father-daughter relationship. It shocks human conscience when the sanctity of father and daughter relationship is ravaged in such a sordid manner and the protector becomes the violator. In such a case the offence assumes a greater degree of vulnerability which shall not go unpunished. There can never be a graver heinous crime than the father being charged of raping his daughter. It is the gravest sin, where the most platonic relationship is shattered by an extreme pervert and shameful act of nonetheless but one's own father. The moral values of individuals of the society have gone down to such a level that every day we hear similar news which shudders our mind and soul. We have become accustomed to saying that females are not safe outside the house but in few cases, it is seen that they are not even safe inside their homes, where the epitome of God's beautiful creation, a child is ravished by her own father for his momentary sexual needs and pleasure which is heart-rending and odious.*
>
> *The change would not merely come from increasing policing, giving harsher punishments etc. but the required change lies in upgrading the moral values inside all of us and imbibing an essential value that women are not an object of sexual gratification.*
>
> *"Above all, be the heroine of your life, not the victim." – Nora Ephron. A very beautiful quote by the American Novelist exemplifying the status of a woman in the society. Beautiful creation of God, A woman who plays an array of roles in one's life, she is a daughter, a wife, a mother, above all a human just like any other, deserves to be respected, adored and valued. It is said and we believe that a girl child is more close to his father and nothing can subside the relationship shared between a daughter and a father. Researches show that a girl's father is one of the most influential people in her life, from infant to toddler to teen. A father's influence in his daughter's life shapes her self-esteem, self-image, confidence and opinions of men. But behind the scenes as they say lies a harsh*

reality which has become a common practice in a few houses and is majorly noticed in lower stratum of the society, a father raping his own daughter, shattering her faith, desolating her self esteem, her beliefs and making her life a curse. A father who shares an equal responsibility of bringing her to life, kills her insight at the very instance of a few minutes pleasure, and a little girl left with no option surrenders. There cannot be a bigger sin than the sin of raping or molesting one's own daughter. It is beyond imagination that how any father can stoop down to a level of satisfying his sexual lust with his own daughter? The father is considered to be the protector, fortress and refuge of his daughter and is looked upon by the daughter for protection from any kind of onslaughts taking place in the outside world. No doubt that the offence of rape is grave by its very nature but it is more horrendous and despicable when the perpetrator of the crime is none-else but her own father ravishing the chastity of his own daughter."

While disposing the two criminal appeals, *i.e.*, Crl. A. No. 846/2010 and 1079/2010, the Supreme Court gave certain suggestions to the concerned Ministries of the Central Government and the Lt. Governor, Government of NCT of Delhi to take some effective steps to create mass awareness so that the common masses get to know about all the relevant laws and statutes concerning women and children.

".....there is a total revolution in the field of communication and through various means every individual can be easily accessed to make him aware about sex related offences and the severity of punishment provided for such offences. Despite the recent mass protest after Nirbhaya murder case, which led to the setting up of Justice J.S. Verma Committee and consequent amendments introduced by the Parliament through the Criminal Amendment Bill, 2013 to make sex related offences more stringent, yet no deterrence can be seen to bring down the ratio of such sexual crimes being perpetuated on the women and child. There is thus an urgent and imperative need to sensitise the people through various mass awareness campaigns and social programmes to make them aware about the stringent laws and severity of the punishments provided for committing such ghastly crimes. This would ensure the confidence of women in the system and they would be in a better position to voice their concern. We are disappointed to note that none of the Government Bodies have come forward to give proper response to our suggestions".

In the instant case, by way of a separate order dated 12-3-2014, Justice Gambhir had asked the UOI and GNCTD to file affidavits apropos the steps taken to create awareness and sensitization about existing laws and latest amendments dealing with various sexual offences and the punishments provided for such offences. In the affidavit it was found that a lot many steps were mentioned and that some of them had been implemented but he was of the view that a lot needed to be done keeping in view the enormity and gravity of the issues involved. And he was distressed to find that things were not moving at the required pace. And he went onto say, that if such a situation persisted, then the odds of achieving the required results are few and far between. He also took note of the PM's Independence Day speech wherein the PM had expressed serious concerns about the increase in rape cases and about the obligation of the parents and the society in general in tackling the monstrous problem.

He further noted that in our country there is a serious dearth of awareness and gender sensitization and that it was disheartening and agonizing to see the perpetrators of crimes walk away freely.

He held that the 'severity and rigorousness' of the law should act as a deterrent to the 'prevalence of flouting and infringement of laws' and that people are not fully aware of the punishments.

He came down heavily on the authorities who merely harped upon that they suggested various steps to be taken to create public awareness but that the things should be seen getting practical implementation. He said, one or two advertisements in any newspaper in a year or six months was not sufficient. And that public awareness has to be constant on war footing.

Justice Gambhir expressed his displeasure at the apathy and insensitivity of the UOI and GNCTD for having failed to take steps to produce even a single documentary to educate the people of Delhi, about the nature of sexual offences concerning women and child and create awareness amongst them about the existing laws and punishments provided against such offences.

While hearing an appeal against the judgment sentencing a rape accused he observed:

> *"In contrast, one individual, a British filmmaker, could make a documentary film on the brutal gang rape that has managed to kick up a storm and trigger a furore in India. We are totally aghast and saddened to find the steep increase in the cases of crimes against women, the shocking testimony to this fact being the latest statistics from the National Crime Records Bureau (NCRB), which says that on an average 93 women are raped every day in India. According to NCRB data, there is a gradual increase in the number of rapes reported in India from 24,923 in 2012 to 33,707 in 2013. This is*

despite the initiation of various steps by the Government and also the passing of the Criminal Law (Amendment) Act, 2013"

Making note of the increasing incidents of violence against women, despite newer stringent laws, he criticised the depressing trend of educated people holding high positions making irresponsible and vile statements that were detrimental to the interests of women and opined:

> *"What is in bad taste are the irresponsible and vile statements made very often by erudite people who hold reputable positions and place in diverse fields, and show no signs of shame while voicing their warped and misogynistic ideals".*

He further noted that the freedom of expression guaranteed under the Constitution was not absolute as:

> *"Clause (2) of Article 19 of the Indian Constitution enables the legislature to impose certain restrictions on free speech. And, these reasonable restrictions should be kept in mind by one and all before giving vent to their opinions and views".*

Vide order dated 9-4-2015, Justice Gambhir rapped the Delhi Government and Delhi Police and denounced the helpline 181 number and Delhi Police safety app for women "Himmat" as "disappointing".

The Bench consisting of Justice Gambhir and Justice Sunita Gupta expressed their shock, when the helpline could not be accessed by the lawyers. And they were forced to wonder if a victim—*"needs to die before the helpline calls back or reaches them."*

'181' helpline number was launched by Department of Women and Child Development (Delhi Government) in December 2012 for women in distress. The bench said:

> *"Advocate, present in Court were allowed to use the said helpline and see whether in fact somebody picks up the said helpline and if not, whether they immediately respond to the phone or not. Shockingly, the phone rang and an automated message informed the caller that they had reached the helpline. But the phone went unanswered. The victim would succumb to death by the time they respond and help reaches her. Although, when ... again dialled the said helpline number, the same was answered. Even the women safety app "Himmat" launched by the Delhi Police is a total disappointment. The moment anyone dials the helpline, they should respond as a woman victim may not be in a position to speak later."*

He also hauled up both the Governments *i.e.* at the Centre and the State for its insensitivity in creating awareness among people about laws and punishment for offences against women and children. It asked the governments to approach Amitabh Bachchan and Aamir Khan and request them to make a small documentary on women's safety.

The Division Bench headed by Hon'ble Mr. Justice Gambhir also rapped the Ministers who are seen on the posters which are issued in public interest.

In a comparable situation Justice Gambhir heading a Division Bench brought out the declivity of moral values of our society to limelight in *Beeru* v. *State NCT of Delhi,* 2014 (1) JCC 509. He went onto observe that:

> *"The Criminal Law Amendment Act, 2013 has given a new ray of hope to the women and teeth to the law and should act as a deterrent. The need for every person to know the legal ramifications of his vicious acts is important, especially that of rape. The most potent tool is to educate the public of the new law and create awareness about the rights of the victims and at the same time the severity of the punishment of the offence committed. The men folk need to be gender sensitized from the very beginning from school to colleges to treat women not as sex objects but as an equal human being. The emboldening of the law should act as a deterrent to the prevalence of flouting the law with impunity. This can only be done through mass awareness and the media has a big role to play in this movement of great change in society. The print and television media, both public and private participants have to be partisans of this change. The government has to be the torchbearer to create the fear of law in the minds of the people that they have to think a million times before committing this immoral act. The common man should be daunted by the law and it can only come by ingraining in them the repercussions of their acts. Much has been achieved by the showing of the clipping in theatres of the harmful effects of tobacco and we suggest the same should be done to apprise the people of the new law relating to sexual offences. Such programs should be run on television and radio also. Everyone today has a mobile phone. Be it a rickshaw wala or a jhuggi dweller to the top-notch people in the society and, therefore, the people can be educated about these laws through SMSs as well.*
>
> *The barbarity of the offence of rape cannot be overemphasized, especially when we have witnessed the most gruesome and horrific instances of the same in the recent past. The indifference that was created towards feral men with the quotidian reporting of rape was followed by a furore bringing the heinousness and depravity of the offence once again into the forefront, awakening the yet hitherto*

dormant attitude of the society. On flipping of the pages of the newspaper or the channels of the television, the only resonating sound is a new incident of rape. The argument being advanced is that the incidents of rape have increased manifold but in reality it is also due to the metamorphic change the society is undergoing, that of the new found willingness of the survivors to report the offence rather than being hapless victims like before. However in the face of this positive development, we cannot turn a blind eye to the fact that the consequences of this monstrous act remain as devastating as ever, but may be the societal prism which shamed and blamed the survivor has changed angles. The women as a whole, cutting across status, class, culture, creed or sex are a vulnerable group but a minor child is most susceptible of the lot. The tender years of innocence where the children are taught to have faith in the goodness of humanity and nurturing relationships with trust fall apart when the same child becomes a prey in the hands of the lusty and unscrupulous men. It is also brought to light by the recent statistics that the rapists are strangers also but are more often than not people known to the family or in a position to trust with the survivor. The present case is a sordid story of both the factors at play where the minor girl was raped by her own uncle. The beastly act of ravishing a child for exerting his position of male dominance and violating her physical and mental well-being, is attitude of a savage tribe and not of a civilized society. To fathom the aftermath of the sentience of the happening of such tormenting act on the person is to add yet another monumental blow to her dignity. In most cases that this court comes across, the offender is the sole bread winner of his family with parents, wife and children etc. to take care of. The remorse that sets in after the realization of the dastard act committed by him is put on a back burner and what is vociferated are the so call mitigating circumstances. The criminal who dared to indulge into such a venomous act now wants to walk way as he has to take care of his family and provide for them.

We are hopeful that once the people are aware of the law and its reach, the attitudes towards women will also change. The price that one pays for one moment of pleasure to assert ones masculinity and violating the woman's self-respect is too great; a life behind bars. The opprobrium that was reserved for the fairer sex has now been reserved for these criminals. The social ostracisation, disgrace and the destitution of the family left behind and of himself should be the reason enough for not committing a crime. The shadow of this can darken the entire future of a person and his family and thus we urge the people to be more gender sensitized and the government and the society at large to take initiative to curb the menace.

One can visibly see the growth of the country in all spheres keeping a pace with the modernization, advancement, science and technology but unfortunately the only front which is on the decline is the moral values. In the recent past, the country has witnessed too many horrifying and heart rendering incidents of rapes and many of such cases were so brutal and barbaric, that they jolted the society to ponder whether such beastly acts can be committed by a human being on the other. Amongst such horrifying incidents, sexual assaults involving minor children are the worst and amongst the worst, the cases involving sexual assault of minor children by none other than their own family members, relatives and friends. An astonishing increase has been seen in the number of cases where children are sexually assaulted by none other than their own family members, relatives and friends on whom they once relied, as their protectors to be protected from the evils of outside world. Such kind of sexual assaults at the hands of family members, relatives and friends is abhorrent as it not only harms the innocent child but it completely destroys and ruptures an innocent soul that has yet not attained enough consciousness even to understand the nature of the act committed upon her. Such cases show as to what extent a person can stoop down just to satisfy his lust for sex. In a society where the custodian of the trust betrays the same and the protector of the dignity and honor becomes the violator, it would not be wrong to say that no one can easily be trusted. Such offences pollute the sanctity of relationship which were said to be made in heaven. A momentary pleasure out of lust for sex leaves an indelible scar not only physically but also emotionally on the victim. Taking note of such an extremely odious and debased offence, the Legislature recently by way of Criminal Law Amendment Act, 2013, incorporated a new clause under section 376(2) IPC as clause (f) to cover cases where rape is committed in a fiduciary relationship. The sole object of this provision is to visit with a more severe penalty to the persons in near relation and position of trust and authority who more often than not commit sexual assault on the members of the family or unsuspecting and trusting young persons.

The mindset of the common man that the law cannot touch him and nothing will happen. This notion of the law being feeble and the offender being actually punished being remote is what needs a tectonic shift. The Criminal Law Amendment Act, 2013 has given a new ray of hope to the women and teeth to the law and should act as a deterrent. The need for every person to know the legal ramifications of his vicious acts is important, especially that of rape. The most potent tool is to educate the public of the new law and create awareness about the rights of the victims and at the same time the severity of the punishment of the offence committed. The men folk need to be gender sensitized from the very beginning from school to colleges to treat women not as sex objects but as an equal human being. The emboldening of the law should act as a deterrent to the prevalence of flouting the law with impunity. This can only be done through mass awareness and the media has a big role to play in this movement of great change in society. The print and television media, both public and private participants have to be partisans of this change. The government has to be the torchbearer to create the fear of law in the minds of the people that they have to think a million times before committing this immoral act. The common man should be daunted by the law and it can only come by ingraining in them the repercussions of their acts. Much has been achieved by the showing of the clipping in theatres of the harmful effects of tobacco and we suggest the same should be done to apprise the people of the new law relating to sexual offences. Such programs should be run on television and radio also. Everyone today has a mobile phone. Be it a rickshaw wala or a jhuggi dweller to the top-notch people in the society and, therefore, the people can be educated about these laws through SMSs as well.

Hence the appropriate Government Authorities are advised to consider our aforesaid suggestions and we earnestly hope that in the larger societal interest they will take effective steps in this direction or other steps as they find suitable to sensitize people and create awareness amongst them about the latest amendments and other laws dealing with the various sexual offences and the punishments provided for such offences. The Registrar General of this Court is directed to send copy of this order to the Secretary, Ministry of Information and Broad Casting, Secretary, Ministry of Woman and Child Development and Lt. Governor of NCT of Delhi for necessary action at their end.

We are hopeful that once the people are aware of the law and its reach, the attitudes towards women will also change. The price that one pays for one moment of pleasure to assert ones masculinity and violating the woman's self respect is too great; a life behind bars. The opprobrium that was reserved for the fairer sex has now been reserved for these criminals. The social ostracisation, disgrace and the destitution of the family left behind and of himself should be the reason enough for not committing a crime. The shadow of this can darken the entire future of a person and his family and thus we urge the people to be more gender sensitized and the government and the society at large to take initiative to curb the menace."

False Promise of Marriage and Charge of Rape

Law is an instrument of social change and is more often than not a result of the need of the hour. But there is always the peril of its misuse and the courts have the task of seeing the unadulterated truth so that no party is wronged in the process of justice dispensation. With the growing awareness of the new laws, is growing abuse and one such is the cry of rape to clothe failed relationships and vengeance. But these broken relationships between consenting adults, trivialize the gruesome offence of rape and should be dealt with caution.

In the present case of *Mohd. Iqbal* v. *State,* Bail Application No. 2145 of 2009 it was the allegation of the prosecutrix that she is a household lady and the petitioner being her neighbour used to be in awe of her and told that he liked and loved her very much and wanted to marry her. The prosecutrix fell in his trap, and allowed the petitioner to keep physical intimacy with her, but the petitioner time and again backed out from his promise and also threatened that the whole family of the prosecutrix would be killed if any action is taken against him. The prosecutrix based on the above facts lodged a complaint alleging rape by the petitioner several times on the false promise of marriage. Whilst dealing with this case, Justice Gambhir held:

"There is an old Jewish saying "if you are close when you should be distant, you will be distant when you should be close". It is for both man and woman to restrain themselves and not to indulge in intimate activities prior to the marriage. Undoubtedly it is responsibility, moral & ethical, both, on the part of men not to exploit any woman by extending false promise or through devious acts to force or induce the girl for sexual relationship. But ultimately, it is woman herself who is the protector of her own body. Promise to marry may or may not culminate into marriage. It is the prime responsibility of the woman in the relationship or even otherwise to protect her honour, dignity and modesty. A woman should not throw herself to a man and indulge in promiscuity, becoming source of hilarity. It is for her to maintain her purity, chastity and virtues."

Rape and Consensual Sex

Consenting adults are expected to know that relationships don't always work out. Equating failed relationships with rape, disadvantages genuine rape victims by diluting the seriousness of the crime.

The court expressed anxiety over the recent spurt in rape cases that appear to have been filed by the petitioner in unfulfilled relationships. He has not once, but on numerous occasions expressed similar apprehensions when it was observed that rape cases were increasingly being used as a weapon for vengeance to harass and even force a man to marry. Such a trend not only militates against justice but also represents a clear danger to the legal framework regarding gender crimes.

In *Rohit Chauhan* v. *State NCT of Delhi*, 2013 (200) DLT 380 a similar fact situation as the previous one where the girl filed the charges of rape against her ex-boyfriend for three years. Demarcating rape from consensual sex, Hon'ble Justice Gambhir held as under:

> *"Rape is a crime against one's mind, psyche and reputation. Rape leaves a permanent scar on the life of the victim and it becomes horrendous for the victim of rape to lead a dignified and well respected life in the society. It is very unfortunate that there is a high increase in the rape instances and ravenous maniacs are not even sparing the girls of a very tender age. Some of the recent rape cases have been so horrifying that the entire nation protested to condemn these barbaric acts and raised a voice to curb the said menace by inflicting more severe punishment. The Government also promptly appointed Justice J.S. Verma Committee to review laws on crimes against women, which recommended certain dramatic changes in the Criminal law relating to offences against women.*
>
> *Undoubtedly there is a manifold increase in the crime concerning rapes, but all the rape cases which are filed have their own individual story and factual matrix. While most of the cases may be genuine, wherein the girl is a victim of this horrifying crime, or has been forced, blackmailed, threatened to enter into physical relationship with a male on the false pretext of marriage with the sole intent to physically exploit the girl but there may be cases where both persons out of their own will and choice, develop a physical relationship. Many of the cases are being reported by those women who have consensual physical relationship with a man but when the relationship breaks due to one or the other reason, the women use the law as a weapon for vengeance and personal vendetta to extort money and sometimes even to force the boy to get married to her. Out of anger and frustration, they tend to convert such consensual sex as an incident of rape, defeating the very purpose of the provision. There is a clear demarcation between rape and consensual sex and in cases where such controversies are involved, the court must very cautiously examine the intentions of both the individuals involved and to check if even the girl on the other hand*

is genuine or had mala fide motives. Cases like these not only make mockery of the sacred institution of marriage but also inflate the statistics of rape cases which further deprecates our own society."

Sexual Exploitation in the Garb of Sanyaas

Justice Gambhir viewed that in recent times, Gurus and Godmen have been embroiled in controversies surrounding their morality and character, bringing to attention the sudden rise in their numbers and their relevance in society. The case of *Anuj Kumar* v. *State NCT of Delhi*, Bail Appln. 579/2013 is an example where such an incident came to light where the petitioner developed physical relations with the woman and promised to marry her and later put on the façade of being a sanyaasi thereby compelling her to file rape charges against him, while dealing with this case Justice Gambhir ardently held:

"The institution of marriage is considered pious where two individuals agree to spend the rest of their life with each other and support the other through thick and thin. There are a vast number of cases where a man exploits a woman in the pretext of sham promises of marrying her later which is highly unethical and absolutely intolerable. In the present case, the applicant has contended that he is a highly spiritual person who does not wish to enter into any type of physical relations as he is following the principle of sanyaas and wishes to attain salvation. It is apparent that the applicant sexually exploited the complainant on the pretext of marrying her and is now trying to take shelter by professing his spiritual inclination and belief in the principle of sanyaas. With a view to sexually exploit the complainant, the applicant also put vermilion in her hairline to convince her of his commitment towards her so that she would have sexual relations with him without restraint. The complainant has placed on record the transcripts of the conversations between the applicant and the complainant and some parts of the transcripts clearly reveal that the applicant was enjoying sexual relations with the complainant and stated his wish to continue having sexual relations with her. These words seem very bizarre coming from a person who is so committed to the sanyaasi principles. Surprisingly, the Counsel for the applicant has himself referred to certain portions of the transcripts but has denied those portions that are damaging to his case and expose the applicant in a bad light.

Sanyaas is popularly perceived as renunciation. It is the instrument of spirituality used for the evolution of the inner conscience. Through spirituality, a person can lead a better life in harmony with nature and his fellow human beings. But it cannot be used to escape from the shackles of law.

Spirituality and religion are often used as synonymous in our country. However, in the literal sense, anything done for ones inner growth and advancement is spirituality. Being spiritual in every facet has a very profound meaning. Even if one is leading a usual life but at the same time is following the path of spirituality, it strongly encourages them to hold their values and teachings intact but does not, by any stretch of imagination encourages a person to lead a self centred, vainglorious or self seeking life. Rather it is about showing respect to all living beings, animals, bees, rocks and even water and to lead a positive and healthy life. Its purpose is to be compassionate, caring and loving to one and all. The great spiritual personalities and gurus have time and again evangelized the same to their followers as well.

It is revolting to see sanyaas and spirituality being used as an excuse for such deplorable acts and this Court strongly condemns it. These fake contentions achieve nothing but unfortunately succeed in making a mockery of the Courts. Manipulating or exploiting a female in the garb of spirituality is against what our ethics dictate. Using a female's body for deriving pleasure and hurting her sentiments on one hand and professing principles of sanyaas on the other is indicative of a deceitful and hypocritical personality".

False Case of Rape by Mother through Daughter against the Father

Sometimes, the incidents that come before the court seem to be fictitious. The adage of too good to be true conversely means too bad to be true which happens when the case where a mother made her own daughter implicate her own husband for the rape of his own child. It does seem unbelievable at first, but the court could not begin to fathom the trauma of a man being falsely accused of raping his own flesh and blood. The case of *Atender Yadav* v. *State NCT of Delhi,* 2013 (4) JCC 2962, the mother used the daughter as a tool to wreck vengeance on the accused/her husband and the Division Bench headed by Hon'ble Justice Gambhir observed that:

"Whether the appellant is innocent and has been falsely implicated with such a serious charge of rape by his own daughter at the behest of her mother for wreaking vengeance on the accused, with a view to spite him due to private and personal grudge or the father is such debouch and an evil person, who would not even spare even his minor daughter in satisfying his lust for sex. Truth being the cherished ideal and ethos of India, pursuit of truth is the guiding star of the criminal justice system. For justice to be done truth must prevail. It is truth that must protect the innocent and it is truth

that must be the basis to punish the guilty. Thus the search of truth is the most pious but arduous task entrusted to the courts and this search of truth primarily rests on the evidence adduced by the parties and the other material proved on record during the trial of a case and its dispassionate judicial scrutiny and objective approach of the court. A criminal trial is meant for doing justice to all, the victim, the accused and also the society. The court does not only discharge the function to ensure that no innocent man is punished, but also to ensure that a guilty man does not escape. Both are public duties of the judge. During the course of the trial, the learned Presiding Judge is expected to work objectively and in a correct perspective. Where the prosecution attempts to misdirect the trial on the basis of a perfunctory, motivated or designedly defective investigation, there the Court is to be deeply cautious and ensure that despite such an attempt, the determinative process is not sub-served. In arriving at the conclusion about the guilt of the accused charged with commission of a crime, the court has to judge the evidence by the yardstick of probability, its intrinsic worth and the animus, if any of witnesses.

....The cases of false implication in rape cases are not uncommon and in some cases parents do persuade gullible or obedient daughter to make false charge of rape either to take revenge or for wreaking vengeance on the accused. We are not here suggesting that in every case the testimony of child witness should be looked upon with suspicion, but before the same is believed as a reliable and truthful statement, due care and caution should be taken looking into all the facts and circumstances of the case especially where the accused happens to be a member of the family and there is another member in a commanding and dominating position to influence and tutor the child in getting the case registered against the other for settling his own scores and vendetta.

There is a tremendous increase of rape cases of the children and in many cases astonishingly, the rapist even involved are those who are otherwise revered persons in the society and worst of all a father himself who is instrumental in giving birth to the same very child and then later treat her as an object of his sexual lust and satisfaction.

There cannot be more serious crime than a rape of a minor child and such an offence assumes a degree of severity when committed by none else but by the father of the prosecutrix. The father is supposed to protect the dignity and honour of his daughter. This is a fundamental facet of human life. If the protector becomes the violator, the offence assumes a greater degree of vulnerability. The sanctity of father and daughter relationship gets polluted. It becomes unpardonable act. This is a grievous sin which could be committed by any such parent, who in the lust of satisfying momentarily sexual desire, shamelessly pollutes his pious and sanctimonious relationship with his own daughter.

To this position as stated above, there can hardly be any other opinion but the converse position is also equally sinful and unpardonable where a father or any member of family is falsely implicated with such a serious allegation of rape when nothing of the same has happened and the prosecutrix becomes a tool in the hands of her own mother and other family members inimical to the accused. Moral values in the society have abysmally gone down where even the most unacceptable thing can also happen.

The desire to take revenge is an evolved outgrowth of our human sense of unsatisfied reciprocity. We can trace innumerable instances of revenge in the history and also in our Hindu mythology. The feeling of revenge destroys the rationale and a common sense even in an otherwise wisest person. At times the feeling of revenge is so strong that the avenger himself also fails to realise the impact of his deeds and easily get swayed by his emotions to wreck vengeance. In order to take revenge he does not even mind doing gravest of act. An avenger may use various means to take revenge. One such means can be process of law **i.e.** *by false implication of the aggressor.*

It is true that barbarity of the offence of rape cannot be overemphasized, especially when we have witnessed the most gruesome and horrific instances of the same nature in the recent past. The indifference that was created towards feral men with the quotidian reporting of rape was followed by a furore bringing the heinousness and depravity of the offence once again into the forefront, awakening the yet hitherto dormant attitude of the society. However, this particular case before us has set forth a contrarian maze which has compelled this court to look away, momentarily, at the offence and look upon the impunity with which it has been trivialised by none else but the own mother of the victim. It is unfortunate, that to seek revenge from her own husband, she went to the extent of using her minor daughter as a tool to implicate him of an offence such as rape. The facts and the circumstance of the case make it amply clear that the grudge nursed by the mother of not being adequately compensated during the divorce coupled with the fact that she made to agree for handing once the legal custody of children in favour of her husband and above all the remarriage of the husband capitulated her into plotting this devious cat. The common belief that no women will fabricate an offence such as rape owing to its social and mental ramification is undoubtedly flawed as is exemplified by the present case. However, the plight of one's charged of the false rape cases, however rare, are also abominable to say the least and understanding it would be an affront to decency. The trauma of a man being falsely accused of raping his own flesh and blood is unspeakable and unfathomable. The court is appalled as how the mother for her personal vendetta compromise the wellbeing of her daughter to let her live for a lifetime with such a stigma and scar of being raped by her own father. The question is best left unanswered in the interest of humanity. Undoubtedly, wallowing in the heartburn drove her to unimaginable lengths, in the lifelong shadow of which the man has to live. In overall perspective cases like these are diluting the authenticity of genuine cases obligating the courts to view every testimony of rape survivor with suspicion rather than a gospel of truth and nevertheless it is nothing but a monumental blow to the larger movement of society against the offence of rape."

Rape is innately Heinous and not to be used as Weapon for Vendetta

Justice Gambhir has always been a torchbearer for the cause of elimination of all kinds of crime against women and children. He has always been very vocal about this issue. In the case of *Nirmal Vaid* v. *State NCT of Delhi*, 2013 (3) AD (Del) 170, the prosecutrix had filed an FIR against the accused, for raping her on the pretext of getting married to her. Abhorring the crime, Justice Gambhir has always been of the view that rape is one of the most heinous crimes against women in the history of mankind. Having said that he doesn't clearly rule out the possibility of people misusing this as a tool to get equal with the other person or for settling scores and has observed that nobody should be allowed to play down the severity of the offence. Emphasising on the need for it to be dealt with an iron hand he propounded as under:

"Rape is one of the most barbaric and heinous crimes not only against the victim of the rape but also against the society as a whole. The cases of rape, gang rape and digital rape are on increase and perpetrators of this inhuman and brutal crime are worse than even the beasts and deserve to be dealt with a heavy hand. The entire country is seriously debating this issue and there are proposals coming forth that death penalty should be the answer to deal with the accused involved in such heinous crime. Having said this, I am also constrained to observe here that no one should be allowed to trivialise the gravity of offence by misusing the same as a weapon for vengeance or vendetta."

II. GORY ACCOUNT OF A CHILD WITNESSING GRUESOME MURDER OF HER MOTHER FOR WANT OF A MALE CHILD

The despicable psyche of the average Indian, where the birth of a girl child is considered no less than a bad omen and the desire to have a male child to carry on the progeny is very strong surfaces in more ways than one, especially when in the courtrooms the age old notions and deep rooted notions are demonstrated. The case of *Baljeet Singh* v. *State,* Crl. A. 386/2011; *Nirmala* v. *State of Delhi,* Crl. A. 486/2011; *Rajesh* v. *State of Delhi,* Crl. A. 487/2011; *Pushpa Devi* v. *Rajesh Kumar,* Crl. A. 1080/2011 highlights one such instance wherein the mother-in-law not only mentally harassed but went to the extent of taking the life of the daughter-in-law holding her responsible for not been able to produce the male heir of the family. The court expressed its anguish and displeasure and at the same time questioned the so called progress we, as a nation had made in fighting these age old prejudices when such an incident surfaces and the years of struggle comes to naught. Justice Gambhir poignantly held:

> *"Tum meri beti nahi beta ho (You are not my daughter but my son), a statement often heard by way of giving a compliment to a daughter who has made her parents proud, but look closely and you will find that this ironic statement is nothing but a reinforcement of every stereotype that women have fought against till date. The so called compliment shrouds the deep rooted prejudice that daughter is a liability and a son an asset and only a male child can do his parents proud, it does nothing but perpetuate the gender discrimination which we had started to believe does not exist anymore.*
>
> *It is an open secret that the want of a male child is one of the biggest manifestations of gender discrimination that pervades all sections of the society, whether urban, rural literate, illiterate, rich or poor. It is understandable that in the past, societal conditioning for wanting to have a male child in a time where women were treated as a second class citizen having a deplorable quality of life was the norm of the day, but it is a disheartening fact that what was treated as an obsession in the bygone era still exists and does not only thrive but drives people to go to unimaginable lengths, the case at hand being a prime example.*
>
> *What monstrosity of a desire would have imbued through the mind of the woman that she was compelled to murder her own daughter-in-law for being unable to give a male heir to the family is unfathomable to this court. Domestic violence, frequent abortions, physical and mental abuse, psychological pressure, all is to be endured like a*

> *penance for the sin for failing to birth a male child. What is the reason for this insatiable urge to have a male child? The reasons commonly postulated which come to mind are that the son is the bread winner of the family, the one to perpetuate the lineage of the family, caste or clan or he is the one to give light to the funeral pyre of the parents, but are not all mere hollow beliefs having no real consequences today. The women of this country have fought a long dogged battle to fade out the gender divide, to break social mores and to overcome social barriers that were regarded as their so called limitations to make a mark in this world, but when viewed from the prism of the reality of the cases like the present one, it all seems to be a mirage. The aim with which progressive legislations such as the PNDT are passed every now and then to curb such social evils becomes toothless in the face of such ghastly acts. It is a scientific fact that the male chromosome is responsible for determining the sex of the child, why is then such savagery reserved for the women who have been granted the privilege to procreate and to continue the human race.*
>
> ....
>
> *At the end we are pained to observe, the more things change, the more they remain the same, and this has never ringed true than in today's time and age. We, the world's largest democracy are touted to be the most progressive nation, proud of our rich cultural heritage, but are we also proud of our deep rooted biases? The present case is a manifestation of the bitter ostensible truth of our society where words like women liberation and gender equality seem to be overrated but have yet to attain their true meaning. There is a huge chasm that needs to be bridged between fact and fiction, to make the women masters of their own circumstance and not vice versa and to falsify the age old adage of "Putrathe Kriyathe Varja" that "we marry with the sole aim to have a son to keep the clan progressing".*

In the same judgment Justice Gambhir discussed the issue of child witnesses and said that children are the most vulnerable faction of the society and by reason of their tender age definitely are considered to be pliable witnesses. With the increase of offences involving children of tender age he opined that competency of child witnesses should not be tested by the age but by the degree of understanding he or she appears to possess. He Held:

> *"………. The Indian Evidence Act, 1872, does not prescribe any particular age as a determinative factor to treat a witness to be a competent one. On the contrary, section 118 of the Evidence*

Act envisages that all persons shall be competent to testify, unless the Court considers that they are prevented from understanding the questions put to them or from giving rational answers to these questions, because of tender years, extreme old age, disease-whether of mind, or any other cause of the same Kind. The only precaution which the Courts should bear in mind while assessing the evidence of a child witness is that the evidence must find corroboration and his/her demeanour must be like any other competent witness and he/she should not be a tutored witness. Another precaution which the Court has suggested in the case of child witness is that as a rule of prudence, it would be desirable to have the authentication to such evidence from other dependable evidence on record. The legal position concerning the testimony of child witness has been a subject matter of discussion in catena of judgments of the Hon'ble Supreme Court as well as the various High Courts of India and abroad. It would be apt to refer to some of the important decisions on the subject.

Children are the most vulnerable faction of the society and by reason of their tender age definitely are considered to be pliable witnesses. There is no denying the fact that each child is different and possesses varied level of interests and intellect. In today's fast paced world, where children are exposed to media, one cannot doubt their cognition levels. Not every child possesses sufficient understanding of nature and the consequences of his acts, but the same cannot negate the intellect capabilities of those who can, very well grasp the state of affairs and maintain a vision of the same in their minds.

One of the issues marring the growth of our country is the evil of child sexual abuse which we hear very often. The POCSO Act, 2013 was therefore formulated in order to effectively address the heinous crimes of sexual abuse and sexual exploitation of children. There lies no iota of doubt that it takes great amount of grit and courage to distinctly explain the horrendous incident that a child is made to go through because of certain ruthless section of the society. A child however even at a tender age does possess the ability to answer the questions put to her/him spontaneously if she/he was present at the site of crime or if he/she has been a victim herself. It is even the courts duty to be sensitive towards the child as the courtroom proceedings are alien to him and it may have a more stressful and terrifying effect which may create a fear in his mind rendering him unable to speak about the incident. It is for the court to adjudge the grasping abilities of children, their tendency to fantasise and their susceptibility to coaching, which are certain factors that need careful examination on case to case basis. Therefore, the court must be satisfied that the attendant circumstances do not show that the child was acting under the influence of someone or was under a threat or coercion. Careful evaluation of the evidence of a child witness in the background of facts of each case in context of other evidence on record is inescapable before the court decides to rely upon it.

As can be seen from the broad principles laid down in the aforesaid legal pronouncements, the competency of a child witness to give evidence is not regulated by the age but by the degree of understanding he/she appears to possess. Undoubtedly, the Court should examine a child of tender years only after it has fully satisfied itself that the child is mentally capable of understanding the questions and also understands the duty of speaking the truth, then only such a child should ordinarily be examined. It is thus imperative for every Court to first test the testimonial intelligence of the child before a child is put in the witness box to testify and where the Court finds that the child does not possess sufficient understanding to distinguish between the truth and falsehood and also lacks the requisite testimonial intelligence, the Court may not examine such a child at all."

III. DOWRY DEATH AND BRIDE BURNING

Dulhan Hi Dahej Hai!

While dealing with the criminal roster, Justice Gambhir had umpteen occasions where he came across cases involving dowry, dowry death and bride burning, he has always been very vocal about the need to abhor all kinds of violence against women. Present was a case being *Santosh Devi* v. *Madan Lal*, FAO No. 80/2001 wherein waxed eloquent about the menace that dowry is, and where the wife due to the demand of dowry or harassment due to bringing insufficient dowry has been compelled to leave the matrimonial home which she enters to leave only at the time of death and the relevant excerpts from the said judgment are reproduced as under:

"Before parting with the judgment, this court would like to observe that an umpteen number of cases, like the present one, must have come before every court sometime or the other, where the wife due to the demand of dowry or harassment due to bringing insufficient dowry has been compelled to leave the matrimonial home which she enters to leave only at the time of death. Dowry has been a despicable word for quite sometime in the society with slogans that adorn buses and walls of public buildings which say "Dulhan hi dahej hai" to convince the public that the menace has been abolished

by legislations and stringent actions would be taken against the ones crossing the line. This court is distraught to observe that dowry is the elephant in the room, more so in the urban and well read strata of the society; we know it exists, it is pervasive, rooted, baneful, pernicious and we do not talk about it and even do not want to believe it exists. This malefic practice which leads to evils like bride burning has exterminated many and is still plaguing many. How ironic that the same fire which is revered as God in our culture and in the presence of which the sacred bond of matrimony is established is used to do a horrific and sordid act like bride burning. It is time that the society has a reality check of its value systems and practices which are overpowered by greed and avarice".

Dowry: An Albatross Around the Neck

Dowry death is a menace that of being extinct by today's time is still permeating the social fabric and eroding it. The pervert mindset of extracting money from the family of the bride and putting her through hell in the process should make the societal conscience to shudder. The instant case of *Raj Kumar* v. *State (NCT of Delhi)*, Crl. A. 664/1999 was one such unfortunate incident where the in-aws tortured the bride for dowry, ultimately resulting in her death and the court was not only saddened but remarked on this horrific practice with great disdain. Expressing his anguish Justice Gambhir held:

"Dowry death and bride burning are social evils which have marred the very concept of marriage being a sacramental and revered union. It is like an albatross around the neck. Ours is a country which is on the verge of development and it is heart wrenching to see that with the nation's development what is also rising is the increasing number of cases relating to dowry deaths and bride burning, and if the National Crime Records Bureau's statistics are something to go by, then one woman dies every hour in the country. It is a crime that is so rampant in our country, where newly wed brides are often harassed for getting more dowry. However, perhaps the primary reason for the spread of this cancer has been the serious dearth of any public campaign or sensitization against it for the past 25 years. As a result, girls are considered a burden on their parents, families go bankrupt trying to get their daughters married off, choice in forming relations is frowned upon and thousands – may be lakhs – of young women suffer brutality quietly behind closed doors, because of an ancient tradition that is still prevalent in most Indian families. The material needs of the society like lust for money or sex etc. ravishes the very basis of this sacramental union called 'Marriage'. No doubt that there are many social & economic

factors, governing the standard of living of various households, yet we feel that it is the righteous and moral duty of a husband that he fully discharges his matrimonial obligations for the sustenance of the family and does not aim to lead a laid-back life at the mercy of his wife's family, by making unwarranted demands or seeking financial backing.

In today's times when women walk shoulder to shoulder with men, pestering newly wedded females for dowry is still spreading like wild fire in every nook and corner and ruining a number of marriages, disbanding our faith in the social and cultural values. It's a curse which the society is facing. Crimes like suicide, bride burning have become common in poor and middle echelons of the society. In most of the cases, such acts are committed to satisfy one's unquenchable and insatiable greed for money and other material needs. In fact, these types of social crimes interfere with the entire societal fabric. The present case involves one such woman, for whom marriage became manacles of depraved windfall which ultimately took away her life."

CHAPTER 2

DACOITY AND MURDER

Observations Regarding Dacoity/Robbery and Murder Cases

The incidents of robbery, dacoity, theft, murder don't even seem to perturb us anymore today as it has become usual for us to hear them on news or read the newspaper with dozens of them being reported every day. But what leads these crimes to happen, what can be done about them? In the case *Naresh Kumar* v. *State,* 2013 (203) DLT 758 the Court dealt with such an incident and heading a Division Bench Justice Gambhir remarked the following:

> *"Honesty pays, but it doesn't seem to pay enough to suit some people"—F.M. Hubbard.*
>
> *The aforesaid quote rightly reveals what persuades people to indulge into unlawful acts, corrupt and criminal means to acquire riches, it is the quest for money but one cannot ignore that honesty and hard work are the verisimilitude of life that enables oneself to survive even in adverse conditions. Majority of people even today imbibe virtues of hard work and honesty in them, but the only gap that needs to be abridged is the difference in the thought process which varies from one man to another. All life demands struggle. Those who have acquired riches by corrupt means cannot brook the same for lifetime ignoring the clutches of law.*
>
> *Tremendous increase in cases of robbery and dacoity has been noticed especially in the metropolitan cities. Robbery is considered as the easiest way to grab money, jewellery and valuable articles of others. To way lay people on deserted places, on highways and other isolated roads has become a very common practice for these criminals. Usually while committing offence of robbery or dacoity, these criminals end up committing more serious and horrendous offence of eliminating the victim of his life or attempting to murder such victim or causing grievous hurt. It is also an acknowledged fact that these criminals keep committing these crimes as their normal routine job till they are convicted and appropriately sentenced and even thereafter. A wave of these grisly crimes is sweeping across swathes of urban and small-town India. The continually rising graph makes us queasy. National*

Crime Records Bureau (NCRB) statistics show that incidents and rates of violent crimes—murder, kidnapping, dacoity, robbery, arson, dowry deaths – have gone up dramatically in the past five years. Although 2010-2011 itself witnessed a 5-6 per cent spurt (National Crime Records Bureau). These numbers are also growing because it is one of the easiest ways to satisfy one's lust for money. Cases like chain snatching and pick pocketing have become so prominent in almost all the localities and neighborhoods. Undoubtedly, the State has to share its blame for not being able to provide good education to its citizens and to secure proper job opportunities or to settle the unemployed youth in small time avocations but at the same time the hard reality is that such kind of persons develop the habit of making easy and fast money instead of putting any hard work for their sustenance and livelihood. It is high time that the State should adopt some kind of measures to educate and sensitize the methods in regards to these criminals who keep indulging and repeating these crimes to earn their livelihood and also to start with some employment avenues and schemes for their proper rehabilitation so that they do not indulge or repeat such dreadful acts".

Son; Turned A Beast in Disguise, Destroyed His Own Creator

"An eye for an eye leaves the whole world blind" is frequently attributed to M.K. Gandhi. At the root of the non-Biblical form of this principle is that one of the purposes of the law is to provide equitable retaliation for an offended party. However law defines and restricts the extent of retaliation.

The old adage "like father, like son" has in the present world shifted to "like mother, like son." For the mother-son connection determines to a great extent not only what sons think about themselves but also what they think about women in general. But the present case is one such example which depicts how brusquely the appellant debauched the core of motherhood and laid all notions as phony.

It is abysmal to note that a woman who gave birth to him was made to succumb to a disastrous end of life by her son for nothing but mere property and monetary issues.

In the instant case of, *Jitender Singh* v. *State of Delhi,* Crl. A. 464/1999, 2014 (210) DLT 48 the Appellant, was convicted for killing none other than his own mother.

The case against the appellant was woven around the dying declaration given by his mother. The brutality of the crime and the grotesque way it was committed was discussed by Justice Gambhir while sitting in a Division Bench. Taking a commiserating view, he noted:

"The case in hand depicts the most gruesome and barbaric act of killing a woman by throwing acid on her head by none else but her own son. It is hard to fathom that one's own blood would commit such a ghastly act of killing his own creator that too out of greed to get the property in his own name. A mother who keeps a child for nine months in her womb, who makes all the sacrifices and bears all the pain without any mope or anguish to bring him to life cannot in her wildest dreams imagine that the same child would one day devastate or ravage her sanctity in such a petrified manner for his sheer crude motives, just for a mere property right. It shakes the very basis of humanity, it kills the faith and emotional bonding borne in the relationship of a mother and his son. It is a dismal truth that acid attacks are quite common in our country, no wonder that any man or woman with malicious intent to take revenge, disfigure and harm the person, commit such a sick act, but committing such an offence with none else than your own mother, tarnishes the very creation of the society as a whole. It causes excruciating pain and terror. The victims are left mutilated and scarred for the rest of their lives, and a few relent."

Set Ablaze, in a Fit of Rage

In a land where we worship goddess 'Durga', it is duplicitous and fills one's heart with dismay to note that the women are treated in the most atrocious manner which is a sacrilege.

In the case of *Manoj Kumar* v. *State,* 2014 (7) AD (Del) 631 the appellant was allegedly set ablaze, on a mere altercation for just Rs. 200. Dealing with such an instance where the very being of a woman was denigrated, Hon'ble Justice Kailash Gambhir presiding over a Division Bench, held as under:

"To commit a murder is brutal in itself, but it is most dehumanizing and bestial when one fellow human is set ablaze by the hands of another human in a moment of rage. There can be various reasons which may drive a person to commit a crime. There exists no logic or rationality which may excuse any crime irrespective of its magnitude. Moreover, in no circumstances an action as nefarious or inhuman as burning a person alive may be justified. The acts of a man is the mirror to his mind and it is a dark reflection of his soul that we see when he loses his rationality and reason and is overcome by emotion so extreme as to turn into a barbaric criminal. None else but the victim alone undergoes horrendous pain, agony and trauma due to burn injuries which cause irreversible damage even if the victim survives. In the present case, the question before

this court is that whether the given facts and circumstances result in a similar situation of inhumanity."

Criminal Trial is a Voyage in Quest of Truth for Public Justice

Undoubtedly, Prosecution plays a pivotal role in establishing the morsel of truth and a sketchy investigation is what defeats the purpose of fair decision making. A good legal system would rather let nine "guilty" men go, than incarcerate one innocent one.

The case of *Kapoor Singh @ Kale* v. *State (NCT of Delhi)*, 2014 (4) AD (Del) 746 is one such glaring example wherein the appellant was let scott free. Hon'ble Justice Gambhir presiding over a Division Bench held as under:

> *"Every criminal trial is a voyage in quest of truth for public justice to punish the guilty and save the innocent person unconnected or unrelated with the crime. To prove any person guilty of a crime is thus not an easy task. Much depends upon as to how and with what perfection the investigation of any crime takes place. Further how the case is prosecuted before the court to prove each and every incriminating evidence as collected by the Investigating Agency is of vital importance. Then comes the dispassionate and objective analyses of the evidence and other material produced on record by the learned trial court which has to be gone into meticulously.*
>
> *It is a settled legal position that in offences as serious as that of murder, the investigation has to be carried out with full diligence and with utmost fairness and honesty leaving no gaps and loose ends to leave a room for the defense to raise any kind of suspicion to claim benefit of doubt. The task of the investigation undoubtedly is undaunted and becomes quite challenging, more so when our investigation machinery suffers from scientific techniques and requires expertise."*

CHAPTER 3

CRIMINAL MISCELLANEOUS

Delay in Disposal of Criminal Cases Due to Shortage of Public Prosecutors Condemned

Justice Gambhir while sitting in a Division Bench came down heavily on the Government while deciding cases exercising constitutional powers. Be *suo motu* considered the aspect of delayed payments to Government counsels by the department and non-filling up of vacancies of Public Prosecutors. Hon'ble Justice Gambhir issued various directions to the Government in *Court on its own Motion* v. *State,* 2014 (4) AD (Del) 429.

Justice Gambhir's relentless efforts aimed at improvising the criminal justice system so that the justice is delivered speedily, which is the need of the hour. While looking at the ignoble situation of the prosecution agency in delaying criminal trials, an Amicus Curiae was appointed in this matter and gave various directions to the Government of NCT of Delhi to put in place an appropriate mechanism for filling-up all the vacancies of Public Prosecutors each year on the basis of existing and anticipated vacancies as on a particular date. Justice Gambhir with his adept experience gave time bound directions for filling the vacancies of APPs on contract basis resultantly the orders have been complied with in true letter and spirit without committing any default as the criminal justice system cannot be made to suffer in the absence of assistance of PPs/APPs.

> *"One of the pre-dominant cause for delay in disposal of criminal case is due to shortage of public prosecutors. It is quite shocking to learn that some of the public prosecutors have been burdened to take care of the work of two criminal courts. This lackadaisical and apathy of the Government in not filling up of the vacancies on the posts of Assistant Public Prosecutors/Additional Public Prosecutors is quite intriguing and appalling. Recently, the Hon'ble Supreme Court of India has given directions for completing the trial of all MPs/MLAs facing criminal prosecution within a period of one year after the charges are framed. But how can any criminal court function in the absence of a public prosecutor attached with the court. It is the statutory obligation of the State to ensure that every criminal court*

whether be of Metropolitan Magistrate or the Sessions Court has the assistance of an able and competent public prosecutor. It is also the duty of the State to ensure that the public prosecutors so appointed have all the requisite facilities for their efficient functioning to discharge their day to day duties."

"This court has already expressed its dissatisfaction and dismay over the conditions in which the public prosecutors have been working. The court has also given various directions for timely appointment of public prosecutors so that the criminal justice system does not suffer due to the absence of the public prosecutors in any criminal court. It is a matter of great concern that for the timely appointment of public prosecutors, this court has to give directions from time to time to GNCT of Delhi. The only anxiety of the court is that no criminal court should be deprived of the assistance of public prosecutors. The Government of NCT of Delhi should get to know in advance as to how many new posts of Judicial officers are going to be created and filled-up in various District Courts of Delhi. It will be taken as a case of gross negligence on the part of the concerned Ministry/ Department, especially the Home Department of the Delhi if they do not take prompt steps in filling up the vacancies of Assistant Public Prosecutors/Additional Public Prosecutors to ensure that all public prosecutors are assigned the duties with such new criminal courts, be that of Metropolitan Magistrates or the Sessions Courts. It is thus made clear to the GNCT of Delhi that this court will take strict view, if at any stage it is found that due to any lapse or negligence, timely appointment of public prosecutors have not taken place. The back-up of 10% of the strength of the public prosecutors in each and every district shall also ensure that during certain exigencies also, the criminal courts will not go unrepresented with these public prosecutors."

So far as the payment of Government counsels is concerned, it was directed that all the administrative departments of the Government of NCT of Delhi shall make the payment without committing any default within a period of two months from the date of receipt of the Bills. It was made clear that so far as the past pending bills of the counsels were concerned, even where the BTFs have not been issued by the Law Department, the payment shall be made by these departments on the certification of the concerned Standing Counsel on the bills.

"While hearing the same matter, on 14-3-2014 Justice Gambhir directed that he did not see any difficulty arising in the settlement of pending bills of government counsels. However, it was also made clear that serious view shall be taken by the court if even after certification

done by the Standing Counsel, GNCT of Delhi, the payments would not be cleared and we may be constrained to impose heavy costs on the concerned Principal Secretary/Secretary/HODs for not clearing the bills of the Government Counsels and that said costs will be directly deducted from their respective salaries. The Government Departments and other Departments of the Government must appreciate that most of the lawyers who represent the Government as Standing Counsels/Additional Standing Counsels/Panel Lawyers are normally not engaged by the private parties, especially where the Government is one of the contesting party and therefore the timely payment of their professional bills should be on top priority of the Government and its other departments."

That Wrongful Approach of Summoning Persons to Court, Irrespective of their Involvement in Incriminating Act: Be Contained

Justice Gambhir observed that in the cases of dishonor of cheques punishable under section 138 of the Negotiable Instruments Act,1881 there has been a practice of summoning all the officials who are not even the signatories to the dishonoured cheques and are not even covered by the provisions under section 138/141 of Negotiable Instruments Act, 1881, meaning thereby the officials who were not in charge of, and were not responsible to the company for the conduct of the business of the company at the time of issuance of the cheque are also summoned, which causes harassment to such persons and with a view to set right this jeopardous state of affairs in the matter of *Sudeep Jain* v. *M/s. ECE Industries Ltd.*, 2013 (201) DLT 461 Justice Gambhir while explaining the sections 138/141 NI Act gave directions to the subordinate judiciary, for saving the innocent, from harassment on account of having to appear in the court without any role to play in the offence committed by the company. He held as under:

"The prime objective of this Court is to remind all the Metropolitan Magistrates in Delhi to carefully scrutinize all the complaint cases being filed under section 138 read with 141 of the Negotiable Instruments Act, 1881 against the accused companies at the pre-summoning stage and make sure that notice be directed only to those directors or employees of the company who satisfy the principles laid down in the aforesaid judgments. Summons must be issued only after giving due consideration to the allegations and the materials placed on record by the complainant. Undeniably, as per the aforesaid legal pronouncements, Managing Director and the Joint Managing Director are deemed to be vicariously liable for the offence committed by the company because of the position they hold in the company. Problem arises in cases where all the persons holding office in the

company are sought to be prosecuted by the complainant, irrespective of whether they played any specific role in the incriminating act. It is surprising to see that in plethora of cases, the complaint contains allegations even against those persons who might have been Directors at any point in time in the accused company, but had resigned from such company much prior to the period when the alleged offence was committed. Issuing summons to all persons named in the complaint mechanically, without ascertaining whether they played any actual role in the transaction, not only pesters the innocent directors/ employees named in the complaint, but also upsurges the load on the High Courts as the Magistrates once issuing the summoning orders against the accused, are precluded from reviewing their summoning orders in view of the decision of the Apex Court in Adalat Prasad *v.* Rooplal Jindal, *(2004) 7 SCC 338: AIR 2004 SC 4674: 2004 Cr LJ 4874. One can also not lose sight of the fact that once such innocent persons are summoned, they have no choice but to seek bail and face the ordeal of trial. Many of such persons also approach the High Court under section 482, Cr.P.C. to seek quashing of the summoning order and the complaint filed against them and this further increases the burden on the already overburdened Courts.*

With a view to ensure that the Metropolitan Magistrates dealing with the complaint cases filed under section 138 read with section 141 of the Negotiable Instruments Act have a clear and complete picture of the persons arrayed by the complainant so as to hold them vicariously liable for the commission of the offence by the accused company, I am inclined to direct that the Magistrates must seek copies of Form 32 from the complainant to prima facie satisfy the Court as to who were the directors of the accused company at the time of commission of the alleged offence and on the date of filing of the complaint case. In addition to the above, the Magistrates must also seek information as given in the following table which is to be annexed by the Complainant on a separate sheet accompanying the complaint:—

a. Name of the accused Company;

b. Particulars of the dishonoured cheque/cheques;

Person/Company in whose favour the cheque/cheques were issued

Drawer of the cheque/cheques

Date of issuance of cheque/cheques

Name of the drawer bank, its location

Name of the drawee bank, its location

Cheque No./Nos.

Signatory of the cheque/cheques

c. *Reasons due to which the cheque/cheques were dishonoured;*

d. *Name and Designation of the persons sought to be vicariously liable for the commission of the offence by the accused Company and their exact role as to how and in what manner they were responsible for the commission of the alleged offence;*

e. *Particulars of the legal notice and status of its service;*

f. *Particulars of reply to the legal notice, if any".*

Duty of the Bar Council against the Erring Members

To dawn the robes and be an officer of the court is a privilege and for many a dream come true. Regarded as a noble profession, it is disheartening to see advocates resorting to unscrupulous practices and playing fraud upon the court. In the case of, *Sharad Kumar Aggarwal* v. *State,* Bail Application No. 1158/2009, Hon'ble Justice Kailash Gambhir while exposing the misdeeds of the petitioner advocate who filed a fictitious case, denounced the inability of the Bar Council to curb such misconduct.

Justice Kailash Gambhir debunked the abominable and detestable conduct of the Advocate, an officer of Court and also pointed out to the Bar Council of Delhi its inactivity to deal with the conduct of this Advocate at their level. He observed as under:

> *"The allegation of filing of fictitious case with fictitious names, fictitious addresses, forged documents, misusing and abusing the process of the court, no doubt constitutes very serious acts and deserve strongest condemnation especially when they are allegedly committed by none else but by those on whose shoulders the edifice of administration of justice rest. This court would have certainly appreciated had the Bar Council of Delhi by now would have taken some decision either to bail out the petitioner from the said serious charges or had thrown out the petitioner from the rolls of the counsel, if such allegations are proved correct. It is a high time that Bar Council of Delhi must rise to the occasion to deal with such cases very strenuously and effectively without siding for unscrupulous lawyers. Stream of justice has to be kept clean and pure and any one spoiling its purity must not be spared howsoever well connected he or she may be, so that the message goes down to one and all that no one can be permitted or spared to undermine the dignity of the court or to interfere with the administration of justice".*

Lackadaisical Approach Adopted by Government Bodies while Launching Criminal Prosecution

Sometimes the overzealous government bodies and its instrumentalities without due diligence adopt the iron-hearted and merciless approach to launch criminal prosecution. It is a sorry state of affairs with such bodies transgressing their powers.

The case of *Parivar Seva Sanstha* v. *The State*, Crl. M.C. No. 1459-64/2006 clearly divulges the callous and lackadaisical approach of the government departments while launching criminal prosecution against the innocent. It was opined as follows:

> *"The Government Body and its instrumentalities who are empowered with the authority to launch criminal prosecution have to be very careful, cautious and confident that the persons complained of are in clear breach of some penal provisions and sufficient material need to be placed with clear averments in the complaint, disclosing commission of cognizable offence on the part of the accused persons. Indisputably, criminal prosecution not only leads to cause serious harassment to such persons but certainly tarnish the image of such persons besides placing them in lower esteem in the society, and therefore, every care must be taken by such government bodies before launching any criminal prosecution against the citizens or the other juristic and legal entities. The DDA projected an irresponsible and a casual behaviour unnecessarily causing hardship to the petitioners by not disclosing the facts..."*

Quintessence of Fair Trial

Fair Trial ensures the separation of the guilty from the innocent and accords protection against injustice. Without this right, the public faith in the rule of law and the judicial system shall collapse. The Right to Fair Trial is one of the cornerstones of a just society. In the case of *Prashant Jain* v. *State*, 2014 (207) DLT 752, reaffirming the virtue of fair trial, Justice Gambhir sitting in a Division Bench observed as under:

> *"The learned trial court perhaps had forgotten that fair and proper trial is at the core of our judicial system to reach the ultimate goal of dispensation of justice between the parties. It is first and foremost duty of every court to see that neither any innocent man is punished nor any guilty person escapes from the clutches of law. Both are public duties of a Judge. During the course of the trial, the learned Presiding Judge is expected to work objectively and in a judicious manner. A watchful and a diligent trial Judge, before whom every piece of evidence is placed by the prosecution and the defence, has to be a protector of the rights of both the victims and the accused*

and nothing should escape his sight which can unduly benefit either of them. While appreciating the evidence on record the Court is expected to be fully cautious and ensure that the determinative process is not sub-served. For truly attaining the object of a 'fair trial', the Court should leave no stone unturned to do justice and protect the interest of the society as well."

Duties Cast on Magistrate when the Witness is Not Speaking the Truth

The litigants have often used the adage that they did not have a fair trial if the decision in a matter is not swaying their way or in their favour. Transfer petitions are preferred consequently taking one pretext or the other, at times finding fault with the conduct of the judicial officer concerned. In the case, of *Madhu Devi* v. *State,* TR.P. (Crl.) 7/2013, such a transfer petition was filed on account of denial of right to fair trial.

Justice Gambhir seizing the transfer petition explained the role of a Judge to be not that of a mute spectator and encouraged the Judges to take up the role of a referee and not an umpire while stating:

"A mere warning given by a judicial officer to the witness so as to depose correctly or to answer the questions put forth by the examining counsel in a proper manner cannot be termed to be as a threatening action against the witness on part of the judicial officer. A judge is expected to play an efficacious role while conducting trial of the case......

Thus, the Presiding Officer of the court has every right to step-in and interfere at any stage of the trial proceedings where he finds that a particular witness appearing is not deposing honestly or when the version put forth by it appears to be tainted, as after all, he is not expected to be a mute spectator but play an active role in trial proceedings in order to bring home the truth and administer proper justice.

Having said this, it would not be appropriate to accommodate a mere plea on behalf of a petitioner that the presiding judge acted in a biased manner on the grounds of over-questioning or personally examining a particular witness. Strong reasons with cogent proofs are required to be given in order to claim transfer of a petition to another court. Paying heed to such skimpy pleas without any cogent proof in respect thereof would lead to drastic consequences. It would not only impede the independent functioning of the courts wherein the judges are given ample space and powers to act in a way they want so as to fulfil their ultimately objective of culling out the real truth from the parties/witnesses but would also disparage and undermine the confidence of the judicial officers as well."

Terrorism – A Severe Blow to Mankind

Terrorism is a serious danger to humanity and we have lost many lives in the wake of such attacks. Unsolved terror cases embolden terrorists to take chances with the law enforcement agencies and hence the police should be given a free hand while investigating cases pertaining to terrorist activities. In the case of *Mohammad Shakeel* v. *State,* Crl MC No. 3374/2008 & *Zeeshan Ahmed* v. *State,* Crl MC No. 3375/2008, Justice Kailash Gambhir elucidated in his observations as to how the scores of terrorist activities go unexposed if police is not given a free hand in investigation on a matter of terrorist attacks and serial bomb blasts. It was held as under:

> "...........*All these accused persons have been charged under sections 302/307/121/121A/120B IPC, 23/4/5 Explosive Substances Act and 13 Unlawful Activities (Prevention Act) and all the five accused persons were arrested on 15-10-2008. Linked with Delhi blasts, the Maharashtra Police and Uttar Pradesh Police had also arrested 21 accused persons, members of Indian Mujahideen. It would be thus evident that these petitioners are facing highly serious and grave charges and they are not simply accused of some ordinary crimes. These serial blasts in Delhi have claimed 30 lives of innocent persons and resulted 130 persons receiving serious and minor injuries. The entire city on that date was thundered and shaken by one after the other blasts at its various prime commercial locations. Before the Delhiites could overcome the said trauma, 10 terrorists on 26th November, 2008 created havoc in the city of Mumbai by their well planned attack at Hotel Taj, CST Railway Station and Cama Hospital, which led to the killings of 173 and injuries to 308. The terrorists attack at the commercial city of Mumbai not only made our leaders on their tenterhooks but also shocked the world leaders who in one voice have condemned such ghastly, barbaric and inhuman attacks. Although this court is not dealing as such with the issue as to how the blasts at Bombay had taken place but certainly these frequent terrorist attacks have traumatized and created a sense of fear and panic in a common man. About 1202 persons have been killed in 23 terrorist attacks in the country since the first barbaric blast in 2001 and thereafter at various metropolis of the country and attack on our Parliament, the seat of largest democracy of the world. The issue of terrorism concerns each one of the citizen of the country and therefore, the blasts at Delhi cannot be viewed in isolation. How these young persons staying at Batala house could indulge themselves into such barbaric and dastardly acts, from which sources they were getting aid, whether such sources are available*

in the country or in the neighbouring country, from where the financial aid came forth, from where the guns and explosives were supplied, from where the mobile phones were procured, from where the fake degrees, identity cards were obtained and who gave them the accommodation to stay, whether the neighbourers or other persons living in the vicinity were aware about their antecedents and their activities, what were their exact motives, aspirations and why being living in this great secular country their loyalties still remains with the neighbouring country. To what organizations do they belong, whether such organizations are based in India or in the neighbouring country. These may be broad aspects and many such other aspects which the investigating agency has to probe so as to unearth the entire conspiracy behind the said serial blasts and to apprehend the actual culprits/offenders involved in such murkier and inhuman acts. The task before the investigating agency in such a case is not only uphill and gigantic but is of great responsibility. It is a well known fact that the actual offenders at whose instance the terrorist acts are committed rarely gets apprehended some times because they are not named even by the person apprehended and if named because of their presence in the neighbouring country. Sometimes also it is not known that how many layers exists in any conspiracy and up to which layer of conspiracy the culprits apprehended had access and sometime one set of culprits may not have any knowledge of other set of culprits committing the same offence at the same place or at some other place and therefore, to unravel these layers of conspiracies the investigative agency has to only trace and collect material from various States but transcending boundaries as well. The period of 15 days as prescribed under section 167 of Cr.P.C. for police remand would not be enough to probe these accused persons involved in all these serial blasts. The police has to be given a free hand to carry out the investigation, so that the police is able to apprehend all the culprits involved in such terrorist attacks so as to expose and unmask the kingpins and real culprits behind such dastardly and cowardice acts."

Directions and Guidelines for Dealing with Offences under Section 498A-406, IPC to Police Authorities, Lawyers, Courts, Social Workers/NGO

Justice Kailash Gambhir had already anticipated a situation as to how section 498A could be misused against the parents-in-law of the women and he had deprecated how the Police was blindly arresting innocent in-laws who were framed in such false and manipulative cases, much before he dealt with the case of *Chander Bhan* v. *State*, 2008 (151) DLT 691.

Prior to this decision of Justice Gambhir there were no law/guidelines/directions in matters of such a nature and now after about 6 years the Supreme Court has laid guidelines for such cases in *Arnesh Kumar* v. *State of Bihar*, AIR 2014 SC 2756: 2014 Cr LJ 3707: 2014 AIR SCW 3930 decided on 2/7/2014 in Criminal Appeal No. 1277 of 2014 @Special Leave Petition (Crl.) No. 9127 of 2013. Nevertheless, the observations/directions given in the year 2008 by Hon'ble Justice Gambhir are as under:

> *"...Before parting with this case, I deem it expedient and in the larger interest of saving matrimony of the couples and to restore peace between the two hostile families of husband and wife who once must have celebrated the marriage of couple with great zeal, fervour and enthusiasm but when faced with many facets and stark realities of life entangled themselves to fight a long drawn legal battle instead of building confidence, trust, understanding, mutual respect for each other and their respective families.*
>
> *The offence of cruelty by husband or relatives of husband (section 498A) was added in 1986 to curb the vice of subjecting women to coerce them or their relatives to meet unlawful demands for dowry. Since its enactment, this provision has been subjected to systematic and sustained attack. It has been called unfair and responsible for the victimisation of husbands by their wives and her relatives. No doubt there may be many deserving cases where women are being subjected to mental and physical cruelty at the hands of the avaricious in-laws. But such cases have to be distinguished from other cases where merely due to trivial fights and ego clashes the matrimony is facing disaster. What is not comprehended by young minds while invoking the provisions of the likes of section 498A and 406 of IPC is that these provisions to a large extent have done incalculable harm in breaking matrimony of the couples. Despite the western culture influencing the young minds of our country, still it has been seen that Indian families value their own age old traditions and culture, where, mutual respect, character and morals are still kept at a very high pedestal.*
>
> *It has been noticed in diverse cases, where the brides and their family members in litigation find the doors of conciliation shut from the side of groom and his family members only on account of there having suffered the wrath of Police harassment first at the stage when matter is pending before crime against women cell and thereafter at the time of seeking grant of anticipatory or regular bail and then the ordeal of long drawn trial. Daily, matters come before this court seeking bail and for quashing of FIRs registered under sections 498A/406 of the IPC. This court is of the view that it is essential to lay down some*

broad guidelines and to give directions in such matters in order to salvage and save the institution of marriage and matrimonial homes of the couples.

Guidelines:

1. Social workers/NGO

There is no iota of doubt that most of the complaints are filed in the heat of the moment over trifling fights and ego clashes. It is also a matter of common knowledge that in their tussle and ongoing hostility the hapless children are the worst victims. Before a wife moves to file a complaint with the Women Cell, a lot of persuasion and conciliation is required.

(a) The Delhi Legal Service Authority, National Commission for Women, NGOs and social workers working for upliftment of women should set up a desk in crime against women cell to provide them with conciliation services, so that before the State machinery is set in motion, the matter is amicably settled at that very stage. But, if ultimately even after efforts put by the social workers reconciliation seems not possible then the matter should be undertaken by the police officials of Crime against Women cell and there also, serious efforts should be made to settle the matter amicably.

2. Police Authorities

(a) Pursuant to directions given by the Apex Court, the Commissioner of Police, Delhi vide Standing Order No. 330/2007 had already issued guidelines for arrest in the dowry cases registered under sections 498A/406, IPC and the said guidelines should be followed by the Delhi Police strictly and scrupulously.

- *(i) No case under section 498A/406, IPC should be registered without the prior approval of DCP/Addl. DCP.*
- *(ii) Arrest of main accused should be made only after thorough investigation has been conducted and with the prior approval of the ACP/DCP.*
- *(iii) Arrest of the collateral accused such as father-in-law, mother-in-law, brother-in-law or sister-in-law etc should only be made after prior approval of DCP on file.*

(b) Police should also depute a well trained and a well behaved staff in all the crime against women cells especially the lady officers, all well equipped with the abilities of perseverance, persuasion, patience and forbearance.

(c) FIR in such cases should not be registered in a routine manner.

(d) The endeavor of the Police should be to scrutinize complaints very carefully and then register FIR.

(e) The FIR should be registered only against those persons against whom there are strong allegations of causing any kind of physical or mental cruelty as well as breach of trust.

(f) All possible efforts should be made, before recommending registration of any FIR, for reconciliation and in case it is found that there is no possibility of settlement, then necessary steps in the first instance be taken to ensure return of **stridhan** *and dowry articles etc. by the accused party to the complainant.*

3. Lawyers

Lawyers also have a great responsibility in this regard.

(a) While drafting pleadings/complaints, the lawyers should not unnecessarily suggest incorporation of wild allegations, or in character assassination of any of the parties or their family members whatever the case may be.

(b) Lawyers are also to endeavour to bring about amicable settlement between the parties as they are expected to discharge sacred duty as social engineers in such cases instead of making them target for monetary considerations by multiplying their cases.

4. Courts

Subordinate courts, be it trying civil or criminal cases concerning bail, maintenance, custody, divorce or other related matters shall in the first instance, in every case where it is possible so to do consistently with the nature and circumstances of the case, to make every endeavour to bring about reconciliation between the parties:

(a) The first endeavor should be for possible reunion and restitution of the parties and as a last endeavor to bring about peaceful separation.

(b) If possible extra time should be devoted to such matters to restore peace in the lives of rival parties be it by re-uniting them or even in case of their parting ways.

(c) Conciliatory proceedings by the court should preferably be held in camera to avoid embarrassment.

(d) Wherever, the courts are overburdened with the work, necessary assistance of Mediation and Conciliation cells should be sought.

Apart from above directions it would not be out of place to ask parties also to themselves adopt a conciliatory approach without intervention of any outside agency and unless there are very compelling reasons, steps for launching prosecution against any spouse or his/her in-laws be not initiated just in a huff, anger, desperation or frustration.

Marriage, Marital Obligation and Crime

While heading a Division Bench, Justice Gambhir expressed its intolerance towards the malaise of dowry deaths in the case of *Mahesh* v. *State,* Crl. A. 654/2010. Justice Gambhir by way of the instant case poignantly noted how we as a nation have come so close to the goal of removing gender discrimination and yet are so far away from it at the same time. The confluence of varied moralities, the varying sense of right and wrong and ethics has to be fine-tuned to achieve justice for all. In the instant case it was observed that:

> *"Marriages are made in heaven, where two souls unite with love and devotion. But the material needs of the society like lust for money or sex etc. ravishes the very basis of this deific union. No doubt that there are many social & economic factors, governing the standard of living of various households, yet we feel that it is the righteous and moral duty of a husband that he fully discharges his matrimonial obligations for the sustenance of the family and does not aim to lead a leisurely life at the hands of his wife's family making prodigal demands or seeking financial backing. However, in today's times when a women walks shoulder to shoulder with men, harassment to newly wedded females for dowry is still spreading appendages in every nook and corner and ruining a number of marriages, pulverizing our faith in the social and cultural values. It's a curse which the society is facing. Crimes like suicide, bride burning have become common in poor and middle stratum of the society. In most of the cases, such acts are committed to satisfy one's unquenchable greed for money and other material needs. In fact, these types of social crimes meddle the entire social fabric. The present case involves one such woman, for whom marriage became shackles of debauched boon which eventually took away her life."*

Judicial Temperament

Justice Gambhir swears by the mantra that justice should not only be done but should also seen to have been done. He has always stuck to the hallmarks of a great judge namely fairness, sensitivity, cool temperament. He is of the firm belief that Courts are the temples of justice where vengeance, arbitrariness, perversity can't be allowed to seep in. Judges ought to decide the case based on merits and not become whimsical and biased. Throwing light on this issue he further elucidated in the case of *BSES Rajdhani Power Ltd.* v. *State NCT Delhi,* 2009 (157) DLT 252, that:

"No order of the judicial officer should give a slightest reflection of anger, insensitivity, unfairness and hastiness. Besides the above hallmarks, the most important personal qualifications required are moral vigour, ethical firmness and imperviousness to corrupting or venal influences, humility and lack of affiliations, judicial temperament, zeal and capacity to work. Judicial temperament of a judge besides possessing qualities of honesty, integrity besides adequate knowledge of law, skill and legal soundness must also possess the qualities of compassion, fairness, diligence, decisiveness, high order of emotional stability, firmness, serenity, ability, endurance and open-mindedness. Totally free from any biasness, perversity and arbitrariness with the overt commitment to the sense of justice. Our system of justice depends on the faith of the citizens. Out of respect for the justice delivery system and the position of a judge in this system, judges have been accorded respect traditionally by our citizens. The Citizens in return expect their judges to decide their cases fairly and impartially with no anger or sense of any biasness or arbitrariness. I feel that the Special Judge has not done his job till the parties and counsel get a feeling of satisfaction that they have had a fair hearing of the dispute regardless of the ultimate decision of the case.

The courts are temples of justice where there is no room to radiate vengeance. In the instant case, the Learned Special Judge unmindful of the basic philosophy of Justice Delivery System and in a spree of fury dismissed 29 cases. It is only where the complainant tries to protract the matter or adopts dilatory tactics to harass the accused the power under section 256, Cr.P.C. should be exercised by a Judge and not out of ferocity and anger."

Roads – Life-Blood of a Nation

Good roads are essential for the development of a country. Roadways are the lifeblood of any nation. We should in this regard ape the Romans, who are celebrated and acknowledged for their roads. A country's road network should be competent in order to capitalize on economic and social benefits. The innovation of motor vehicles has made it unproblematic to transport goods from one place to another. These vehicles, nevertheless, require good and not bumpy roads to travel faster. It is common knowledge that the better the roads are, the more goods can be transported from place to place. Thus, trade is enhanced.

It is a sorry state of affairs to see how due to rains, the roads collapse, cause traffic snarls. An imminent need to re-carpet rough, uneven and pot-holed roads is the need of the hour. It's the public money that gets spent to maintain roads. It is a very genuine and legitimate expectation that any commuter on the road has, he expects the roads to be in motor able condition. In this fast paced life, a smooth and effortless ride is what a person looks for.

It is a dismal picture that gets shown every time, the roads cave in, their situation worsens and they can't even stand a single spell of rain.

Whilst deciding the case of *Rakesh Tyagi* v. *State*, B.A. No. 2068/2008 Justice Gambhir held as under:

> *"...........The report filed by the MCD itself shows total apathy and lackadaisical attitude of the MCD towards the poor maintenance of road. It is a well known fact that the city roads are not built on international standards and most of the roads are in shambles. The roads of the 'National Capital' are bumpy, full of potholes and uneven which are perennial source of giving nightmarish experience to the vehicle owners. Besides, such worsening road conditions lead to frequent traffic jams. Mostly it is on account of use of sub-standard and inferior quality of material by the contractors which results in the poor construction of road and essentially in the process the complicity of the officials of the MCD cannot be ruled out............ it is a daily experience of Delhiites that the roads are not worthy of use and lot many accidents take place because of the potholes and uneven roads. The MCD and other agencies taking care of constructions and maintenance of roads in Delhi should now be on their tenterhooks because Delhi being the host of Common Wealth Games. What image the capital of the country would project if the roads are not built on the international standards and remained in such poor and worsen conditions.........."*
>
> *"The MCD is responsible for the constructions and maintenance of 94% of roads in Delhi* **i.e.** *around 41,000 k.m. of roads. Day in and day out the people experience difficulties to drive on some stretches of uneven, broken and bumpy roads of Delhi. It is a nightmare for the citizens of Delhi to drive through these uneven roads, more particularly when they get stranded in long traffic jams due to potholes in the middle of the roads and uneven stretches. The situation gets more worsened during the rainy season and post rainy season. The respondent MCD shall prepare a time bound Schedule to ensure that these roads are constructed at international standards and these roads are kept properly maintained and wherever any repair is required the same is carried out within a fastest possible time. The MCD should have emergency mobile staff to carry out immediate repair on the roads as it is done in all the advanced countries."*

"Roads are symbols of the prowess of the nation state seems like an oxymoron in the context of the capital of the country today. Despite various directions given by this court, the picture appears to be more dismal than what is being shown to the court through the affidavits. In one short spell of rains Delhi has experienced total chaos at many places. Roads have caved in due to water logging and most of the main roads resulted in long traffic jams bringing the city to a standstill. With the Common Wealth Games in the offing, with this situation, passing the roads would then be kettles of fish for this city. .... One area where in all the seasons the roads appear to be in perfect motorable condition without there being any potholes or unevenness is the area surrounding the Embassies **i.e.** *near Chanakyapuri. The question is why all the roads in Delhi cannot be built or maintained at the same standards and in the same fashion standing the test of all seasons. The Delhi Government charges a very high amount towards the road tax but in return it does not provide smooth and worthy roads to the citizens of Delhi. Why should the common man expect to have good roads only before an international event. The situation is also distressing for the motorists as they do not get optimal use of their vehicles because the life of the vehicles also gets shortened after the same are driven on bumpy and uneven roads. Looking at the present state of affairs, the capital of the country with its mega city dream, it seems has an uphill task ahead unless it provides smooth, even and quality roads without any potholes. It seems that the job of construction of the road is shoddily executed as most of the roads do not even sustain the pressure of one spell of rains and therefore after every rainy season the condition of the roads worsen and they degenerate to their sorry state.............It is a well known fact that lot many accidents take place on account of these uneven and bumpy roads and also because of the existence of potholes on these roads.*

Time and again this Court has expressed deep concern on the deplorable quality of roads wreaking havoc in the lives of citizens of Delhi, who day in and day out have nightmarish experience while travelling on the bumpy roads of Delhi, especially, within the jurisdiction of the MCD. But despite several directions given by this court the condition of many arterial/main roads especially within the jurisdiction of the MCD have not shown much progress. The poor condition of roads is primarily due to the sub-standard material used by the contractors in building such roads and also because of the nexus between the contractors and the engineering staff and there being no proper mechanism in place to fix responsibility of guilty staff and contractors. Frequent digging of the roads by various Government and non-Government agencies mainly Delhi Jal Board further compounds the situation from bad to worse. Some of the roads do not even sustain one heavy down pour and the bitumen can be seen washed away from many places creating potholes and large patches. The growth of any city can be measured by the condition of its roads. Undoubtedly, the city has undergone a monolithic makeover in the last decade, particularly with the construction of fly-overs which has indeed eased the congestion on the main roads, giving smooth driving experience to commuters, but shockingly the condition of some of the main roads in Delhi/New Delhi has not improved for the reasons well known to the concerned authorities. Poor maintenance of the roads with potholes not only leads to causing accidents but the same leads to many other troublesome consequences such as long traffic jams, excess consumption of fuel, increase of pollution, reduction of life of the vehicles. Certainly, there is now greater mobility system in the city and massive augmentation of the public transport system, but there is still a large scope for a lot to be done for giving solace to the harried commuter."

".........It is the statutory duty of these authorities to provide high quality roads to its citizens. Citizens are not expected to suffer on account of bad planning, lack of coordination of the multiple authorities in Delhi. The officers from junior to high level of these authorities are either not taking their job seriously or some of these officers are hand in glove with the contractors in laying or relaying of substandard roads. An effective and proper mechanism needs to be in place. This court does not intend to say that these authorities are not taking any steps for the construction of better and durable roads but nevertheless in any case the progress is not only very slow, but in some areas it cannot be even visibly seen making the patience of the common man reach the boiling point. Some of the roads of New Delhi and Delhi have not been part of any development plan and are as lamentable as they were many years ago..........

.........The task, no doubt, is gigantic not only because lots of issues involved; right from the stage of awarding the contracts for the relaying and maintenance of the roads, strict observance of the laid down norms under the CPWD manuals, certification by various accredited laboratories about the quality of the material used, life span of the re-laid roads, prompt repair of the re-laid roads by the same contractors, imposition of penalties and legal actions against the defaulting contractors, fixation of responsibility of the engineering and another staff of the authorities, design of the roads, technique

of digging of roads, coverage of drainage and cleaning of drainage, special measures to be adopted before the onset of rains and so on and so forth. Also, responsible for the present chaos and complete mess is multiplicity of various authorities responsible not only in the task of relaying and maintaining the roads but the various authorities who do not adhere to the laid down norms and keep digging and re-digging the roads."

Re-union of Pakistani Woman Made Possible by Court on EID

Separation from family is painful but adding to the woes is the forced separation on the ground of unnecessary legal and administrative technicalities. In the instant case HMJ Gambhir while sitting in Division Bench directed that a Pakistani woman, who has been languishing in a beggars' home, be released, saying she had lawfully married an Indian here in 1983 and allowed her to reunite with her family to celebrate Eid. In the case of, *Nuzhat Jahan* v. *Govt. of NCT of Delhi*, 2013 (7) AD (Del) 61 the Bench ordered for *Nuzhat Jahan's* release, by allowing the *habeas corpus* filed by her husband, for her release. The relevant excerpt of the said judgment is:

"Undeniably, we do not find any justification in detention of the petitioner in a solitary confinement in the Beggar's Home, Nirmal Chhaya Parisar, Delhi as persuasive when, indisputably, the petitioner had lawfully married Mohd. Gulfam, and was holding a valid passport and valid Long Term Visa. No doubt, the Pakistan authorities did not renew the passport of the petitioner and there is a possibility that on that account, the visa of the petitioner was also not renewed by the Indian Government, however the petitioner did take necessary steps to seek renewal of her passport and extension of her Long Term Visa. ....

We also direct the concerned authority that upon receiving any such application, the concerned authorities shall take a decision on the request of the petitioner within a period of three months from the date of receipt of the application. We further direct that depending upon the said decision of the concerned authorities on the said application of the petitioner for regularisation of her stay and further grant of Long Term Visa, the Ministry of Home Affairs shall also take a decision thereon, for the grant of Indian citizenship in terms of the Citizenship Act, 1985 and other guidelines, as are applicable.

In the light of the aforesaid view taken by us, we direct the release of the petitioner from the Beggar's Home, Nirmal Chhaya Parisar, Delhi, forthwith, considering the fact that the important Muslim festival 'Eid' is around the corner, so that the petitioner is able to celebrate such a pious and important festival with her family members, as it would be too asperous on our part to confine the petitioner in isolation, away from her husband, children and even grandchildren, in the Beggars Home on the joyous and much awaited feast of Eid. The said release of the petitioner shall be subject to the petitioner and her husband furnishing an undertaking before the DCP, Special Branch, Delhi, that they will not leave the country without prior permission from the office of the DCP, Special Branch, Delhi till the final decision is taken by the Government of India on the said Citizenship application of the petitioner. The petitioner and her husband are also directed to immediately communicate to the office of the concerned DCP, if they intend to change their residential address."

Registering of FIR – Whether Mandatory?

The canons of justice are violated in a twofold manner when there is a refusal to file an FIR for not only the criminal is allowed to escape but also the doors of justice are shut on the face of the victims and their families. In a recent study that was conducted on the 'Image of Police' in India it was observed and ridiculed that this malpractice of refusal to lodge a complaint is at an all time high. Justice Kailash Gambhir gave his views on the same much before the five-judge bench decision of the Apex Court was rendered. It is now a settled position of law that disciplinary action shall be initiated against those police officers who wrong those who have already been wronged.

In the case of *Radha* v. *State,* 2011 (179) DLT 810, the court entertained a petition filed by one Radha, whose brother was found dead on August 6, 2007, under mysterious circumstances in a waterlogged park in Rohini and she sought the filing of a First Information Report in respect of the charge of murder and probe against the suspect. Radha and her family made several complaints to police officers of different ranks between 2007 and 2008 but to no avail and a complaint before a magistrate also yielded no result. Such deplorable state of affairs is what is appalling, more so because we repose faith in the instrumentality of Police.

Justice Gambhir stressed on the necessity of setting the criminal machinery into motion in the following words:

"The 'First Information Report' sets into motion the process of criminal machinery. The Hon'ble Apex Court and various High Courts of the country through various authoritative legal pronouncements have time and again taken an unequivocal view that where a complaint is made to the police officer which discloses commission of a cognizable offence, it is the statutory duty of the police to register an FIR and then proceed to hold investigation in the complained offence, but unfortunately the voice of various

> *High Courts and even the Highest Court of the land has fallen on deaf ears of not only the lower officials but also of the rank of Joint Commissioner of Police, Additional Commissioner of Police and the top Cop of the Delhi Police as well. To give a reminder of the same to the Delhi police once again, it has become imperative to reiterate the dicta of law laid down by the Hon'ble Supreme Court through various pronouncements."*

He cleared the fallacy that registration of FIR mandates arrest, by segregating cases wherein arrest would lie. He observed herein:

> *"It is a misconception that the registration of an FIR must necessarily lead to an arrest of the suspect of the crime as it entirely depends on each case as there may be cases where the arrest of the accused maybe essential and others where the police may require more incriminating evidence for apprehending the accused. It is thus a settled law that mere registration of an FIR in every case may not result into arrest of a person accused of the offence. It would be useful to refer here to the recent pronouncement of the Apex Courts in* Siddharam Satlingappa Mhetre *v.* State of Maharashtra, *(2011) 1 SCC 694: AIR 2011 SC 312: 2011 AIR SCW 3813 where while laying down parameters for anticipatory bail the court regarding arrest held that:*
>
> > *129. In case the arrest is imperative, according to the facts of the case, in that event, the arresting officer must clearly record the reasons for the arrest of the accused before the arrest in the case diary, but in exceptional cases where it becomes imperative to arrest the accused immediately, the reasons be recorded in the case diary immediately after the arrest is made without loss of any time so that the court has an opportunity to properly consider the case for grant or refusal of bail in the light of reasons recorded by the arresting officer."*

He spoke of the cardinal duties that attach to the office of Police by holding that:

> *"Hence, in the given facts of the case, the police can always postpone the arrest of the person accused unless it is prima facie satisfied that the accused named in the complaint or the accused/suspect of a crime under the given circumstances cannot at all be involved in the commission of the crime or in a case where prompt action to arrest if not taken will result in jeopardizing or sabotaging the course of investigation. But certainly the police cannot postpone the registration of an FIR where the information laid by the complainant before it clearly discloses commission of a cognizable offence. The*

police is expected to take fair, impartial and sincere steps whenever any crime is committed as the prime function of the police is to protect the lives of the people and also to maintain the law and order situation to ensure a crime-free society. It would be useful here to refer to the observations of the Hon'ble High Court of Punjab & Haryana in the case of Amrik Singh v. State of Punjab, *1983 Cr LJ 1405: 1983 (10) Cr LT 416 where it was held as under:*

17. The duty of the police is to prevent and detect crime and to bring the accused to justice. Lord Denning, Master of the Rolls in his book titled "The Due Process of Law", 1980 Edn., in Chapter I of Part Three, has observed about the role of the police as follows:— "In safeguarding our freedoms, the police play a vital role. Society for its defence needs a well-led, well-trained and well-disciplined force of police whom it can trust; and enough of them to be able to prevent crime before it happens, or if it does happen, to detect it and bring the accused to justice. The police of course, must act properly. They must obey the rules of right conduct. They must not extort confessions by threats or promises. They must not search a man's house without authority. They must not use more force than the occasion warrants."

Hon'ble Justice Kailash Gambhir also spoke of the duties that enjoin upon an investigator during the course of investigation by holding that:

"The investigation in the present case had been tainted and aimed at to save the appellant and not to bring him to justice. Under the law the investigator is enjoined upon to unearth the crime and as soon as he receives the information about the crime, he is to proceed to the spot, ascertain the facts and circumstances of the case and arrest the suspected offender, collect the evidence relating to the commission of the offence, examine various persons including the accused, reduce their statements into writing, to search the places and take into possession the things considered necessary for the investigation and to be produced at the trial and then to form his opinion as to whether on the material collected any accused is to be placed before a Magistrate for commitment and to file a charge-sheet under section 173, Cr. P.C. In the nature of things, an investigator has to have and is clothed with many powers by the Jaw for the purpose of conducting investigation and where a murder has taken place, it is the duty of the investigator to send the special report to the illaqa Magistrate at once."

Justice Gambhir also denounced the conduct of the Delhi Police and spoke of the sacrosanct objectives of the Police. He held:

"Thus, the conduct of the concerned officials of the Delhi Police in the present case is highly deplorable and an astonishing spectacle was the action of the senior officers upto the rank of the Commissioner of Police who came out in defence of the shoddy inquiry instead of coming forward to rectify their reprehensive conduct of not registering an FIR in such a case involving murder of a young boy of 22 years. It is a harsh reality that despite numerous police reforms yet the common man shirks and hesitates to freely walk into the police station to lodge a complaint as he is still afraid and fearful that he will not be treated well and perhaps would be subjected to harassment for reporting any crime, which otherwise is his legitimate right. It is the notion that the police procedures are veiled, slow paced and uncertain in outcome which has further plummeted the public trust in the police. The Delhi police motto states "Citizens First" and a part of its Mission statement reads as:

"The objective of Delhi Police is to Uphold the law fairly and firmly; To prevent crime; to pursue and bring to justice those who break the law; To keep the peace in partnership with the community; To protect, help and reassure the people;......"

But these promising words seem to have no verisimilitude.

They seem so hollow especially in the present case, where they have whittled down to become nothing but a teasing mirage."

Since in the present case the petitioner and the entire family of the deceased are the hapless victims who not only had to pass through the galling and traumatic period due to the sudden death of their beloved but they were further forced to file one case after the other just for seeking the registration of a simple FIR into the alleged murder case, therefore, the cost of Rs. 2 lakh is imposed upon the Delhi Police for their illegal, contemptuous and defiant approach in not following the law of the land. The said amount shall be paid by the Delhi Police to the petitioner within a period of one month from the date of this order."

Inordinate Delay by the State in Filing Criminal Leave to Appeal against Order of Acquittal Denounced

Justice Gambhir while sitting in the Division Bench dealing with the subject of Criminal Leave to Appeals came across number of Criminal Leave to Appeals preferred by the State under section 378, Cr.P.C. much beyond the prescribed period of limitation. Taking a very strong view of such lackadaisical approach on the part of the State the Division Bench of Justice Gambhir in the case of *State* v. *Lal Bahadur*, Crl. L.P. 413/2012 gave various directions to the Government of NCT of Delhi and Commissioner of Police so as to devise a proper mechanism to streamline the system in filing such leave petitions by the State within the prescribed period of limitation and the direction given by the Division Bench could result in the introduction of a comprehensive procedure by the Home Department of Government of NCT of Delhi and the Commissioner of Police and as a result thereof now hardly any delay takes place in the filing of such leave to appeals by the State. Relevant excerpts are as under:

> *"In this batch of Crl. Leave Petitions preferred by the State, there is a delay on the part of the State in filing the petitions. In some of these cases, the state has already filed affidavits and even additional affidavits giving reasons for the delay in filing the respective petitions. In the present case, the delay is for 939 days and as per the affidavit filed by Mr. Sanjay Kumar, Additional Commissioner of Police, the file remained pending with the Inspector ATO Rajesh Johri for a period of 24 months. In the other connected matters, delay period ranges from 522 days (as in the case of State* v. *Neeraj) to the extent of more than 1381 days (as in the case of State* v. *Wajid). In some of the cases the State has not even filed an affidavit. Where the requisite affidavits have not been filed by the State, let the same be filed by the State through Dy. Commissioner of Police of the concerned district explaining the delay in filing such petitions.*
>
> *In State* v. *Surender @ Sunder,* Crl. L.P. 638/2013, *the Commissioner of Police has filed his own affidavit taking a view that steps are being taken to devise a proper mechanism to streamline the system in filing such leave petitions within the prescribed period of limitation and the direction has been given to the Commissioner of Police to place on record the newly devised mechanism for curbing such delays. In the said case, Commissioner of Police has also issued displeasure notices to the three officers comprising of one DCP and two Additional DCPs of the concerned District besides that the departmental action has also been directed against the concerned SHO and the Additional SHO."*

In compliance with the directions given by Justice Gambhir, the Commissioner of Police filed an affidavit of compliance and apprised the Court that now the system is in place and inquiries have been initiated against the erring police officials, the relevant excerpt of which is as under:

> *"The Commissioner of Police has filed his affidavit in compliance with the direction given by this Court vide orders dated 7th February, 2014. In the affidavit Commissioner of Police has stated that after issuance of the circular dated 26-3-2014 by the Government of NCT of Delhi and circular dated 26-3-2014 issued by the Special*

Commissioner of Police Law and Order now the comprehensive procedure is in place and reoccurrence of any such situation of delay in filing petitions/appeals, as have arisen in these matters would be obviated. The Commissioner has further stated that adequate checks and responsibility has been set out in the said circulars to ensure filing of petitions/appeals within the period of limitation. It has also been stated that in 13 cases the Joint Commissioners of Police are conducting enquiries against the erring police officials, who are found responsible in causing exorbitant delays in filing the appeals against the orders of the acquittal."

In response to the said affidavit Justice Gambhir directed the commissioner of Police to file an affidavit stating the Departmental action taken against the erring police officials:

"Considering the fact that the enquiry has been conducted in 13 Criminal Leave Petitions, whereas the similar enquiries are required to be conducted in all other cases of delay, let the Joint Commissioners of Police conduct enquiry in all the cases which are fixed before this Bench. A compliance affidavit shall be filed by the Commissioner of Police within a period of eight weeks. In the affidavit to be filed by the Commissioner of Police it shall be clearly spelled out about the departmental action being taken against the erring police officials in the said 13 cases and the other cases of delay listed before this Bench.

We make it clear that it is only in those cases where the delay on the part of any erring police official irrespective of his rank is inordinate and unreasonable and also where such delay is found to be unjustified and unexplainable by the erring official, the Commissioner of Police shall proceed to conduct an enquiry against the erring police official and not in other cases where the Commissioner finds that there is no undue delay and explanation given by the erring official is found satisfactory. However, it is also made clear that in the affidavit to be filed by the Commissioner of Police, it will have to be spelt out that what reasons have been given by the concerned police official for the delay and on what basis Commissioner of Police/Joint Commissioner of Police felt satisfied finding the ground to be justified for the delay."

Justice Gambhir's prime objective in dealing with this batch matter was to put the entire mechanism in place so that no delay takes place on the part of the State in filing the appeal as inordinate delay on the part of state in deserving cases put the offender to an advantageous position. Justice Gambhir also observed that Police Officials are doing arduous jobs much beyond their duty hours, therefore, he directed the

Commissioner of Police to take liberal view against the police officials against whom actions had been initiated. While arguing this matter, the Senior counsel for the State submitted that now a complete mechanism has been devised for filing State leave to appeal against order of acquittal within the prescribed period of limitation and wherever delay takes place appropriate action shall be taken against delinquent officials. The relevant excerpts are:

> *"An affidavit has been filed by the Commissioner of Police in compliance with the directions given by this Court vide order dated 29-4-2014. In the affidavit, it has been explained that a copy of the order dated 29-4-2014 passed by this Court was sent to all the concerned Joint Commissioners of Police/Ranges and Special Branch, Delhi for meticulous compliance of the said directions* **vide** *Delhi Police Headquarters U.O. letter No. 2/Misc./14/HC/3443-49/Court Cell (DA-1)/C and T Branch/PHQ dated 20-5-2014. A copy of the said order was also forwarded to the Commissioner of Police. The Joint Commissioners of Police/Ranges, Special Branch, Delhi had conducted the necessary enquiries into the cause of delay in filing these leave to appeals by the State in respect of 33 Criminal Leave Petitions pending adjudication before this Court and the details of all the enquiries, case wise have been detailed in this affidavit. These 33 Criminal Leave Petitions are in addition to the 13 Criminal Leave Petitions details of which have been annexed in Annexure R-2 of the present affidavit. As per the details given in this affidavit filed by the Commissioner of Police, a departmental action has already been initiated against the erring/delinquent police officials in over 15 cases, where delay in filing the criminal leave petitions was primarily on the part of the concerned police officers/officials. In rest of the cases delay was on the part of the other agencies such as Prosecution Branch, Law Department/Govt. of NCT of Delhi and in some cases the delay was on the part of the concerned Standing Counsel (Criminal)/Prosecutors. As per the list of other 13 Criminal Leave Petitions, the details of which have been given in Annexure R-2 of the affidavit debarring two cases, i.e., Criminal Leave Petition Nos. 600/2013 and 428/2012, in rest of the cases departmental action has been initiated against the erring/delinquent police officials.*
>
> *Mr. Siddharth Luthra, the learned Sr. Counsel appearing for the Delhi Police submits that at present, a system is in place pursuant to the directions given by this Court vide order dated 14-2-2014 in Criminal Leave Petition No. 638/2013* (State v. Surender @ Sunder) *whereafter the necessary orders were passed by the Special Commissioner of Police, L and O, Delhi vide Circular dated*

26-3-2014 and vide Office Order dated 26-3-2014 by the Govt. of NCT of Delhi, Home (Police-II). He also submits that now a complete mechanism has been devised for filing State leave to appeal against the order of acquittal within the period of limitation or also where the State seeks to challenge an order on sentence passed by the learned Trial Court and wherever the delay takes place, appropriate action will be taken against the delinquent/erring officials. The learned Senior Counsel also submits that both the said Circulars have been placed on record in Criminal Leave Petition No. 638/2013 and after issuance of the said two circulars, the experience has been that the State leave to appeals are being preferred within the time period of limitation.

Various directions were given by this Court in Criminal Leave Petition Nos. 638/2013 and 413/2012 and other such petitions which came under consideration before this Court, the need for the same arose because of the fact that a large number of cases in which Criminal Leave Petitions were being preferred by the State under section 378, Cr.P.C. same were much beyond the prescribed period of limitation. In some of the cases, delay was as inordinate as more than 1000 days. The State has been conferred with a statutory right to file an appeal to challenge an order of acquittal under section 378, Cr.P.C. This right, later through amendment introduced by Act 5 in 2009 w.e.f. 31-12-2009 in section 372, Cr.P.C. has also been given to the victim/complainant to prefer an appeal to challenge an order of acquittal or lesser sentence or imposing inadequate compensation. However, with regard to the decision as to where such appeal to challenge an order of acquittal should be filed, is vested with the State Machinery which includes the Delhi Police and this process starts from the concerned Prosecutor who handles the matter before the learned Trial Court and the same passes various stages and then finally reaches to the office of the Standing Counsel (Criminal) or Public Prosecutors for filing an appeal. This entire procedure is administrative in nature. Till the issuance of office order dated 26-3-2014 and Circular dated 26-3-2014 which came into effect pursuant to the directions given by this Court in Criminal Leave Petition No. 638/2013, there was no proper mechanism in place to ensure that such appeals are filed within the prescribed period of limitation. When the system itself was not in place, it often, resulted into inaction, lapses, negligence and in some cases taking advantages of such system, the officers involved deliberately caused inordinate and undue delays. The prime objective of the Court in giving directions in such cases was to put the entire mechanism in place so that in future no delay takes place in such kind of cases. Inordinate or unexplained delay even on the part of the State in a given fact situation of the case creates a valuable right in the other party. Non-filing of appeals by the State in deserving cases or delay in filing of the appeal by the State can put the offender to an advantageous position.

.... Considering the fact that now the Home Department of Government of NCT of Delhi, Delhi Police and Prosecution Branch have streamlined the entire procedure and devised a full proof mechanism for timely filing of the State appeals and also the fact that wherever a delay takes place without any sufficient reasons, stern action will be taken against the erring/delinquent officials, we need not pass any further direction in these matters. Another aspect which is equally important, on which we are inclined to give certain directions, concerns the disciplinary action initiated by the Disciplinary Authority against the erring police officials and in some of the cases such departmental action has resulted in the passing of punishment orders including that of censure orders. On perusal of the details placed on record regarding all these 46 cases, we find that in many cases delay has taken place on the part of agencies other than the police and this Court has not recommended any action against the officers who were heading these agencies. We also find that the action by the Disciplinary Authority have been initiated only out of 46 cases while there may be many more cases where lapses either on the part of the police officials or other agencies can be more serious. Another glaring fact which we find is that the actions have been mostly recommended or initiated against the officials below the rank of DCP although every District is headed by the DCP. We cannot lose sight of the fact that at time these officials are doing arduous jobs much beyond their duty hours. Looking into all these circumstances, we hereby give the following directions:

i. Commissioner of Police or Disciplinary Authority shall take a liberal view against the police officials against whom show cause notices for censure or other actions have been initiated or even sought to be initiated.

ii. Wherever the departmental actions have been culminated into passing an order of punishment, Disciplinary Authority shall revisit their order to award a lesser punishment as they deem fit in the circumstances.

iii. Copy of this order be made available to all the officials against whom departmental actions have already been taken or is under contemplation."

CHAPTER 4

MOTOR ACCIDENTS AND CLAIMS

Lawyers Representing the Claimants, owe a Special Responsibility, not only Legal but also Moral, to take Prompt and Urgent Steps at the Service Stage and then at the Evidence Stage

The short issue that came up before Justice Gambhir in the case of *Hukum Singh* v. *Shri Avdesh Singh,* 2011 (121) DRJ 735 was as to whether the order of the Tribunal dismissing the claim petition filed by the appellant can be justified simply because the appellant had failed to adduce his evidence even after taking three dates in this regard. Counsel for the appellant contends that the appellant could not adduce the evidence before the Tribunal as he had applied to obtain certified copy of the criminal court record, but the same were not made available by the Copying agency of the Distt. & Sessions Judge. Counsel therefore, contends that there were bona fide reasons for not adducing the evidence before the Tribunal.

Justice Gambhir taking note of the issue at hand held that lawyers representing the claimants owe a special responsibility not only legal but moral also to take prompt and urgent steps at the service stage and then at the evidence stage. Relevant para of which is:

> *"Indisputably, it is an unfortunate situation that the claim petitions filed by the claimants invariably gets delayed either at the service stage or at the evidence stage due to fault of the either counsel representing the claimants or claimants themselves. This unnecessary delay which takes place adversely affects the insurance companies as they are made liable to pay the interest even for the period of delay caused in the matter due to the sole negligence of the claimants or their counsel. Such delay also affects the claimants themselves as the final disposal of the case gets delayed and they get deprived of the award amount at an early stage. In such scenario, the lawyers representing the claimants owe a special responsibility not only legal but moral also to take prompt and urgent steps at the service stage and then at the evidence stage so that agony of the victims of the accidents and dependent members is not prolonged. This would not only help speedy disposal of the cases fixed before the Tribunal but*

would also be beneficial to the claimants who will be able to get the compensation amount with promptness."

Drunkard Driver is no less than a Live Human Bomb; Need for a Scientific Investigation and Guidelines to Avoid Road Accidents and Role of Media

Justice Gambhir believes in the fundamentals of a good judgment, and he is of the firm belief that judgments should not just involve legal jargon, but should also be able to touch a chord, to move people to ponder and eventually make the society a better place to live. He likes to give out social messages and/or directions and guidelines to the actors/ stakeholders in the judicial system, public at large, government agencies and even the media. *Sanjeev Nanda* v. *The State,* Crl. Appeal No. 807/2008 is a much talked about decision, where Justice Gambhir expatiated on a number of issues; observations were made on the need for scientific investigation; Guidelines to avoid road accidents; explained the Role of Media and addressed the growing menace of drunken driving & road traffic accident[1] and while doing so he held:

1. *"The miracle is not to fly in air or to travel to the moon, but to walk on the earth", says a Chinese proverb.*

The increase in vehicular traffic along with the population of Delhi has grown much faster since the time Maruti Company has flooded the market with their brand of cars for the middle class of the society. Although the capital of the country is dominated by the middle and lower class, but the presence of rich and affluent is no less visible when one looks at the roads of Delhi to find large number of high class luxurious cars, including the Mercedes and BMWs. The traditional mode of travelling by tangas, bicycles, rickshaws, two wheelers is coming to gradual extinct except in the interiors of some localities.

Except for a few hours between midnight to dawn, one cannot see even a patch of earth but vehicles and vehicles either running or stranded in traffic jams on Delhi roads. This ever increasing vehicular explosion in traffic is due to the rapid increase of human population primarily due to continuous migration of people in search of their livelihood from adjoining states and from far flung areas. In this unmanageable crowd, what we have lost is humanity, morals, our age old rich culture, tradition, ethos and path of truthfulness and righteousness as shown to us by saints and scriptures. Of all the maladies afflicting India, the malady of inner decay reigns supreme. There is a weakening of our moral fibre and ethical values. Corruption, red tapism, callousness, casualness and crumbling moralities dominate our public life instead of much needed culture of care, compassion, empathy, and catholicity.

Drunken driving, insensitivity and apathy of the Government for public safety on roads; poor, faulty and ill equipped police investigation; growing interference of media in criminal trials; media hype; hostile and dishonest witnesses; falling standards of legal profession, filthy use of money power by rich and mighty; unholy nexus between defense counsel and State appointed Special Public Prosecutors are some of the issues that cropped up in this infamous case known as the BMW case.

He stressed on the need for scientific inputs and held "Scientific inputs help the investigators in solving a number of cases of crime. The latest state-of-the-art equipments are the need of the hour considering the escalating rates of acquittal in India due to faulty and defective investigation.

With the advancement in science and technology, it is high time that the novel & scientific methods of investigation by a team of well-trained experts and not merely through an ill equipped overburdened and constrained team of Investigating Officers...

...Today, India is making a mark in the world map due to myriad reasons but the internal situation of the country when it comes to public safety is gloomy. It is high time that government should become sensitive to the plight of the citizens and come up with stringent laws and better planning to curb

Contd. on next page

"........... Except for a few hours between midnight to dawn, one cannot see even a patch of earth but vehicles and vehicles either running or stranded in traffic jams on Delhi roads. This ever increasing vehicular explosion in traffic is due to the rapid increase of human population primarily due to continuous migration of people in search of their livelihood from adjoining states and from far flung areas. In this unmanageable crowd, what we have lost is humanity, morals, our age old rich culture, tradition, ethos and path of truthfulness and righteousness as shown to us by saints and scriptures. Of all the maladies afflicting India, the malady of inner decay reigns supreme. There is a weakening of our moral fibre and ethical values. Corruption, red tapism, callousness, casualness and crumbling moralities dominate our public life instead of much needed culture of care, compassion, empathy, and catholicity.

.... Drunken driving, insensitivity and apathy of the Government for public safety on roads; poor, faulty and ill equipped police investigation; growing interference of media in criminal trials; media hype; hostile and dishonest witnesses; falling standards of legal profession, filthy use of money power by rich and mighty;

Contd. *from previous page*

drunken driving and such other menaces in the society which are reasons for fear in the mind of the pedestrians, each day, when they move out of their homes, whether they would safely reach home. In this regard, following guidelines are recommended:—

1. *Proper and strict implementation of the excise laws for minimum age for consumption of liquor;*
2. *Proper lights on the streets and better maintenance of roads so as to reduce occurrence of any kind of accidents;*
3. *Improvement in the methods of investigation so as to make it more scientific.*
4. *To introduce and implement the system of Native Citizen cards as being talked about, maintain complete data of citizens as the country which will facilitate checking of persons and their records.*
5. *Installation of CCTV cameras on major roads.*
6. *Random checking by the police to prevent the menace of drunken driving specially near pubs, five star hostels, discos etc.*

While deciding the present case, he also deliberated on the role of media especially in criminal trials. "No doubt the media has an important role in disseminating information, creating public opinion in matters which are of vital concern to the society, exposing misdeeds of high and mighty but it is being exceedingly felt that while doing so in some cases particularly relating to crime and punishment, the media is going over board. Many a times, an accused who is yet to be tried and convicted, is pronounced guilty by the media by referring to such evidence which is not even admissible in evidence, such as, confessional statements made before police officers. The various channels of electronic media in order to outdo each other repeats an incident ad nauseam little realising that it has the effect of generating public opinion against the culprit even before he is found guilty. Let not the media forget that judges are also humans and like any other human sometimes even they can err because of the hype created in relation to a particular incident. Like all other wings of our democratic set up such as executive, judiciary and legislature who are supposed to remain within their bounds, Media, which is the fourth estate, must also not cross the "Laxman Rekha". If it abides by this principle, it will be doing more good to the society and to the administration of justice.", he said.

unholy nexus between defence counsel and State appointed Special Public Prosecutors are some of the issues that cropped up in this infamous case known as the BMW case.

.... It is no time for slumber. It is high time that we wake up and act for the protection of the citizens who appear before the courts to testify so as to render a helping hand in the dispensation of justice. Best Bakery case, Jessica Lal murder case and many other like cases, if repeated, would shatter the strength and credibility of our criminal justice system. Every country is expected to make laws to meet the situations prevalent in that country. However, there is nothing wrong, rather it is wise, in imbibing the spirit shown by other countries in the matter of witness protection. No nation can afford to expose its righteous and morally elated citizens to the peril of being haunted or harassed by anti social elements, for the simple reason that they testified the truth in a court of law. If the State continues to turn a blind eye to the ground realties, the plight of an honest witness will be pathetic and calamitous. Not only the honest witnesses need full protection of the State, but at the same time dishonest witnesses need to be dealt with an iron hand. No leniency and indulgence should be shown to such a witness who with impunity has the audacity to utter falsehood after taking oath. Such a witness derails the trial which can result in miscarriage of justice and consequently bring miseries to victim of crime. Present is not the only case where witness has adduced false evidence in misleading the Court and thus causing interference in the due discharge of justice. This evil of perjury has assumed alarming proportions in cases depending on oral evidence and in order to deal with this menace effectively in a given case the Courts must take re-course to section 340 Cr.P.C. (summary procedure for trial for giving false evidence) more frequently. Therefore, the State must give serious thought to protect the interest of witnesses and to introduce suitable legislation in this regard at the earliest so that the witnesses are not discouraged to come forward to give evidence for fear of harassment, humiliation and danger to their lives.

.... Indisputably, one's heart goes out, the way the accident had occurred resulting into piercing the body parts of some of the innocent victims. At the time of passing interim order, this Court had observed that the site looked like a scene of bomb blast, had it not known that the occurrence was as a result of accident involving a car. Lot many deaths take place in various metropolitan cities in our country due to the accidents caused by the drunken drivers and in most of the cases the spoilt brats of rich families are involved.

The necessary amendment in the Indian Penal Code and the Motor Vehicles Act is the only solution as suggested by the Parliamentary Standing Committee on transport, tourism and culture in its 139th Report on the Motor Vehicles (Amendment) Bill, 2007 to effectively deal with this growing menace of drunken driving, and in the absence of any proper legislation in the place, neither the prosecution nor the courts should venture to convert the accident cases resulting into deaths from section 304A of IPC to section 304(I) or (II) of IPC unless the fact situation clearly proves intention or knowledge on the part of the accused as held by the Apex Court in the case of Shankar Narayan Bhadolkar's case (supra). So long as the law is not suitably amended, the State should take stringent measures to deter drunken driving, but ultimately this menace can be curbed only by means of legislation.

.... At this juncture, it is worthwhile to discuss the role of prosecution and the importance and need for scientific investigation.

Every man is presumed to be innocent until he is proved guilty. This is the cardinal principal of criminal law. In recognition of this right of the accused the burden of establishing the charge against the accused is placed on the prosecution.

Courts have quite often observed that though they are convinced that the accused is guilty but they have to acquit him by giving benefit of doubt due to failure of the investigators in properly conducting the investigation.

The investigation of a criminal case, however good and painstaking it may be, will be rendered fruitless, if the prosecution machinery is indifferent or inefficient. One of the well-known causes for the failure of a large number of prosecutions is the poor, faulty and unscientific investigation.

Although the Public Prosecutors are appointed by the State, the prosecutor's sole aim is not to seek a conviction. A number of court judgments have emphasized that the Prosecutor is a 'minister of justice' who should place before the court all evidence in the Prosecutor's possession, whether in favour of or against the accused. This is seen as proper prosecution, as opposed to single-minded persecution in seeking a conviction regardless of the evidence.

Investigation and prosecution are two different facets in the administration of criminal justice. The role of a Public Prosecutor is inside the court, whereas investigation is outside the court. Normally, the role of a Public Prosecutor commences after the investigating agency presents the case in the court on culmination of investigation. Its exception is that the Public Prosecutor may have to deal with bail applications moved by the parties concerned at any stage. Involving the Public Prosecutor in investigation is injudicious as well as pernicious in law.

.... Since our country follows the adversarial system of criminal justice, it is essential for bringing the culprits to the books that the prosecution is strong and well fed by the investigating agencies.

Police and other investigating agencies are at the heart of the criminal justice system of India. The foundation for the Criminal Justice System is the investigation by the police. When an offence committed is brought to the notice of the police, it is their responsibility to investigate into the matter to find out who has committed the offence, ascertain the facts and circumstances relevant to the crime and to collect the evidence, oral or circumstantial, which is necessary to prove the case in the court. The success or failure of the case depends entirely on the work of the investigating officer.

Scientific inputs help the investigators in solving a number of cases of crime. The latest state-of-the-art equipments are the need of the hour considering the escalating rates of acquittal in India due to faulty and defective investigation. In plethora of cases, the Hon'ble Apex Court has pointed out the need for scientific investigation by the investigating agency and deprecated the practice of failure on the part of the investigating agencies in collecting relevant evidence resulting in the acquittal of the accused due to inefficient and untrained Investigating Officers, who take the investigation in a very casual, careless and traditional manner.

With the advancement in science and technology, it is high time that the novel & scientific methods of investigation by a team of well-trained experts and not merely through an ill equipped overburdened and constrained team of Investigating Officers."

While dealing with Crl. M.B. No. 1232/2008 in the same case, where the petitioner sought suspension of his sentence during the pendency of the appeal preferred by him sir refused to grant bail to him, as he was convicted for running down six persons while driving his BMW in an inebriated state almost a decade ago, whilst doing so he held:

"......... I would like to touch upon the social ill of drunken driving. Alcohol has been successful in making a distinct niche in daily lives of humans since the centuries of the recorded history. Alcohol has been found to play a major role in social ills in almost all countries across the world, but foremost amongst the ills produced by alcohol

is its role in traffic crashes. It is a stark reality of every metropolitan city where lot of deaths take place due to the megalomaniacs in drivers' seat driving the vehicle while venturing on the road in inebriated state. The spectacular increase in the number of motor vehicles has created a major social problem more particularly when large number of road accidents take place due to excessive intake of alcohol endangering the precious lives of citizens mostly belonging to poor strata of society. It is a matter of common knowledge that excessive intake of alcohol adversely affects the sensory organs and also sometimes leads to blurring of vision, decrease of sense of equilibrium, impairs ability to judge and take spontaneous, rational and logical decision. The drunkard driver not only risks his life but endangers the lives of others as well. Such a drunkard driver is no less than a live human bomb prepared to blast himself and innocent people on roads and pavements including friends and relatives riding in his vehicle. In the light of the aforesaid, this court is of the view that it is high-time that legislature undertakes a re-look at the present laws so as to prevent drunken driving which is taking toll of precious human lives".

Practice of Lawyers Soliciting Filing Claim Petitions in Cases of Motor Accidents Deprecated

The present case dealt with the sheer avarice that lawyers can showcase, and how two lawyers can resort to filing two separate claim petitions arising out of the same accident, get the grieving family members to sign the petitions even before they successfully recuperate from the trauma the loss of a kin has cast in their lives, by luring and promising to get them hefty compensations.

HMJ Kailash Gambhir in the case of *Baby Rinki* v. *Surender Singh*, 2008 (147) DLT 660 unmasked the sordid conduct of two lawyers, who succeeded in getting two separate claim petitions signed from the widow of the deceased and a mother of three minor children and went onto observe:

> *"Before parting with the present case, I strongly deprecate the practice of some unscrupulous lawyers who against all legal ethics, approach the family members of the victims of the accident or the victim themselves so as to solicit filing the claim petitions on their behalf. The unwary citizens sometimes get entrapped, when alluring offers of grant of hefty compensation amount is assured by such advocates that too at that point of time when the family members of the victims are still under the state of shock and are not able to form a rational opinion of taking a particular decision.*

To curb this menace prevailing amongst handful of lawyers who ultimately become instrumental to defame the entire legal profession, the Bar Council of Delhi, a statutory body of lawyers, is requested to issue proper guidelines and statutory warnings in the case of any lawyer found indulging into such illegal and unethical act of soliciting a compensation case. The Delhi Legal Advisory Board is also directed to carry out some publication especially in Hindi newspapers educating the public not to fall prey at the hands of such unscrupulous lawyers."

Urbanisation, Industrialisation, Vehicular Accidents and Role of Insurance Companies

Justice Gambhir by way of the instant judgment famously remarked that, *"the life of a human is not cheaper than a NANO* **car".** With the advent of urbanisation and industrialisation, there has been an alarming rise in the number of road accidents. As if the agony of losing a dear one isn't enough, the families of the deceased have to undergo a lot of harassment from the unfortunate death till the award of compensation. Shifting his focus to the serious indifference and apathy, which makes the lives of the family members of the deceased even worse, he threw light on the irony of this country, where the insurance companies are overzealous about solving and settling the claims of the insured vehicles, but don't give a second thought for resolving the miseries of the poor victims. He was of the view that no pains are taken by these insurance companies to compensate the victims of the accidents in the injury cases or to the dependent family members in fatal accident cases. Understanding the importance of providing immediate succour to the family of the deceased, Justice Gambhir noted that insurance companies should make a serious endeavour to settle the compensation cases preferably at pre-litigation stage and if not at pre-litigation then at least at the earliest possible stage before the Claims Tribunals and in any case at the time of passing of the interim award at least in those cases where there is an admitted liability of the insurer to pay the compensation amount. Excerpts from the judgment in the case of *Sh. Narinder Bishal* v. *Sh. Rambir Singh,* 2008 (5) AD (Del) 178 are as follows:

"With the massive progress in urbanisation and industrialisation in the recent times, we have switched from fast to faster vehicular traffic which has come as a boon to many and as a bane to some. There has been an acceleration in automobile traffic, which concomitantly has resulted in escalating statics of motor vehicular accidents culminating in to casualties of human lives. There has been an alarming increase in the road accidents. Accidents on Indian roads are perhaps the second highest in the world and about ninety six thousand people

were killed in road accidents in the year 2005 itself. As per the recent data released by Delhi Police, a total of 8270 accidents had occurred in the capital in the year 2006, in which about 2050 people were killed.

The blue line buses are the major killers as far as Delhi is concerned. These killer blue line buses have played havoc on Delhi roads and every year many precious lives get sacrificed by these blue line buses who have unleashed a kind of death drive putting in danger the lives of delhiites on the roads of the capital. Death of any person in a family torments and shatters the entire family more particularly when it is death of a sole bread winner. No amount of compensation can bring back the family to the same position. The victims of accident and their family members not only undergo the traumatized and harrowing experience of losing a family member but also they are made to suffer greatest humiliation and embarrassment right from mortuary till the award of compensation. The apathy and insensitivity of various government and other agencies involved in the process instead of lending a helping hand place all sorts of hindrances to make the life of victims and their families worst and miserable. It is a great irony in this country that the insurance companies are prompt in settling the claims of the insured vehicles for its damage but create all sorts of obstructions and bottlenecks in settling the claims of victims of the accidents. The precious life of a human being is of little concern in comparison to settlement of a claim for the damaged motor vehicle in the estimation of these insurance companies. On reporting damage to a vehicle, immediate steps are initiated by the insurance companies to appoint an investigator/surveyor and photographer etc., for assessing the damage caused to the vehicle and practically no time is lost to get the vehicle repaired and restore the same to original condition. The insurance companies have tied up arrangements with various car manufacturers and the leading auto workshops to help out the insured for immediate delivery of the vehicle after the same is met with an accident. Atrociously, no similar pains are taken by these insurance companies to compensate the victims of the accidents in the injury cases or to the dependent family members in fatal accident cases.

....

In this scenario, the Court is of the opinion that insurance companies should make a serious endeavour to settle the compensation cases preferably at pre-litigation stage and if not at pre-litigation then at least at the earliest possible stage before the Claims Tribunals and in any case at the time of passing of the interim award at least in those cases where there is an admitted liability of the insurer to pay the compensation amount. The payment of compensation amount can be made tentatively to the claimants taking in view the broad legal principles settled by the Apex Court and High Courts. The realities of life cannot be overlooked. The victims of accident and their family members should not be made to wait for the compensation amount to reach after spending long years in courts, making them vulnerable to come under heavy debts for meeting day to day expenses of life. This exercise by the insurance companies will not only provide speedy justice to the victims and dependent family members of the victims of the road accidents but will also considerably help the insurance companies to save millions of rupees which gets paid by these companies due to the accumulation of interest amount on the compensation amount to be ultimately awarded by the Tribunal due to time consuming trials before MACT courts. Such payment of compensation at the early stage would also be of immense help to the victims of the accidents, especially, in those cases where the life of a lone breadwinner is lost. This court hope and trust that all the insurance companies shall immediately take suitable steps in this direction so as to provide immediate succour to the dependent family members of the deceased or the victims of the accident in the same manner as they swung into action to settle the claims in respect of the damaged vehicles. The MACT Tribunals are also directed to ascertain from the insurance companies through their respective counsels at the first available opportunity as to whether the insurance companies are ready and willing to pay some reasonable amount of compensation tentatively as per their own assessment in all those cases of admitted liability and then take on record the response given by the insurance companies to such a query of the MACT court. In any event, life of a human being is not cheaper than a 'Nano' car. In any given case where concerned officials of these insurance companies do not initiate action in this direction, then suitable explanation may be called for by the high-ups of the same company or by its regulating authority **i.e.** *Insurance Regulatory & Development Authority, as non payment of legitimate compensation amount at the initial stage will ultimately unnecessarily burden the company to pay interest amount for the entire trial period."*

CHAPTER 5

CIVIL MISCELLANEOUS

Self Effacing Parents: Ungrateful Kin!

The family tree being hit at its very root and part by part falling in the Courtrooms as a sorry state of affairs has become the norm. The increasing trend of litigation amongst blood relations has marred the very fundamentals of an ideal Indian family, which was once known for its togetherness and oneness and judgment in the case of *K.D. Mathpal* v. *State,* 2006 (91) DRJ 406 is a testament to that. He felt that there is a grave need for this bitterness to be dissuaded and the lawyers can play an active role in this regard. Justice Gambhir laid emphasis on the sacrosanct and revered status that parents always held in our society which of late is going down the drain. He stressed that the moral values which we pride ourselves on and hold close to our hearts are fast diminishing, and held as under:

> *"It is most unfortunate that for the past few years there is manifold increase in the litigation amongst the blood relations. The father who once must have derived utmost pleasure, happiness and joy taking his own small child in his lap or giving a ride on his shoulder or on his back, now feels the same child, when grows-up becoming a trespasser in his house. Same may be the position with the mother who must have enjoyed every moment of her life on becoming a mother and even after the child is born in the family. Now, she also considers the same child as trespasser in the house and a subject of hatred. Why such a situation has arisen and who is responsible for this? Nobody is oblivious of the fact that with the fast deterioration in moral values in the society the children are not giving due respect to their own parents and elders which they deserve. Parents have high hopes from their children, especially, from the sons, at the time of their advanced age. It is an irony of fate when the parents need utmost care and attention, they are neglected and discarded by their own blood. The grievance made by the petitioner in the present case may or may not be correct as there are counter-allegations made by the son and his wife as well, respondents ...... of harassment at the hands of the petitioner and the eldest son,.... The respondents ...... in their counter-reply have also stated that ......he had received*

serious injuries on his head when a pipe blow was given by the petitioner and he was taken to Lal Bahadur Hospital, Khichripur, New Delhi. It is, thus, evident that there are allegations and counter-allegations between the petitioner and his eldest son on one side and the youngest son........and his wife on the other side and once the criminal process starts it is bound to result in cross criminal cases amongst the members of the same family which will further create embitterness, hostility and acrimony amongst blood relations. We, thus, feel that it is the solemn duty of the Courts to see that in the ever increasing disputes amongst the family members, due care and caution is taken so that there is no misuse and abuse of process of the criminal law. The lawyers being the officers of the Court also must discharge their noble duty of putting every endeavour to dissuade such clients from launching any sort of frivolous litigation against their kith and kins or blood relatives."

Advocate cannot Act in Dual Capacity that of a Constituted Attorney and an Advocate

The profits steering this profession has made the lawyers comprise on various grounds and one such is the trend of advocates donning various hats *viz.* that of constituted attorney and an advocate at the same time, which amounts to professional misconduct. The legal profession is growing by leaps and bounds and professional misconduct by the officers of the court would taint the very system. Justice Gambhir while deciding the case of *Baker Oil Tools (India) Pvt. Ltd.* v. *Baker Hughes Ltd.*, 2011 (47) PTC 296 remarked that, foreign companies and firms must respect the laws of this land and that the solicitors and law firms are equally not expected to discharge their duties as clients for these foreign companies/ firms. Relevant paragraphs of which are:

"In the wake of globalization and increasing international trade, India has become one of the biggest commercial hubs which has consequently led to a spurt in the volume of litigation in the country, making the Indian legal fraternity a much sought after lot. It is undoubtedly a golden period for the lawyers and law firms in India which are being engaged by the foreign companies and multinationals, but at the same time it has but brought an insalubrious trend, that of the lawyers wearing two hats; of an attorney and of a client at the same time. The Advocates Act, 1961 and The Bar Council of India Rules prescribe rules for professional conduct and ethics for lawyers. Rule 13 of the Bar council of India states that:

"13. An Advocate should not accept a brief or appear in a case in which he has reason to believe that he will be a witness, and if

being engaged in a case, it becomes apparent that he is a witness on a material question of fact, he should not continue to appear as an advocate if he can retire without jeopardizing his client's interest."

Thus as is manifest from the said rule, it would be a professional misconduct if a lawyer were to don two hats at the same time. However not only that, the partnership firms have a hurdle for acting in the said two capacities even under the Partnership Act, as every partner in a partnership firm is an agent of another and if one were to be acting as an advocate for a client, the rest would also be in the same capacity by virtue of agency and the same would be the situation in case of a an advocate acting as a client. However, it cannot be forgotten by any who has ever been graced with the honour of wearing the robe that the lawyer is first an officer of the court and his prime duty is to assist the court in the administration of justice. The rules of conduct as per the Bar Council of India Rules may act as a guardian angel for ensuring the moral conduct of the lawyers but the legacy of the traditions of the Bar cannot be bedaubed by a few for the lucre of commercial gains. A lawyer cannot forget that this is called a noble profession not only because by virtue of this he enjoys an aristocratic position in the society but also because it obligates him to be worthy of the confidence of the community in him as a vehicle of achieving justice. The rules of conduct of this profession with its ever expanding horizons are although governed by the Bar Council of India Rules but more by the rich traditions of the Bar and by the cannons of conscience of the members of the calling of justice of being the Samaritans of the society. Thus the foreign companies and firms must respect the laws of this land and the solicitors and law firms are equally not expected to discharge their duties as clients for these foreign companies/firms. Law is not a trade and briefs no merchandise and so the avarice of commercial gains should not malign this profession. Hence there can be no divergent view on the legal proposition that an Advocate cannot act in the dual capacity, that of a constituted attorney and an advocate."

That Banks as Lessee should not Indulge in Frivolous Litigation

Banks are one of the most rock solid financial institutions on which a common man depends. The simplistic expectation that they wouldn't do any wrong and take advantage of the situation of the person has been shattered by the aggressive approach of dog chasing resulting in not only the faith of the people but wasting of precious judicial time. Feeling aggrieved with the same, in the case of *Oriental Bank of Commerce* v. *Shri Ram Prakash Sehrawat*, 2010 (10) AD (Del) 478, the appellant preferred the present appeal. Justice Gambhir gave a stern message by putting the spotlight on Banks and by mentioning as to how they are considered as reliable establishments and how it should steer clear from entering into frivolous and vexatious litigation and not compel lessor to chase it for payment of his dues. He held:

> *"When an ordinary citizen leases out his property to a Bank or a Company as opposed to a private individual, it is with the view that these organized institutions are hassle free to deal with. It is a common perception that the Banks are reliable establishments which do not harass the lessor for trivial and inconsequential issues. But in the event of the circumstances like that of the case at hand, this court is constrained to observe that the Scheduled Bank like the appellant has embroiled itself in frivolous litigation on trivial issues leading to vexatious and galling litigation resulting in waste of judicial time. It is rather expected of a Bank, like the appellant, not to compel the lessor to chase it for payment of his dues and then hassle him to approach the court of law. This attitude of the bank is certainly deprecated by the court and it is expected of the bank to conduct its dealings more responsibly in future."*

Oath, Purpose of Oath – False Affidavit

Apart from a fine sense of judgment, the case of *Court on its own Motion* v. *Farah Khatoon*, 2014 (1) JCC 662 delineates how Courts of trodden road by following a strict and customary method of achieving justice (Balanced verdicts).

Justice Gambhir while sitting in a Division bench dealt with the instant case and held as under:

> *"We are not prepared to accept the plea raised by the counsel representing the Respondent in the contempt proceedings that the Respondent is not well versed with the law and relevant procedure of the court because of her appearing in court for the first time and it was due to social pressure, she took false stands of denying the marriage with the petitioner. The Respondent is an educated girl and employed as a teacher in MCD School* i.e. *Marginal Bandh, Old II, Selampur, Delhi, therefore we cannot believe that the lady who is employed as a teacher at least is not aware of the fact that she has to be truthful before the Court of Law even though unrepresented by a lawyer or under social pressure. The entire conduct of the Respondent is contumacious as in the face of the court she kept telling lies after lies and also she had the audacity to take a false stand*

when her statement was recorded in court on oath. The conduct of the Respondent is unpardonable. The Respondent is thus held guilty of committing the contempt of court in terms of section 12 of the Contempt of Courts Act.

With regard to the quantum of punishment, taking into consideration the unqualified apology tendered by her and the other reasons given by her in the said replies, we impose a fine of Rs. 2,000 on the Respondent which amount shall be deposited by the Respondent with "Mahatma Gandhi Trust" within a period of one week. Respondent is further directed to repent her sin by offering prayers at Rajghat **i.e.** *Samadhi of father of the nation who is worshiped because of his cherished principles of truth and non-violence from 21st December, 2013 and shall sit there for at least four hours a day for a period of one week. The area Police Station shall monitor that she sits there and offers her prayers in silence to feel remorseful about her such conduct."*

Justice Gambhir while dealing with a similar case titled *Mohd. Shamim* v. *Shahnawaz Khan*, 2012 (193) DLT 520 relating to false affidavits was of the view that seldom is the Court faced with a situation where the act of the litigant strikes at the edifice of justice delivery system and leaves the Court to ponder at its sanctity to the common man. Truth before anyone be it Court of law or the Court of God is nothing but the Truth alone but when man differentiates between them, it shakes the conscience of the Court and the society alike. The instant case showcased the audacity of the petitioner to lie with impunity before the Court swearing on false affidavit but his conscience awakened before his maker where he felt accountable.

Constrained to call in question the efficacy of the oath administered, Justice Gambhir held:

"It is a matter of great concern that litigants so often swear false affidavits, give false statements on oath being confident of the fact that no consequences would follow at the end of the case as one party would win and the other loose. The present circumstances have constrained this court to call in question the efficacy of the oath administered. The practice of taking an oath has been in existence in our country since times immemorial and the Indian Oaths Act, 1873 lived for almost a century. Oath is administered because it is believed that it has the strongest hold on the conscience of a man either he believes that God will punish him if he lies on oath or that it deters him to lie in the presence of God. Oaths have existed in India since the essence of time in almost all religions. The Hindu scriptures contain narrations as to how the conscience of a man

pricks him, what rewards await the truthful witness here and in the next world and what sin and terrible torments in hell are in store for an untruthful witness. In Muslim Law "Lian" was the testimony confirmed by oath and accompanied with an imprecation. The Quran says:

"Violate not your oaths, since ye have made God a witness over you.."

And also that: "Verily those who plight their fealty to thee do no less than plight their fealty to Allah: the Hand of Allah is over their hands: then anyone who violates his oath, does so to the harm of his own soul and anyone who fulfils what he has covenanted with Allah – Allah will soon grant him a great reward."

The purpose of oath is not to call the attention of God to man but the attention of man to God, not to call upon him to punish the wrong doer, but on the witness to remember that He will assuredly do so............. But commonly it is believed that the oath is administered as the main sanction behind oath is the fear of God. The Oaths Act, 1969 as it is in the present form was enacted after the report of the 28th Law Commission of India. The Law Commission in its report discussed the various forms of oath taken by people of various cultures and it would be of value to cite a few of the observations in this regard. The Chinese are usually administered oath by the ceremony of breaking a saucer, with an admonition: "You shall tell the truth and the whole truth the saucer is cracked, and if you do not tell the truth your soul will be cracked like the saucer.".................. Hence in all the forms, whether across countries or religions, oath is a means of reminding the witness of the presence of the Almighty to put him in a state of mind in which he would utter only the truth.

....

Thus for the believers of God, He is present in every form, all pervasive, ubiquitous, in the mosque as well as in court alike and more importantly in our hearts. What is however lamentable and pricks the conscience of this court is that the decree holder differentiated between the court and the mosque as if God is present only in the mosque and not in Courts. For those who do not wish to swear in the name of God, the Oaths Act provides for making an affirmation but the decree holder in the present case took the oath in the name of God. It is often said that courts are temples of justice and if that being the position how one can be untruthful before the temple of justice and be truthful standing at the place of worship. The decree-holder while swearing in the name of God in the courtroom not once but twice spoke untruth but while in mosque he spoke the truth which has not only perverted the course of justice but also questioned the sanctity of the oath administered in the court."

The Stand taken by Law Enforcement Agencies Found in Contravention of Various Municipal Laws

The environmental jurisprudence of this country has been majorly developed by the rulings of the Courts. For a considerable time now the care and concern that was the duty of the civic authorities has been shown by the Courts and at times even *suo moto*. The case of, *Green Park Extension Residents Association* v. *Municipal Corp. of Delhi*, 2008 (150) DLT 614, is one where the authorities turned a blind eye to an unauthorized construction and encroachment done by the officer of Chief Election Commission, where the Hon'ble Judge expressed his displeasure at the indifference of the law enforcement agencies.

He held that the illegal activities by the respondents were in gross violation of the municipal laws and in contravention of the designated purpose of the lay out plan.

Casting serious aspersions on the working of the law enforcement agencies, he was of the view that the situation becomes more grave and alarming when you find that the law enforcement agencies themselves are indulging into committing such gross illegalities and these authorities should have at least spared the locality known as Green Park by not depriving the people of its greenery, he held. The relevant paragraph of the said judgment is:

"It is also not a case set-up by the respondents that no other site was available for setting up of the office of the Chief Electoral Officer or there was any kind of compulsion on the part of the Chief Election Commission to set-up their office in the green area, at the cost of the residents of the said locality. Uprooting of trees, removal of swings which were meant for tiny tots, dismantling of badminton court by these statutory bodies clearly exemplify that these bodies have scant regard for the rule of law. The situation is more serious and alarming when you find that the law enforcing agencies themselves were indulging into committing such gross illegalities. These authorities should have at least spared the locality known as Green Park by not depriving the people of its greenery. The illegal acts committed by the respondents are in gross violation of the municipal laws and in contravention of the designated purpose of the lay out plan. It has recently been learnt that Delhi Cabinet has given an approval

for setting up of society to be headed by the Lt. Governor as Chief Patron under the name of 'Delhi Parks and Gardens Society', to undertake the task of ensuring maintenance of parks and greening activities in the city. I feel that when the said society is in place then the same shall certainly ensure that at least no green area or park in the city is under encroachment of the Government body or instrumentalities of the State."

Plight of Petitioners Who Became Migrants in Their Own Homeland

Discussing the plight of 8 Kashmiri migrants, in the case of, *Manoj Kumar* v. *Delhi Development Authority,* 2008 (150) DLT 143, who were residents of Jammu & Kashmir and were migrated to Delhi under forced circumstances arising out of the militancy in the state in the year 1990. They were forced to leave their State due to threat to their lives and migrated to Delhi with a hope that they will return back to their homes after the situation gets normalized. Alongwith other Kashmiri migrants, the petitioners were given a place in one of the migrant camps in New Delhi, where they resided for 13 years almost. All the Kashmiri migrants were requested to apply for allotment of the flats under the housing scheme launched for the rehabilitation of Jammu & Kashmir migrants.

Justice Gambhir expressed his displeasure at the plight of these innocent migrants and also remarked that these petitioners became migrants in their own homeland, owing to the serious lack of empathy by the powers that be and how these authorities instead of extending them a helping hand, caused more trouble for them.

He specified that there is a standard by which an Indian citizen needs to be treated with and makes clear how these migrants fall under the same class. He also berates the inhuman stance taken by the authorities which had the contrasting task of rehabilitation of these migrants. Uprooting you from your home and hearth is as it is very devastating but what added insult to injury in the instant case was the excuse of technical unsuitability of the petitioners by the authorities wherein Justice Gambhir observed:

"These Jammu and Kashmir migrants certainly needed better treatment. The authorities instead of extending a helping hand to these citizens who became migrants in their own motherland caused more trouble and trauma in their lives.

These authorities remained totally insensitive and unconcerned with the woes of these helpless petitioners, who were made to suffer firstly at the hands of militants then at the hands of these authorities, who are least concerned with the miseries, traumas and humiliation undergone by these citizens after they were uprooted with lock, stock and barrel from their home land. These authorities have really committed a great sin in not considering the case of the petitioners sympathetically and instead of wiping out their tears they made them weep more in their struggle to get the allotment of flats under the scheme which was exclusively meant for the Kashmiri migrants. These authorities did not appreciate that once living in a paradise on earth surrounded by mountains, cool breeze and meadows the petitioners were thrown out from their sweet homes and jobs and were placed in inhabitable camps. The situation which these citizens would have never dreamt of but instead of assuaging their feelings these authorities have not only thrown them out from their camps but also inflicted another major blow in their lives by discarding their claims for allotment of a flat under the scheme."

Footpaths – Are they meant for Walking or Hawking?

In the recent years, the problems of overpopulation and overcrowding have added to the misery of the pedestrians, who have, time and again been denied their right-of-way over footpaths. It is often seen that the hawkers encroach upon the footpaths by way of shops/kiosks/pan tharas etc., thus, compelling the pedestrians to walk on the roads amidst heavy vehicular traffic. In a mushrooming city like Delhi where there has been a significant increase in traffic, this right of the pedestrians has to be ardently protected.

In *Suman Lata* v. *NDMC,* LPA 685/2014, the appellant and the erstwhile licensee had breached the terms of the license granted by NDMC. It is the case of the appellant that hazardous material in the form of gas cylinders was stored by him and provided protection to an encroacher.

Hon'ble Mr. Justice Kailash Gambhir heading a Division Bench vehemently opposed such violation by the Appellant and deprecated the inaction on part of NDMC. He propounded that:

"We have perused some photographs which have been placed on record by the appellant alongwith the present appeal. The same depicts a highly objectionable, indeed horrifying state of affairs, as the occupants of the kiosks/pan tharas are carrying on various kinds of activities on the pavements far beyond their allotted spaces, they are blocking spaces meant for pedestrians. By definition, footpaths are meant for pedestrians, and the latter have a first right over these paths. In the name of providing livelihood to hawkers in the metropolises the rights of pedestrians cannot be compromised. Orderly streets and footpaths are the hallmark of an organized and civilized society. Commercial interests will have to bow to social

order and public interest and public convenience. The licensees of shops/kiosks/pan tharas on footpaths cannot spill onto or encroach upon public space. Every such infraction will be frowned upon and stringent action should be taken against the defaulters. In an ever-burgeoning city like Delhi with the daily quantum increase in the already heavy vehicular traffic, the rights of the pedestrians cannot be compromised; nay it would need to be zealously protected, lest the innocent pedestrians be compelled to use the main streets? With fast moving traffic, at her/his own peril."

CHAPTER 6

MATRIMONIAL CASES

Condonation of Previous Acts of Cruelty Means Forgiveness

Ours is a nation, where marriages are revered and are considered to be a sacramental union of two souls for eternity. Marriages have always been accorded prime importance. It as an enigma and a saga, which once begins ends only in death. There are far too many vain and petty reasons like being over bearing, jealousy which inevitably result in irretrievable breakdown of what was otherwise meant to be a happy marriage.

In the instant case *Shipali Sharma* v. *Gaurav Sharma, Mat.* App. (F.C.) 52/2013, the decree of divorce was not granted as according to the court the acts of cruelty by the appellant were condoned by her husband. Talking of cruelty Hon'ble Justice Gambhir presiding over a Division Bench observed:

> *"Marriage as a social institution is an affirmance of civilized social order where two individuals, capable of entering into wedlock, have pledged themselves to the institutional norms and values and promised to each other a cemented bond to sustain and maintain the marital obligation. It stands as an embodiment for continuance of the human race. Despite the pledge and promises, on certain occasions, individual incompatibilities, attitudinal differences based upon egocentric perception of situations, maladjustment phenomenon or propensity for non-adjustment or refusal for adjustment gets eminently projected that compels both the spouses to take intolerable positions abandoning individual responsibility, proclivity of asserting superiority complex, betrayal of trust which is the cornerstone of life, and sometimes a perverted sense of revenge, a dreadful diet, or sheer sense of envy bring the cracks in the relationship when either both the spouses or one of the spouses crave for dissolution of marriage – freedom from the institutional and individual bond.*
>
> *Every divorce case has its own story to tell. Any petitioner approaching the Court to seek a divorce on the ground of cruelty is required to give specific instances and acts of cruelty which are complained of by him and wherever possible with precise dates and the places where such acts were committed. Any kind of vagueness*

and evasiveness in the allegations will prove fatal to the case of the petitioner. It cannot be proved by mere allegations in the pleadings but the same are to be proved with the help of evidence and if possible, through independent witnesses. It is an undeniable fact that seldom witnesses, who are privy to the marital discord of husband and wife are their own respective family members and therefore the courts ought to be cautious enough while determining the truth behind the depositions of these witnesses.

Another settled legal principle with regard to cruelty is that the petitioner who is claiming decree on the ground of cruelty should not have condoned in any manner the acts of cruelties complained of and if the acts are so condoned, then the petitioner would not be entitled to grant of the decree."

Divorce on the Ground of Irretrievable Breakdown of Marriage

Matrimonial matters are subjects of fragile human and moving affiliation. It demands mutual trust, reverence, respect, love and affection with sufficient scope for reasonable adjustments with ones better half. Marriage requires constant nurturing and understanding. It constitutes the very basis of social organization or the very being in itself. Hindu law regards marriage as a sacrament indissoluble and eternal. It is the foundation of the family and without which no civilization can exist. This sacramental character of marriage has given rise to certain anomalies. There used to be a time when marriages were set to be made in heaven, and it was deemed as a relation of flesh with flesh and bone with bone. So even the thought of separating never crossed one's mind.

The present case *Subhash Chander Sharma* v. *Anjali Sharma*, 2010 (174) DLT 564 dealt with irretrievable breakdown of marriages and justice Gambhir held as follows:

"....It would be important to bring forth that the High Court in the exercise of it inherent powers cannot grant divorce on the ground of irretrievable breakdown of marriage as it is yet not a ground of divorce under the Hindu Marriage Act. Here, it would be pertinent to refer to the recent judgment of the Apex Court in the case of Vishnu Dutt Sharma *v.* Manju Sharma, *(2009) 6 SCC 379: 2009 AIR SCW 2984: AIR 2009 SC 2254 where it was held that:*

On a bare reading of section 13 of the Act, reproduced above, it is crystal clear that no such ground of irretrievable breakdown of the marriage is provided by the legislature for granting a decree of divorce. This Court cannot add such a ground to section 13 of the Act as that would be amending the Act, which is a function of the legislature.

Learned Counsel for the appellant has stated that this Court in some cases has dissolved a marriage on the ground of irretrievable breakdown. In our opinion, those cases have not taken into consideration the legal position which we have mentioned above, and hence they are not precedents. A mere direction of the Court without considering the legal position is not a precedent. If we grant divorce on the ground of irretrievable breakdown, then we shall by judicial verdict be adding a clause to section 13 of the Act to the effect that irretrievable breakdown of the marriage is also a ground for divorce. In our opinion, this can only be done by the legislature and not by the Court. It is for the Parliament to enact or amend the law and not for the Courts.

Hence, we do not find force in the submission of the learned Counsel for the appellant.

Also recently, the Apex Court in the case of Neelam Kumar *v.* Dayarani, *Civil Appeal No. 1957/2006 placed reliance on the judgment of Vishnu Dutt Sharma (supra) and reiterated the same view and held that irretrievable breakdown of marriage is not a ground for divorce as it is not contemplated under section 13 of the Hindu Marriage Act.*

However, it would be befitting to mention here that the Apex Court in the case of Naveen Kohli v. Neelu Kohli *(supra) recommended to the legislature to make 'irretrievable breakdown of marriage' as a ground for divorce. The Apex Court in the said judgment was confronted with a situation where the parties were living separately for a period of more than 10 years. Based on the said recommendation made by the Apex Court in the said case, as also in various earlier decisions, the Law Commission of India in its 217th Report has recently again recommended to the Parliament to introduce an amendment in the Hindu Marriage Act, 1955 and the Special Marriage Act, 1954 to include irretrievable breakdown of marriage as another ground for divorce.*

The relationship between husband and wife is one of the most delicate emotional bonds and needs constant nurturing, tolerance and understanding. This relationship once which was of love and mutual trust when starts to leave a bitter aftertaste bedevilling this bond that it is no more bearable to stay under one roof is when they seek to legally put an end to such a marriage. Divorce on the ground of irretrievable breakdown of marriage might be contrary to common perception and the idea of marriage being a holy union for seven births, but in the bid to preserve the unworkable marriage which has long ceased to be alive is abound to be a source of greater misery for the parties than the divorce itself.

However it is a catch 22 situation as this ground can ease the way for many who are under the burden of a doomed relationship to a breather but at the same time it may give an opportunity to the ones trying to maneuver the alleys of law for their self conceited motives.

There has been a lot of brainstorming with regard to the efficacy and societal impact that this ground would have if it is made as a ground for divorce. On the recommendations of the Law Commission of India, the Legislature in its wisdom would amend the Hindu Marriage Act to bring within its fold the ground of irretrievable breakdown of marriage. However, it is expected that watertight safeguards are introduced so as not to send the message that now divorce has become a cakewalk.

Henceforth, there are some key areas that need to be pondered upon. The ground of irretrievable breakdown of marriage cannot be resorted to as a straitjacket formula leading to the institution of marriage becoming so fragile that the wrong doer abuses it for his selfish ends leaving the other party in lurch. But it is only when the court is satisfied that the marriage has been wrecked beyond the hope of salvage and there is no chance of their coming together should the court open the deadlock of wedlock.

It is an open secret that getting a decree of divorce takes an invariably long time and with the existing grounds available, it leads the parties to level acrimonious allegations antagonizing each other. Consequently, when the decree of divorce is granted then the other party appeals to the High Court, and if unsuccessful, reaches the Supreme Court in the hope for relief, therefore prolonging the already gruesome legal battle. It happens in a lot of cases that in the end during this vicious legal voyage, whatever little hope there is of reconciliation is anyway diminished leading the parties pitiful and penniless.

Adding to the woes, if there are children born out of the wedlock, then they suffer immensely; emotionally, psychologically and even financially, depriving them of proper upbringing and education due to meagre means of one of the spouses. A divorce from a spouse is not a divorce from the children and they should not be punished for the act of their parents. Hence if this ground is added it has to be taken care of that the children do not bear the brunt between two warring adults and that a proper mechanism is in place for taking care of all their needs. The child's well being, who is but a mute spectator and officially not a party to the lawsuit, should be the eye of the resolution.

Also in cases where the wife is the respondent, and the husband orchestrates a breakdown and unilaterally wants to terminate the marriage on this ground, it has to be taken care of that to achieve his ulterior motive the husband on the premise of a deadlock does not leave the wife impoverished or at the mercy of her parents."

Making a Mockery of the Court by Playing Fraud

A person who has the most earnest belief in the judicial system, can't stand the thought of someone trying to take advantage of it and get away with it. Justice Gambhir being one of them, as he believes that no one can be permitted to pollute the streams of justice. According to him fraud on the court makes a mockery of our pious judicial system which is at the mercy of the litigants from whom the courts expect truthful and honest disclosure of facts.

In the present case *Sarabjit Singh* v. *Gurpal Kaur*, 2013 (196) DLT 326, in a zeal to obtain a prompt decree of divorce, the appellant husband instead of filing the petition for divorce on any of the grounds as envisaged under sub-section 13(1) of the Hindu Marriage Act, 1955, resorted to the said fraudulently forged the signatures of the respondent wife on both the petitions and affidavits, brought an imposter before the Court instead of the actual respondent & produced a fake Advocate to achieve his sinister design of obtaining a fast decree of divorce so that he could marry some other lady.

Justice Gambhir while deciding the present case came down heavily on the increasing tendency of parties/litigants to be daring enough to mislead the court, making it to believe in its concocted, cock and bull story and inducing it to pronounce judgments based on their untrue submissions. He asked the courts to deal with such dishonest litigants with an iron hand. He further observed that judges being the repositories of justice must play a proactive role to condemn the alarming rise in frivolous and dishonest litigation and held:

"Truth is the foundation of justice and it has to be common endeavour of all to uphold the truth and no one can be permitted to pollute the steams of justice. Fraud, on the other hand, which means deceit, trickery, material misrepresentation, sharp practice, or breach of confidence perpetrated for profit or to gain some unfair or dishonest advantage, is a crime deemed to be fundamentally opposed to the principles of justice. The Fraud on the court makes a mockery of our pious judicial system which is at mercy of the litigants from whom the courts expect truthful and honest disclosure of facts.

It is only when people are convinced that the justice which they seek by submitting themselves to the jurisdiction of the court is based on the foundation of truth, that they would acquire trust & confidence on the judicial system. Therefore, the judges, being the custodians of the justice delivery system must play a proactive role so as to abjure the practice of dishonest litigation and fraudulent intendance on the court. They must ensure that the dishonest and unscrupulous litigants are dealt with sternly to give a clean message that there is no incentive for the wrong doers in the temple of justice. Heavy/ exemplary costs must be imposed on the party/litigant who even dares to show the courage of misleading the court, making it to believe in its concocted story and inducing it to pronounce judgment based on its untrue submissions.

In the present case, in a zeal to obtain a prompt decree of divorce, the appellant husband instead of filing the petition for divorce on any of the grounds as envisaged under sub-section 13(1) of the Hindu Marriage Act, 1955, resorted to the said fraudulent practice by forging the signatures of the respondent wife on both the petitions and affidavits, bringing an imposter before the Court instead of the actual respondent & producing a fake Advocate to achieve his sinister design of obtaining a fast decree of divorce so that he could marry some other lady. The appellant husband has thrown to the winds all norms by affixing the photograph of some other lady in place of the respondent wife in both the petitions. It is quite evident that the appellant husband is not alone in such fraudulent acts and certainly there is some legal brain who must have encouraged the appellant husband in committing such murky and fraudulent acts to pollute the streams of justice.

To ensure that such fraudulent acts are not committed again the matrimonial/family courts and other subordinate courts shall adhere to implement the following instructions:—

(i) All the matrimonial/family courts shall take care that they put their own signatures on the photographs of the parties at the time of recording statements of the parties in the joint motion petitions under section 13B(1) and section 13B(2) of the Hindu Marriage Act, 1955.

(ii) The concerned ministerial staff attached with the matrimonial/ family courts shall ensure that the photographs on the joint motion petitions are pasted and not stapled.

(iii) The ministerial staff attached with all subordinate Courts shall verify that the Power of Attorney filed by any advocate carries

them what they are and the media augments their cause further. These Godmen resort to various methods and each of them claim to be unique and have an individual connection with the Almighty. Let this not be understood to mean that there is dearth of saints who enjoy real spiritual powers and are alleviated souls. Such saints often live a life in oblivion. To quote an example Swami Dayanand Saraswati who was a great spiritual leader and a social reformer found his Spiritual Guru in a blind man, named, Swami Virjanand, who lived in a hut, and after having received lessons at the feet of his spiritual Guru, he asked him as to what he could offer him as Guru-Dakshina - the Guru replied "Spread my message to the world and that will be my Guru Dakshina". Such were the saints that this country have produced and known.

The plaintiff claiming to be a spiritual guru on directions of this court placed on record various videos of the Samagams held by the plaintiff where his devotees have expressed their gratitude to him for making their lives problem free. The videos also depict the various cures and remedies propagated by him. It would be pertinent here to quote at least one of them:

"Baba: puri chhole khaye kabhi? Bakht: ji Baba ji khaye hain.

Baba: Aisa karo puri chhole baba ko yad kar do char garibo ko khila do, prabhu ki zyada kripaa ayegi."

The above instance is only one odd out of the basket and any prudent person with average intelligence would be in rapt disbelief if such a remedy would get him rid of the difficulties he is facing in his life. Prima facie, these do not appear as logical to a rational mind but the whole edifice of this God market and its nuances is based on the belief system of people. This court cannot help but sound a word of caution that this sudden resurgence of the Babas who claims to have mystical powers and give all kind of illogical solutions to overcome the miseries of people has amplified and glorified superstition and has turned the clock back of development in our country.

The media today is the messiah of the masses and it influences people's thoughts, actions and opinions on the most crucial of issues, keeping public debate alive. However, with this power comes the responsibility to verify news and not generate in public; bias, hostility or enmity. However, it cannot shy away from the fact that the media **inter se**, *print, electronic and internet, etc. have cut throat competition and in the bid to outdo each other has tremendous pressure in terms of hits, circulations, viewership, commonly referred to as TRP. In the race to grab eyeballs it sensationalises news and information.*

It will not be incorrect to say that the information revolution has proved to be a double edged sword with its omnipresence and drive to dig into every nook and corner for news and dissect and thereby corrode the lives of public figures. The potent media has the power to massacre the reputation and lives of many and has made many glorified saints and Gods out of nobody in the cloak of informing and creating awareness.

In the present case on perusing through the content of the website of the defendants placed on record, it appears that the defendants have a series of articles against the plaintiff calling him names like "thug Baba", "Chor", "fraud nirmal darbar", darbar as "thug darbar". Not commenting on the veracity of the allegations levelled against the plaintiff, the defendants have in the opinion of this court gone a step ahead of its rights of freedom of press. It also cannot be forgotten that the reach of the internet as a medium is vast and far reaching than print and electronic and the click of a mouse can disseminate in a split second the views of anyone. Having said this, the plaintiff who claims himself to be a Baba and Spiritual Guide and through his Samagams and telecast of his discourses through various T.V. Channels, like other public figures is under constant public and media gaze, should not be sensitive to and rather should be open to criticism and scrutiny. The filing of defamation suit is a right of the plaintiff but the same cannot be allowed to become a lethal weapon in sabotaging the freedom of the press. The print and the electronic media being the eye and ears of the citizens, its freedom cannot be unreasonably trampled upon by resorting to legal processes and unreasonably dragging them to face defamation and contempt cases as it will lead to sounding a death knell for democracy. But at the same time, the press and the media cannot denigrate others with a targeted campaign without any basis and proper verification."

Cinema Representation of Individual and Institution, 2013 (53) PTC 536,

Movies have been perceived as seeds of social revolution. It can't be stressed enough, how many lives, the entertainment industry touches. The plethora of people that can be reached puts a lot of responsibility on these film makers. An incomplete or incorrect view can have grave effects on the reputation of the parties involved and hence should not be taken so lightly, as it is very delicate in nature, something that's very hard to earn yet easy to lose.

The main grievance of the plaintiff against the defendants was for the alleged offending song in their movie. As per the plaintiff, the said song was being used to promote the film on YouTube and the said movie was likely to be released in various cinemas very shortly. As per the plaintiff, the following lyrics in the said song were offending so as to cause serious harm to the reputation and goodwill of the plaintiff:—

> "Birla Ho Ya Tata Ambani Ho Ya Bata, Apne Apne
> Chakar Mein Desh Ko Hai Kata
> Birla Ho Ya Tata Ambani Ho Ya Bata
> Apne Apne Chakar Mein Desh Ko Hai Kata"
> Are humre hi khoon se inka engine chale
> dhakadhak, Aam admi ki jeb ho gai hai safa
> chat, aam aadmi ki jeb ho gai safachat."

While deciding this case Justice Gambhir held:

> *"Since times immemorial, the Indian cinema has not only been a source of entertainment but has also been responsible for bringing to the fore various political, socioeconomic issues. Movies play a very significant role in the life of a common man and any issue based movie leaves a great impact on the minds of the viewers and influences their mind set and attitude. Films have the capacity to galvanize a human mind, as the human psyche is vulnerable and due to being star struck the mind of a common man germinates with the ideas shown in the movies.*
>
> *At omega, this court would like to observe that cinema is not only an entertainment industry but also a potent weapon for social change. From a six to a sixty year old, everyone derives and takes home something from a movie and it has the power to evoke emotions and shape the outlook of the common man towards various issues like none other. The film makers have since yore mirrored social ills plaguing the society which movement continues till date with igniting the minds and being responsible for various social movements leading to monumental changes in the social setup. However, with this responsibility to bring to the public domain the realities of our diverse nation, there comes a duty to act cautiously not to make inroads in the lives and dignity of people and institutions alike in the garb of being the messiahs of social change. Thus the film makers have no unbridled right to tarnish the image and reputation of any individual or institution, that too in the absence of any foundation for the same. One cannot be oblivious of the fact that the main stay of the film industry is not only entertainment but also commercial gains and in this pursuit to earn huge profits the cinema makers have no right to trample upon, disrepute or disparage the reputation of others. To cull out a passage from the famous Othello which states; A good name is worth more than good riches. (Shakespeare's Othello,*

Act-II, Scene III, pp. 167):—Good name in man and woman, dear my Lord is the immediate jewel of their souls; Who steals my purse, steals trash; Its something nothing; T'was mine, t'is, and has been slave to thousands; But he that filches from me my good name, Robs me of that which not enriches him And makes me poor indeed. Thus as rightly said, reputation is the only jewel that cannot be bought and is built over the years and a person who is robbed of it is no less than a destitute."

Infringement of Copyrights Explained, 2012 (193) DLT 593

The plaintiff claimed that use, sale and advertisement of products and services by the defendant under the trade mark/trade name ICRAVE amounts to passing off of the plaintiffs services and use of such similar trade mark by the defendant was nothing but an attempt to wrongfully trade upon the plaintiff's goodwill and is done with the sole intent to mislead the public and to cause confusion and deception in their minds to make them falsely believe that the goods and services of the defendant originated from the plaintiff or at least have some affiliation.

Intellectual Property seems to a lay man as a technical concept and the laws developed have furthered this belief. Simplifying this concept of infringement in the utmost innovative manner in the case at hand, Justice Gambhir explained the origin of the law in a manner intertwined with the basic morality of not cheating or stealing which is ingrained in all as children and held thus:

"World-over, the first lesson that is taught to every child entering the school is that one should not cheat by copying from the answer sheet of the other student. This principle still holds good in every school as philosophy behind this principle is that if one student has prepared for his exam by his hard work and devotion then his work should not be copied by the other student without putting the requisite hard work and devotion by him as well. The students of yesteryear when they enter in the commercial world tend to forget this basic principle and tenets of morality and ethics. What is called when one copies the answer sheet of other student in examination as cheating and when any person engaged in commercial world without putting any hard work and devotion either uses the trade-name or the brand name of the other company or steals any artistic or other performing art of other person or copies designs, logo etc. of other person or company it is called infringement. The said basic principle has been expressed by various courts in different ways through catena of legal decisions."

Advertisement, Sales Promotion and Precautions to be taken, 2013 (200) DLT 563

Advertising is a subset of marketing, a form of communication intended to persuade people to purchase the products or the services of a particular brand. Much capital is pumped into this sector and this medium caters to many people. While deciding the case at hand, he said that in our country, the advertising industry in order to promote a particular product, does not hold back in spending millions of dollars on it.

Judgement on comparative advertising where Defendant Company aired a television commercial which depicted a child being sick because of the alleged use of an antiseptic liquid of the plaintiff's in bathing water whilst promoting the superiority of the respondent's own Soap. The plaintiff filed a suit against the telecast of the television commercial of defendant soap, which was disparaging and denigrating the reputation and goodwill of the plaintiff's product in the commercial market.

Justice Kailash Gambhir decided that the commercial telecast by the respondent indeed disparaged the product of the plaintiff and granted an interim injunction to the plaintiff against the telecast and believed that one had the right to promote one's product but not by trampling own its competitors and reminded them that it is a delicate task and whilst doing so he held:

> *"With the liberalization and globalization of the Indian economy, firms have been aggressively and vigorously promoting their products and services. In a comparative environment, every representation of a product or service is about what others are not. These practices raise questions about candour and fairness of representation of products and services. In our country, the advertising industry in order to reconnoitre and promote a particular product, does not hold back in spending millions of dollars on advertising and marketing. Advertising is a subsection of marketing, a form of communication intended to persuade people to purchase the products or the services of a particular brand. The discerning fact is that in such a competitive market, effective advertising techniques are being incorporated to promote one's product with addition of high profile names like various actors and renowned personalities, nonetheless it is an indubitable fact that we get swayed by the reflecting names in the advertisements and tend to develop a parlous connect with the actors endorsing the products as they are the idol for their aficionados. Through the entire process, television makes a major contribution, beginning with awareness, where it makes its greatest impact. When*

spoken of media boosted awareness, a survey shows that 43% of those questioned said television, as in our society especially the middle class, relates highly to the television promotions. It is one of the influential modes that monitors and captures the major segment of the society. And particularly when the product is being endorsed by a well-known cinestar, the advertisement campaign or visual media creates an immediate impact on the viewers and possibly purchaser's mind. We as mere viewers easily get blind folded and "duped". Therefore, this medium of promotion should be used very carefully and painstakingly, wherein in the garb of promoting one's product, it has no right to disparage or denigrate its competitor's product. Therefore, when any such discrepancy is noticed, the issue in question has to be looked from the view point of an ordinary person of average intelligence."

Urgent Need for World Class Gateway Airport Needed in India, 2013 (197) DLT 567

Justice Gambhir talked about the booming industry of aviation. He took a stance, one of an entrepreneur and was futuristic. He took account of the fact that the aviation industry is complementary to other industries and hence should be developed as much as a utility. In this day and age, the aviation industry is making this world a smaller place, one flight at a time and held:

"Civil Aviation is the fastest growing arm of the India's transport infrastructure. During the last one decade the civil aviation sector has grown at a phenomenal pace and India has emerged as one of the largest civil aviation market in the world. The airport operations in India have expanded considerably not only in terms of domestic passenger volume but also in terms of number of operational airports, passenger handling capacity and air cargos and to meet such an unprecedented growth in aviation sector, improvement of infrastructure facilities on several fronts is the need of the hour. There is an urgent need for India to have world class gateway airports providing aviation services and passenger/cargo facilities of global standards in a safe and secure environment. The government and the concerned authorities need to put an effort towards optimum utilization of the existing airports by addressing the problems of outdated terminal infrastructure, inadequate ground handling systems and poor passenger amenities without compromising on the security and safety aspects."

CHAPTER 8
EDUCATION

Non-Compliance of Directions of the Apex Court by Faculty of Law Criticized

Fathers of our Constitution envisaged the idea of reservation to uplift certain classes, however, over the course of time the utility of reservation has changed. In today's time, with the increase in the number of aspirants, it must be borne in mind that reservations should not be made at the stake of meritorious candidates who are in the general category.

In the instant matter of *Anuj Sharma* v. *University of Delhi*, W.P. (C) 6933/2011 the petitioners sought directions to direct the respondent to convert the OBC category seats, which remained vacant at the time of admissions, to the general category.

Justice Gambhir, appalled by the omission on part of the Faculty of Law, opined that:

> *"It is quite shocking that the non compliance of the directions of the Apex Court is not by any other institution but by a Faculty of law, University of Delhi, which is considered to be one of the premier law institutions in the country. The Admission Committee of the Law Faculty must be comprising of law teachers and how can they who teach and impart education to the students who would become future lawyers, the means of dispensation of justice of the society, ignore the directions passed by the Apex Court of the country is baffling and alarming to say the least. To obey the mandate of the highest Court of the country is the bounden duty of all and by adopting a cavalier approach, the respondents in a most brazen and outrageous manner have given a go by to the directions of the Apex Court.*
>
> *The plea taken by the respondent that the academic session of the LLB first year course has already begun does not cut any ice in view of the fact that the petitioners cannot be made to suffer for no fault on their part. Ordinarily, the mid stream admissions are not the preferred norm, but in the case like the present one where there is a sea of opportunity but is not open to the ones willing to avail, due to the unreasonableness and high handedness of the respondents, the court will lean in the favour where justice can be done and the principles of equity and good conscience are the torch bearers*

The Courts have also consistently held that every endeavour by the University and all other institutions should be made to fill all the seats as wastage of seats is not only at the cost of the public exchequer but at the cost of depriving a number of aspiring students struggling to get admission in coveted institutions and universities such as the Delhi University, which is a dream of many. Hence, considering the aforesaid circumstances, the respondent is hereby directed to hold a special counselling to fill the vacant 50 OBC after converting the said vacant 50 OBC seats into the general category in terms of the directions of the Hon'ble Apex Court in the matter of P.V. Indiresan (supra). The said special counselling shall be conducted by the respondent university after duly notifying the candidates belonging to the general category through notice board and through their website. Atleast seven days time shall be given to the candidates through such a notice inviting them to participate in the said special counselling. The respondent is also directed to publish an advertisement to this effect in a national daily so that the candidates can be made aware that the admissions have yet not been closed so that not only the present petitioners but the other candidates standing higher in rank can try their luck to seek admission against the unfilled vacant seats. It is further directed that after filling the said 50 seats, the Faculty of Law shall conduct special classes for such students so that they can cover their curriculum to appear in their first semester examination."

Admission in Specialised Courses

This judgment throws light upon the system of Entrance examination and its importance for student selection. It is well known in the public domain that entrance examination is conducted for the purpose of maintaining uniformity and to separate the grain from the chaff.

The short controversy involved in the case of *Dr. Hari Nath Yadav* v. *Govt. of NCT of Delhi,* 2011 (6) AD (Del) 162 was that the respondent no.2 selected the petitioner without him having qualified the CET-DNB (Super Specialty) examination, which as per the respondent NBE was the eligibility criteria for admission in a DNB course and therefore the application for registration of the petitioner to the said course was rejected by the NBE *vide* letter dated 3-6-2009.

Hon'ble Mr. Justice Kailash Gambhir relying on various judgments of the Hon'ble Supreme Court held:

"that in the present day and age of cut throat competition, admissions in almost all of the specialized courses is through centralized entrance examinations for giving preference to merit and to have a uniform

standard and method of granting admissions. Today, whether it is the Senior Secondary examinations or the eligibility of MBBS or Engineering degree for pursuing a higher degree, it has become immaterial as to how one fairs in these examinations as the entire thrust is on how well you perform in the entrance examination, which is the gateway for admission in any course based on the merit and position one secures in these entrance tests.

Certainly, Entrance Examinations are a prism for evaluating students on an undifferentiated level and any action to dilute the procedure and standards laid down would be to set the aim and objective of these tests to naught. Thus, any laxity or concession in favour of any student or any misplaced sympathy would not only give leverage to many unscrupulous colleges and institutes but would also result in compromising the merit, which will ultimately lead to a pandemonium and deterioration of standards of education of this country. No undue sympathy can be shown by this Court on account of the fact that the petitioner had undergone the said DNB programme for a period of about 4 months on the date of the receipt of the rejection letter and then continued the said course under the protection of this Court through interim orders. This court is thus troubled not to grant relief to the petitioner as prayed for and no special advantage can be claimed by the petitioner as he continued with the said course at his own peril."

Privatization of Medical Education

What might seem to be a very trivial issue, yet a very pertinent one, was dealt by Justice Gambhir where the various institutes/medical colleges had approached this court to challenge the order of the respondent Medical Council of India/Board of Governors whereby it had rejected the grant of additional intake in the MBBS course in the petitioner institutes/colleges. In *Teer Thanker Mahaveer Institute of Management* v. *Union of India,* W.P.(C) No. 5763/2011 & Cm No. 11723/2011 & *Rama Medical College Hospital & Research Centre, Kanpur* v. *Union of India,* W.P. (C) No. 5917/2011 & Cm No. 11971/2011 & *School of Medical Science & Research, Sharda University* v. *Union of India,* W.P.(C) No. 4920/2011 & Cm No. 9982/2011 whilst discussing that there were only 19 medical colleges in the country at the time of independence and today the number of colleges imparting MBBS education is almost 335, Hon'ble Justice Gambhir held:

"It is indeed a significant rise which should be the sign of the progress and growth of a nation, especially like ours, with a burgeoning population, but whether the increased numbers means higher health care delivery system is still debatable as the number crunching has another story to tell. As per the recent published reports, India

ranks 67th in the list of 133 developing countries with the doctor-population ratio at 1:1700 as compared to the world ratio which is 1.5:1000. The WHO target is to achieve the ratio of 1:1000, which India will be able to do only till 2031 with the existing colleges and state of affairs and it is estimated that there will be still a shortage of 9.54 lakh doctors till then. With the government colleges share being less and the private colleges shouldering more responsibility, there is still approximately only 1 medical college per 38.41 lakh, dismal figures which reflect the acute crisis in the country. The MCI received 104 applications this year for the increase of admission capacity out of which 43 were disapproved on scrutiny, 61 inspected and 33 approved, out of which 18 were in private sector. With the panoramic view of the above statistics, the inevitable conclusion is that the private colleges are the harbingers of hope for the dreaming and yearning India.

At omega, this Court would like to give its observations on the larger issue of the medical education in the country. The doctors of our country are the cynosures of the medical fraternity of the world and for making them a sought after lot, the and for making them a sought after lot, the privatization of the medical education became the need of the hour. But it is a hard hitting reality that this edu-business, as it is now popularly called, has led to the growing merchandising of the medical education, blurring the benefits of privatization and entering the realm of proliferation. This sudden spurt has no doubt contributed to the declining standards of the medical education, with more money being pumped in by charging higher fees but the infrastructure and facilities, more importantly, faculty, is dwindling and inadequate. The mushrooming and setting of medical shops has been in the news quite often leading to the scrapping of the Apex Regulatory body like the MCI due to its tainted practices, the natural corollary of which being more stringent rules and regulations appearing on the statute book and like in the present case, more rigorous interpretations of the regulations being sought in the wake of the regulatory checks and monitoring of the private colleges. There is no two way about the fact that there are colleges which are set up only for the purpose of minting and raking in the moolah, appointing rogue doctors at the time of inspections, an emergency like frenzy for the show day, window dressing, etc but the crucial question is that is it a reason enough to look at all the private colleges through the prism of incertitude.

There were only 19 medical colleges in the country at the time of independence and today the number of colleges imparting MBBS education is almost 335. It is indeed a significant rise which should be the sign of the progress and growth of a nation, especially like ours, with a burgeoning population, but whether the increased numbers means higher health care delivery system is still debatable as the number crunching has another story to tell. As per the recent published reports, India ranks 67th in the list of 133 developing countries with the doctor-population ratio at 1:1700 as compared to the world ratio which is 1.5:1000. The WHO target is to achieve the ratio of 1:1000, which India will be able to do only till 2031 with the existing colleges and state of affairs and it is estimated that there will be still a shortage of 9.54 lakh doctors till then. With the government colleges share being less and the private colleges shouldering more responsibility, there is still approximately only 1 medical college per 38.41 lakh, dismal figures which reflect the acute crisis in the country. The MCI received 104 applications this year for the increase of admission capacity out of which 43 were disapproved on scrutiny, 61 inspected and 33 approved, out of which 18 were in private sector. With the panoramic view of the above statistics, the inevitable conclusion is that the private colleges are the harbingers of hope for the dreaming and yearning India.

The privatization of medical education was aimed at reversing the notion of higher education being the prerogative of the rich and making it universal and attainable. The additional numbers would bring glory if they go through the highest standard of education and training and bridge the gap in the health services in the urban and rural areas. To achieve a balance, between the unprecedented institutional growth today vis a vis skewed doctor-patient ratio, the only solution is to review the entire regulatory mechanism and revitalize the system of checks before this aberration of rot becomes a trend in the country. The MCI requirements for setting up medical colleges focus more on infrastructure and human resources required and less on process and quality of education, with the information sought only from the college administration and not from students, faculty or patients and it is time that the regulations be focused more to foster true medical education and producing a competent cadre of doctors rather than just more number of doctors. It is a national quality challenge and the time for the MCI/BOG to be vigilant and reinvigorate the system to stop the unplanned and unequal growth of mediocre colleges aimed at commercialization of medical education, rather than stop the growth of colleges catering to the needs of the aspirant doctors by giving lopsided interpretations to the regulations. The health care sector cannot be allowed to suffer a trust deficit, and it is time the trust of the common man in the custodians of our health is rejuvenated and strengthened, and that can only be done by monitoring the quality of medical education in the country more stringently by the MCI. It is the time of perils to be addressed before we lose the cutting edge in global healthcare and education."

Non Filling of Seats by IIM Deprecated

In today's time we are faced with yet another problem of incessantly growing number of candidates *vis-à-vis* the limited number of seats at educational institutions and universities. The practice of non-filling of seats by the elite institutions like the IIMs etc. should be curtailed for the primary reason that it causes a loss to the State exchequer. In addition to this the vacant seats can be put to use in a fruitful manner to train worthy minds, who eventually become assets to the nation.

The case of *Rajat Goel* v. *Ministry of Human Resource & Development (Govt. of India)*, WP (C) No. 4834/2011 was filed by an aspiring student, the petition sought to direct the respondents to fill the vacant seats for the batch 2011-2013 and call upon the petitioner for admission in IIM Shillong.

The Court while condemning the complacent attitude of the institute also held that:

"The Indian Institute of Management or IIMs, as they are called, are India's elite business schools and are a brand to reckon with, both in India and abroad. The IIM graduates form not only the cream of India's business bigwigs but are wooed by the foreign companies alike. The tag of being an IIM graduate is for a lifetime and it is a dream of many a lot to be part of this prestigious alumni. IIM Shillong is the younger lot of the IIMs, established to give the IIM experience to more hopefuls. Such a premier institute is expected to act fairly and transparently and justify the money and funds that are allocated for them by the Government. The approach of the respondent no.2 of not filling all the 120 seats for the said course of PGP is whimsical and capricious to say the least. It is not expected of such a highly reputed educational institute to act in an arbitrary manner and had this petitioner not been before the court, the practice of leaving the seats vacant unreasonably by the respondent No. 2 would not have come to light. It is the bounden duty of every educational institute to justify the funds being diverted for them. In the time of cut throat competition today, every seat can make or mar the life of a student and the amount of time and effort that goes to prepare and finally qualify such a competitive examination like CAT

goes down the drain due to the high handedness of the institutes in wasting the seats, despite having world class infrastructure and top notch faculty at their disposal. This court severely condemns the unsavoury and unpalatable practice of not filling the 22 vacant seats of the respondent No. 2 with the admonition that in future its conduct in this regard should not be dubitable. There can be no dispute with regard to the judgments of the Madras High Court, Kerala High Court and Patna High Court cited by the petitioner holding that the seats should not go waste in educational institutes and therefore for wasting the seats and now the time having passed to undertake the entire admission process again, this court deems it appropriate to impose a cost of Rs. 1 lakh on the respondent No. 2 to be paid to the Prime Minister's National Relief Fund (PMNRF) within a period of 4 weeks from the date of this order."

Absenteeism by Student in College

It is a well-known fact that 'absenteeism' from classes reflects majorly on the performance of a student; regularity in the class on the contrary helps in shaping the personality of a student for the better. Not only does one gain more knowledge by virtue of regularity but it also helps in inculcating a sense of punctuality which is the need of the hour especially for lawyers of tomorrow. It is for this reason that the universities mandate bars as regards attendance which have to be met.

Kangana Modi v. *National Institute of Fashion Technology*, W.P.(C) No. 569/2010: (2010) 170 DLT 648

Justice Gambhir by way of an exemplary decision in the above mentioned cases dealt with the recurring issue of absenteeism of students in college. The instant five writ petitions raised a common issue that all the petitioners were detained from appearing in their respective semester examinations on account of shortfall of their attendance.

Setting an example that all the students are treated with principles of equality and fair play, Justice Kailash Gambhir observed that education teaches only those in attendance. He held:

"there is no royal road to education. Absenteeism has become chronic in the present day and it has to be cured by making the students realize that education teaches only those in attendance. Students take admissions in various courses and they are required to fulfil the laid down attendance norms of each University/college or institution. No doubt that because of youthful age, students sometimes do bunk classes or even sometimes due to certain exigencies, medical or otherwise, are not able to attend the classes, but for that the provision of abstaining from 25% in over all subjects and 35% in

the core subjects has already been made by the respondent institute. Further provision of relaxation has already been made if a student is short of attendance in modular subject/non-core subject if due to medical or other unavoidable reasons the student has not been able to attend his/her classes."

In yet another bunch of matters i.e. *Vandana Kandari* v. *University of Delhi,* 2010 (170) DLT 755; *Aarti Meena* v. *University of Delhi and Manas Pegu* v. *University of Delhi; Sukriti Upadhyay* v. *University of Delhi; Rajesh Kumar Gautam* v. *University of Delhi; Sajili Vashisht* v. *University of Delhi; Samiya Singh* v. *University of Delhi; Manpreet Kaur* v. *University of Delhi; Samuel S.L. Serto* v. *University of Delhi,* the petitioners posed a common question as all these petitioners were detained from appearing in the semester examinations on account of shortfall of their attendance.

Justice Kailash Gambhir expressed his views on the same in the following words:

"Eminent jurist Nani Palkhivala once remarked that lawyers education is a process extending over a whole career. It starts with the academic stage, extends through training in courts and continues through a mix of self education and learning from peers for long as a person is involved in legal work. The stress is on the importance of the capacity to learn, which must be developed at the earliest possible stage **i.e.** *the law school. It is this vital capacity, in my opinion, which marks the distinction between getting a degree and having an education.*

Our Colleges of law do not hold a place of high esteem either at home or abroad, nor has law become an area of profound scholarship or enlightened research" observed Dr. Sarvepalli Radhakrishnan some decades ago. But today we have travelled a long distance since then, altering the landscape of legal education in our country. We are just marginally away from the profound scholarship and enlightened research and we must proudly admit that Dr. Radhakrishnan's powerful and poignant words are amenable to radical restatement today. The subject matter of the present petitions is a case of an unfortunately prevalent trend in the now otherwise highly systemized scheme of legal education that exist today, but there is a marked change in the scenario than what it was when the above observations were made. The oft quipped statement that many students enter into the portals of a law college because they cannot be anywhere else seems is far from truth today as law now ranks high in the list of highly preferred professions. But, alas, the problem of absenteeism has taken the face of a chronic disease plaguing the edifice of the legal education system. Those students who do not attend classes have a strong conviction that they are not suffering significantly by their absence and the absenteeism does not affect their clearing the examinations with good grades. But the status of legal profession is directly linked with the legal education process. It is high time that the law students understand that there is no royal road to education and education teaches only those in attendance. Lawyers are always going to be students and the learning does not stop in law school. The quality and standard of legal education acquired at law school is reflected through the standard of the Bar and the Bench and consequently affects the legal system. Hence a student who is habitual to not attending classes in law school would seek adjournments later in his cases thus infesting the whole system.

Carving out an exception for female students unable to attend classes on account of their pregnancy held:

> *Of all the rights of women, to be a mother is the greatest. Long ago, the Universal Declaration of Human Rights, by Article 25 had declared that everyone has the right to a standard of living adequate for the health and well-being of himself and of his family, including food, clothing, housing and medical care and necessary social services, and the right to security in the event of unemployment, sickness, disability, widowhood, old age or other lack of livelihood in circumstances beyond his control. Article 25(2) provides that:*
>
> *(2) Motherhood and childhood are entitled to special care and assistance. All children, whether born in or out of wedlock, shall enjoy the same social protection. In the light of the above discussion, if any female candidate is deprived or detained in any of the semester just on the ground that she could not attend classes being in the advanced stage of pregnancy or due to the delivery of the child, then such an act on the part of any of the university or college would not only be completely in negation of the conscience of the Constitution of India but also of the women rights and gender equality this nation has long been striving for. It is a saying that "Motherhood is priced of God, at price no man may dare to lessen or misunderstand". By not granting these students relaxation, we will be making motherhood a crime which no civilized democracy in the history of mankind has ever done or will ever do. We cannot make them pay the price for the glory that is motherhood.*
>
> *It would not be inappropriate to mention at this juncture the recent rulings of the Apex Court in the cases of* Lata Singh *v.* State of Uttar Pradesh, *AIR 2006 SC 2522: 2006 Cr LJ 3309: 2006 AIR SCW 3499 and* S. Khushboo *v.* Kanniammal, *AIR 2010 SC 3196:*

2010 Cr LJ 2828: 2010 AIR SCW 2770: MANU/SC/0310/2010 where it has given liberty to the live-in relationship from the shackles of being an offence and also in the latter case where it has held that premarital sex is not an offence. The society today is changing at a rapid pace and we must be in tune with the realities and not hold on to archaic social mores. Once such a right, however unpopular, is recognized then it cannot be ruled out that there can be more cases of girl students proceeding on maternity leave when while they are still in college. Law should be an instrument of social change and not a defender of it. Motherhood is not a medical condition but a promise. We all kowtow to our mothers to whom we owe our existence and to punish a woman for becoming a mother would surely be the mother of all ironies.

Bar Council of India, although not a party in the present writ petitions is hereby suggested to make rules for women students claiming relaxation on ground of maternity relief so that they are not deprived of appearing in the LLB examinations due to pregnancy.

College is a time when students are able to grow and mature before going into the real world. At omega, it would be in the right earnest to hope that the students understand that attending college is important in the context of their future plans and goals, not just in terms of grades and academic success. Nevertheless, law colleges would still remain places where pebbles are polished and not where diamonds are dimmed and law students not bottles to be filled but candles to be lit."

Special Care for Persons/Children Suffering

Dyslexia is an impediment in the path of processing symbols by the brain but it does not make one incompetent. Looking at the sad predicament of students troubled with this unnatural complexity, Justice Gambhir in a writ petition suggested that it is the responsibility of the school authorities as well as that of parents of the child to channelize their energies, so that such children can successfully prosper. He encouraged them to make a concerted endeavor by sharing their acclivitous job and not subjecting them to their administrative tyranny leaving them in lurch.

The following case deals with the case of a child who was denied his right to education granted by the Indian constitution merely on the ground of him being dyslexic.

Justice Gambhir in a writ petition bearing W.P.(C) No. 3221/2010 *Master Priyam Kumar* v. *Director of Education*, suggested that it is the responsibility of the school authorities as well as the parents of the child to channelize their energies, so that such children can successfully prosper and to make concerted efforts to share their acclivitous job and not subject them to their administrative tyranny leaving them in lurch.

Dealing with this susceptible issue Hon'ble Mr. Justice Kailash Gambhir distinctly held that:

> *"The petitioner who was diagnosed as a case of Dyslexia and ADHD needs to be given special care by the school authorities instead of meting out such a harsh and inhumane treatment. It is not in dispute that the petitioner had been a student of the respondent school right from Ist standard and that he was being promoted to higher classes upto VIIIth standard. The petitioner also appears to be a creative student and that he had been performing excellently so far co-curricular activities are concerned including in the field of sports. The Dy. Director, DOE has already directed the school to retain the petitioner but adopting an insensitive attitude the respondent school has not reverted its decision.*
>
> *School poses multiple challenges for students with dyslexia, ADHD and such other disorders, but it is the responsibility of the school to provide a friendly and conducive environment to channelize their energies so that such children can successfully thrive in the classroom. They are to be handled with great compassion, sensitivity and offered support by the school and not to be treated in such an abrasive manner like the respondent school has done. Parents of such like children already have an arduous task and the schools are expected to make concerted efforts to share their acclivitous job and not subject them to their administrative tyranny leaving them in lurch. Taking into consideration the aforesaid facts and circumstances, it is directed that respondent no. 3 shall allow the petitioner to continue with his studies in the IXth standard till further directions are given by this court."*

Concept of Fee Concession and Free Ship

This is nothing but abuse of the valuable social legislations and an abuse of the court of law, besides an assault on the opportunities of the ones truly deserving these concessions. Education is a must, it is our fundamental right and no one can deprive us from learning or educating ourselves. But misusing our rights for erroneous purposes is highly unacceptable and felonious.

Justice Gambhir unmasked the deceitful conduct of an educated man who falsely claimed to be a man of no means solely to facilitate the education of his child through legal means in the case of *Shishti Solkar* v. *Mahavir Sr. Model School,* W.P. (C) No. 1659/2011.

The court rapped the attitude of the petitioner and held:

> *"that the concept of fee concession and free ship as envisaged in the two statutes is with the aim and object that those who do not have the means to give education to their children are not deprived, as education has become the necessity for survival in this day of cut throat competition. Education is a right not a luxury in our country and the statutes are to abridge the gap between the goal and the reality. The country has gone through a long struggle to put itself on the world map and be known for its brilliantly trained minds, but this has not been without the struggle that the parents go through for making every possible endeavour to educate their child. Today, education is empowerment and with a view that the economically weaker sections and the disadvantaged groups are not left behind, a social obligation has been cast upon the private unaided schools to provide fee concession to the deserving students, but this does not mean that the parents who have the prime responsibility to provide education to their child put the burden on the school. The parents cannot in any manner shirk away from their duty in the garb of belonging to the weaker section of society and as a matter of right demand concessions from the schools. Indians today are highly aware and informed citizens and the demand for inclusive education has never been as fervent as it is today, and for the State to fulfil the expectation of every common man for providing a better tomorrow to his child through education should no doubt be the ambition of this country, but the chasm that exists between achieving this goal and the reality cannot be overlooked and shied away from. The present is a classic example of the parent, petitioner No. 2 herein, who is educated and is in a profession, but does not wish to pay for the education of his child, and falsely claims to be a man of no means and wants to realize the education of his child through the portals of law, is nothing but an exploitation of the beneficial social legislations and an abuse of the court of law, besides an assault on the opportunities of the ones truly deserving these concessions. The petitioner No. 2 is a compulsive litigator, who has not come to the court with cleanhands, coupled with his recalcitrant attitude of not paying the outstanding arrears of fee to respondent No. 2 discredits him from any relief by this court."*

Equal Opportunities to Disabled Persons

India being a welfare State has a great responsibility to promote overall development of its citizens including those who are differently abled in order to enable them to lead a life of dignity, equality, freedom and justice as mandated by the Constitution of India. Therefore, bringing them in the society and treating them as equals is the need of the hour.

Ranjana Verma v. *AIIMS,* W.P.(C) No. 4465/2011 is a case where a person was not given the benefit for being disabled and Hon'ble Mr. Justice Kailash Gambhir laid stress on the fact that the differently abled persons are also humans and in a soul-stirring manner laid down that:

> *"the Persons with Disabilities (Equal Opportunities, Protection of Rights and Full Participation) Act, 1995 was enacted to give effect to the Proclamation on the full participation and equality of people with disabilities in the Asian and Pacific Region to which India is a signatory. This Act is undoubtedly a beneficial piece of social legislation and its provisions are mandatory in nature. Section 39 of the said Act reads as:*
>
> *"All Government educational institutions and other educational institutions receiving aid from the Government shall reserve not less than three per cent seats for persons with disabilities."*
>
> *Thus the provision was enacted to provide a level playing field to the disabled persons in the realm of education to have an attitude free of preconceived bias against these sufferers of fate. The court is mindful of the fact that the above said provision of 3% reservation in educational institutions cannot be done away with especially by the premier institutes such as the respondents, as it would lead to bringing the spirit and object of the Act to naught."*

Object of the Admission Procedure Involving of a Written Test and then for a Group Discussion, Essay Writing and Interview etc.

As every year passes more and more students come forward for admission in various institutes and thus the selection criteria has also considerably transformed. The applicants have to go through various steps to finally get qualified for admission. This tedious and arduous exercise is performed so as to judge the capacity and merit of the applicant as in today's competitive world only the best can survive. As Charles Darwin said *"It is not the strongest of the species that survive, nor the most intelligent, but the one most responsive to change."*

In *Ritu Aggarwal* v. *Indian Institute of Foreign Trade,* W.P.(C) No. 3620/2011; *Namrata Panwar* v. *Indian Institute of Foreign Trade,* W.P.(C) No. 3618/2011; & *Mayank Gupta* v. *Indian Institute of Foreign Trade,* W.P. (C) No. 3845/2011 the students had been the victim of a clerical error of the institute and hence, when the discrepancy came to light, found them and thus approached the court. Understanding the importance of competitive examinations and that the major aim of this competitive examination is to find out a suitable and meritorious candidate, Hon'ble Mr. Justice Kailash Gambhir poignantly noticed that:

"It is manifest and cannot be overlooked, that the criteria laid down by the respondent for admission consisting of a written test and then for a group discussion, essay writing and interview etc. is with the object to select the best from the lot for the said MBA (International Business) programme. Today in the time of cut throat competition, there are umpteen number of candidates vying for every single seat and it is a hard hitting reality that admission to various colleges, especially to the professional institutes like the respondent have become a Herculean task. It is unlike the bygone days when the marks in the last examination cleared would entitle you to admission in a professional course as now a lot of factors are taken into consideration which are measured by the yardstick of written examination, group discussion, etc. Undertaking a professional course from a prestigious college guarantees the future in the job arena and hence students prepare for months for these exams, enrolling themselves in coaching centers, taking tuitions, so that they are able to make it to the top notch institutes. Merit and merit alone is the mantra today and being able to get admission in the desired college is a dream come true for many. Undoubtedly, the respondent and other such institutes have to be very careful and diligent with the expert staff in place to prepare the correct result of such candidates and any wrong declaration of the result, can jeopardize the career and future of these students. It is no doubt possible that had these petitioners known that they were selected for the Kolkata campus they certainly could have tried their luck to seek admission in some other course or with some other professional institute. Admittedly their ranking in the merit list is much lower than the ranking of the last candidate who secured admission at Delhi, which is a case of one Arnav Kapoor, who secured the rank of 286 and while the last candidate who secured admission at the Kolkata campus was at the rank of 592. Certainly there cannot be any justification to perpetuate such a wrong and that too such a wrong which would demoralize the meritorious candidates. The writ jurisdiction is jurisdiction of equity and this equitable jurisdiction cannot be exercised in favour of those who are not entitled to such a relief. If the case of these petitioners is accepted then even a student having failed in exam but wrongly declared successful in the admission will also claim his admission because of such wrong declaration in his results. The petitioners thus cannot claim any advantage and rather undue advantage because of the error committed by data operator at the time of insertion of their marks."

CHAPTER 9
SERVICE AND LABOUR MATTERS

Morality, Truth and Mahatma Gandhi

Gandhi, was a man worshipped and revered worldwide and aptly given the moniker "Mahatma" for his tryst with the freedom struggle. Of all the moral principles, Gandhi placed truth as first and foremost; He called it "the sovereign principle". Every person is faced with numerous situations where these principles can be compromised or followed thereby proving their relevance. But the beauty of time is that it does not stay the same forever. Being truthful is undoubtedly the idyllic way of life, which should not be worn like a garment, worn and removed at your own whims and fancies with changing time.

Hon'ble Justice Gambhir dealt with these accredits in the case of *Kanhaiya Lal* v. *The Union of India,* 2011 (179) DLT 288, wherein the petitioner who was working as a Chowkidar at the Samadhi of the Father of the nation, failed to follow the alleyway of truth, the principles that he could not emulate and imbibe himself while working at Gandhi's samadhi. The court taking a compassionate view so far as the conduct of the petitioner of his audacity as he lied through his teeth, as an exceptional case, the court directed him to offer his daily prayers for at least two hours for a period of one month to seek penitence for committing the sin of being untruthful to the court of law.

Justice Gambhir making known his anguish and displeasure held as under:

> *"It is quite agonizing and antagonizing at the same time to find that the petitioner who worked as a Chowkidar for a period of about two years to act as a sentinel of the Samadhi of the Father of the Nation, who led us to achieve "Swaraj" sacrificing his life for the cause of a free India without compromising his cherished ideals of truthfulness, non-violence and peace could not emulate and imbibe the said principles himself. The petitioner by taking a false stand of claiming his employment with the respondent from the year 1990 till 1999 has not only committed an act of perjury with the court but in fact has committed a greater sin with his own soul.*

The paradox which this Court is now confronted with is that the petitioner who was a Chowkidar and was rendered unemployed should be proceeded with for committing perjury or should be pardoned following the much revered principles of Mahatma Gandhi, as the petitioner was mercilessly turned out of the employment by the respondent without following the due process of law. Perusal of the records produced by the respondent clearly shows that the petitioner had worked on the post of Chowkidar as a daily wager w.e.f. September, 1997 till 1999 and then suddenly he was thrown out from the employment without any rhyme or reason.

While delivering the verdict he also noted:

Mahatma Gandhi, a man worshipped not only by this country but by the world stood for his cannons of truth and non violence even in the dark times of freedom struggle. He said:

Morality is the basis of things and truth is the substance of all morality. But it is this morality, which today, when the winds of materialism and capitalism are blowing in our society, seems cast in a shadow of despair. It is no doubt true that falsehood is easy and truth difficult, but that does not entail that the virtue of truthfulness be worn like a garment, worn and removed at our own will. It would not be wrong to say that in the time of universal deceit today, speaking the truth seems like a revolutionary act. The soil of this nation is soaked with the blood, toil and principles of the Father of the Nation, and the Samadhi is the repository of his great soul reminding us never to forget the path of ideals he so painstakingly carved for us. The petitioner by falsely deposing has not only failed this Court but also all that that great soul stood for."

Human Rights – Role of NHRC – Periodical Extension in Service

Human Rights means the rights which speak of life, liberty, equality and dignity of the individual guaranteed by the constitution or embodied in the International covenants and enforceable by courts in India. NHRC is playing a crucial role in implementation of human rights, responsible for its protection and promotion. It is the prime duty of the commission to ensure that no citizen of the country is deprived of his personal rights. It is however ironic that how blatantly it refused one of its own employees/a Hawaldar in army from availing the same and that is what triggered the judiciary to echo the commission's responsibility.

There has been a barefaced violation of the human rights of the petitioner, who after putting in about more than 10 years of service was thrown out on the ground that his appointment was *de hors* the recruitment rules.

In the case of *Rajinder Prasad* v. *NHRC*, 2010 (3) SLR 26, the petitioner sought directions for his reinstatement with respondent on the post of Constable and also for declaring his services from the year 1997 to 2006 in the category of re-employment. The petitioner also claimed grant of all consequential benefits after directing his reinstatement retrospectively from 1-9-2006.

Whilst imposing cost, justice Gambhir brought to dock the respondent for such an inhumane conduct and held:

> *"Human rights are those inalienable and natural rights without which we cannot live as human beings. The National Human Rights Commission (NHRC) was set up under the Human Rights Act, 1993 with the objective of safeguarding human rights by investigating human rights violations and punishing the offenders, including those whose negligence permitted the offence. Fortunately, NHRC is playing an effective role in implementation of human rights and sets up right the Government entities but relentless human rights violation of the present petitioner by NHRC, itself has gone unnoticed by it. The claims raised by the petitioner from time to time before NHRC fell to the deaf ears. There has been blatant violation of the human rights of the petitioner, who after putting in about more than 10 years of service was thrown out on the ground that his appointment was dehors the recruitment rules. Such periodical extensions on service ruins one's entire career and at times the employee gets deprived of many opportunities may be because of over age or other factors, which otherwise would have been available if such an employee would have shown the exit door at the earliest possible time. The petitioner must also show the blame for his sufferings as he was fully aware that his appointment was not backed by the recruitment rules. The Apex Court in catena of judgments has held that Courts cannot show undue sympathy or generosity in such cases of illegal appointment as the function of the Courts is to see whether there has been strict adherence to the scheme of the Constitution or Recruitment Rules and other statutory provisions dealing with public employment, which of course have to be fair and transparent for all the eligible persons seeking employment on such posts instead of making way for the few favoured one's who get entry through back doors either with the influence of high ups or through some other extraneous means. Since the respondent Commission failed to protect the human rights of the petitioner concerned, who will be thrown on the road to struggle again to search for a job, the same being in serious violation of his human rights, costs of Rs. 1 lakh is imposed on the respondent for their such an inhuman act. Costs of*

Rs. 1 lakh shall be paid by the respondent to the petitioner within a period of four weeks from the date of this order."

Freedom Movement – Freedom Fighters and SSS Pension Scheme

Freedom fighters, who are responsible for giving us a free country, are to be revered and not discarded, and hence the Government should be a little more considerate and thoughtful while considering cases that involve freedom fighters. We attained freedom almost six decades back and it is so unfathomable to note that people who fought for it, because of whom we breathe the air of freedom today, are made to run from pillar to post in courts for claiming meagre amount of pension from government treasuries. The Delhi High Court considering the plight of one of such persons opined that the Government should deal with such matters on priority basis without languor, with due importance and concern.

The case of *Shri Satish Chandra Mishra* v. *Union of India,* 164 (2009) DLT 172 highlights the hypocrisy of the Government which on one hand launched the SSS Pension Scheme and at the same time denied the same to a valiant freedom fighter legible for the same. Present is a case where the clear lack of empathy on the part of the government loomed large.

While deciding this case and elucidating as to what gave the pension scheme its sanction, justice Gambhir remarkably noted:

"Today as we freely move around in our country without anyone questioning or imposing any kinds of restrictions on us we feel satisfied and contended. But this satisfaction is due to the efforts made by our freedom fighters to free our country from the British rule. It is because of our freedom fighters that today we are enjoying our freedom. Their satyagrahas, sacrifices, and tortures have resulted in the freedom that we enjoy today in our motherland India. Free India is a gift to each one of us from these freedom fighters. As a mark of respect and to pay are gratitude to them the Government started the SSS Pension Scheme. But cases like the present one show the apathy and pithiness of our Government on one hand it launches SSS Pension Scheme and on the other hand it arbitrarily denies the same to such freedom fighters who are eligible for it. The government should not deal with such matters in an arbitrary and shabby manner. These freedom fighters who now are very aged should not be made to run from pillar to post for grant of SSS Pension Scheme for which they are eligible. The Government should be little more considerate and thoughtful while dealing with such cases."

Cost of medical treatment to Government Servant

Cancer is a deadly disease which requires day to day care and treatment. As an employee we are promised to be taken care of, for most of our medical & health related problems and the criteria is set from department to department basis and with cost of medical treatment being on an forever upsurge, it is difficult for a common man to avail the best of medical benefits in that meagre salary. Government plays a pivotal role in formulating such policies as well as executing the same, still there are certain ambiguities which makes access to such facilities sluggish when we require them the most. It is the need of the hour that with the advent of inflation, even the policies formulated are revised as what costed 5 paisa decades ago costs Rs. 15 in today's age and time.

The judgment in the case of *K.K. Kharbanda* v. *The Union of India*, W.P. (C) 6049/2005 is one such example wherein the Hon'ble Justice Gambhir examined the facts keeping in view the law, as well as the need of the petitioner and went on to say that with the change in time, the policies should also be revised and the compensation be given accordingly. The present case is based on peculiar facts and circumstances and the petitioner approached this Court feeling aggrieved with the withholding of the medical reimbursement claim to the full extent as regards the treatment of the wife of the petitioner for cancer for which ceiling limit was removed later on. Whilst deciding the present case justice Gambhir made a mention of the "stark increase in the cost of medical treatment" and held as under:

> *"Be that as it may, health service forms a very important part of existence of an individual. Government servants are provided the benefit of medical aid as within the limited financial emoluments available to them they would be unable to meet large medical expenses which may arise in certain exigencies. The chances of seeking such medical aid increases as the years go by and a person gets older. In fact the better medical facility back-up is required at that age.*
>
> *The cost of medical treatment has been rising over a period of time and respondents cannot deny the actual reimbursement from a Hospital recognised by them for treatment on the basis of the rates as per the previous decision of 1989 herein, which cannot remain static and should be revised regularly. When the policy was adopted in 1989, the rates fixed had nexus with the actual treatment cost charged by the hospitals. When the treatment was taken by the petitioner and his wife in 2001-2002, the hospitals had revised/raised their rates but still the respondents reimbursed the petitioner as per its 1989 policy. The hospitals cannot be blamed for raising the cost of treatment due to the components of treatment becoming costlier. But the Government has to bear the expenses incurred by the Government Servant as the Government servant cannot within his limited earning bear the expenses for the treatment*

of his ailments. In this regard, the Supreme Court had duly noted in State of Punjab *v.* Mohinder Singh Chawla, *AIR 1997 SC 1225: 1997 AIR SCW 1260: (1997) 2 SCC 83 as under:*

The law is therefore, well-settled that right to health is an integral part of life and the Government has constitutional obligation to provide the health facilities to its employees or retired employees and in case an employee requires a specialised treatment in an approved hospital it is the duty of the Government to bear or reimburse the expenses. It is in this context that the Supreme Court in Mohinder Singh Chawla etc. (Supra) observed as under:

It is now settled law that right to health is integral to the right to life. Government has a constitutional obligation to provide health facilities. If the Government servant has suffered an ailment, which required treatment at, a specialized approved hospital and on reference whereat the government servant has undergone such treatment therein, it is but the duty of the State to bear the expenditure incurred by the Government servant. Expenditure, thus, incurred requires to be reimbursed by the State to the employee.

Cancer comes in the category of chronic disease. Even after treatment at the hospital the follow-up treatment continues because of the possibility of relapse of the same. Thus, clearly the expenses incurred upon the wife of the petitioner as an outdoor patient, are reimbursable. Therefore, the issue No. 3 is answered in the affirmative.

When a Government employee puts forth a bona fide *claim for reimbursement of his medical bill, it should not be taken lightly and the approach of the Government in such matters should be justice oriented. Such claims should be treated in a humanitarian manner keeping in mind the totality of circumstances. In view of the foregoing, I feel that EIC by its arbitrary approach made the petitioner to suffer not merely the agony of withholding the medical expenses, which were reimbursable, under the guise of ceiling limit but also made him go through the tribulation of litigation."*

Solitary Act of Corruption will be Sufficient Enough to Award Punishment of Dismissal from Service

Justice Gambhir has time and again spread the message that no leniency or sympathy can be shown to a person who indulges himself in corruption at any level and by all means, corruption has to be uprooted completely from the Indian system. Corruption to whatever extent, is poisonous for our country and no matter how big or how small the act of corruption is, the need of the hour is to treat such acts with equal stringency.

In this case *Shanti Devi* v. *DTC,* W.P. (C) No. 3804/2007 Hon'ble Mr. Justice Kailash Gambhir taking a very stern and unrelenting stand opined that:

> *"no sympathy can be shown to the petitioner who is bound to suffer because of the corrupt deeds of her husband. The past clean record of the deceased would also be of no help to the petitioner as the solitary act of corruption will be sufficient enough to award punishment of dismissal from service. No doubt, it may look harsh and perhaps inequitable to uphold punishment of removal in cases where misappropriation of a small amount of money is concerned, more particularly when the big sharks are seen swimming comfortably without any fear of law and law enforcing agencies. Strangely, corruption is a paradoxical phenomenon as the highly placed corrupt officials, rich and influential, save themselves from the clutches of law by corrupting those whose primary job is to take action against the corrupt people. Henceforth, it is in this way how the evil of corruption is well flourishing and has now, so to say, carved a comfortable niche for itself in the societal framework. It is not surprising that rather than becoming a hard hitting reality to which people should object and frown upon, looking with disdain upon those indulging in such unethical practice, it has gained acceptance as an indispensable virtue and is gradually becoming a way of life. Therefore, no leniency or sympathy can be shown even to a person who indulges himself in corruption even at a small level and by all means, corruption has to be checked and nipped in the bud. It is not the amount but the mind and intention of a corrupt person which has to be checked and the conductor on duty can only indulge in corruption at a small level and one cannot expect him to misappropriate amount of thousands and lacs of rupees as his job is to issue tickets and non issuance of the same can only result into pocketing small amounts on daily basis. However, nevertheless, by that process alone, his daily and monthly earnings sometimes may be more than his official income. Therefore as a society this widespread malpractice has to be de-fenestrated."*

Promotion

"Promotion" is instrumental in encouraging the employees to put earnest efforts while rendering service. Furthermore, increase in competitiveness is also corollary to Promotion. Promotion results in the overall development of not just the employee but also the organisation.

The case of *Captain Bindu Sethi* v. *Union of India,* W.P. (C) 4840/2010 and *Captain Bindu Sethi* v. *R.K. Singh Secretary,* Cont. Cas (C) 475/2012 is regarding a petitioner who was earlier serving in the Indian Army and had joined the BSF Air Wing in the year 1992. The petitioner lost his right of promotion to the rank of Senior Captain only because he could not fulfil the prescribed flying hours and not for any other reason. Considering the magnitude of promotion in service, Hon'ble Mr. Justice Kailash Gambhir observed that:

> *"36. Promotion in any service career is a very important event, which every employee aspires for. Any unjust and arbitrary denial of this right to an employee would be a gross violation of his fundamental right of equality before law and equal protection of the laws as enunciated under Article 14 of the Constitution of India. Once, this right of consideration for promotion has been held to be fundamental, then such right must accrue to the petitioner immediately after any post falls vacant or is created or at least within a reasonable period of time. Any unreasonable or arbitrary delay to such right of an employee would amount to unjust denial of his legitimate right for consideration of his case for promotion and the same would also be in violation of his fundamental rights. It is often seen that in many cases, employees are denied their promotion during their service period and it is only through Court's intervention that a person gets his promotion, often post retirement, just for deriving financial benefits. In the Armed and Para-Military Forces, denial of such right of timely promotion is more agonising, as any unreasonable delay on part of the authorities not only denies a member of the Forces, a higher rank but also the privilege of tenure of service commensurate with the higher rank."*

Restore One's Glory and Honour: Quashing of Suspension Letter

Dignity and honour in the armed forces is not a preserve of mere high ranking officers but the lower ranks deserve to be equally respected. In given situations genuine officials need to be dealt with a compassionate and humane approach.

In one such case *Abrar Ali* v. *CISF*, 2014 (144) DRJ 446, Hon'ble Mr. Justice Kailash Gambhir while sitting in A Division Bench threw light on the aspect of maintaining the dignity of all the officials of the armed forces irrespective of their rank and vividly held and observed as follows:

> *"Undeniably there cannot be any compromise so far the question of maintaining discipline, honesty, devotion and professional sanctity is concerned of all the persons employed in the Indian Armed Forces and in the other Paramilitary forces but at the same time the senior officers should always take care that the honour and dignity of even the officer of the lowest rank is not hampered. Ultimately one*

must realize the fact that all the members of these forces serve the country even when they are posted in far flung and hard areas, far away from their families and other near and dear ones. Being humans, we must say that in given situations they also deserve the compassion and concerns for their genuine problems. In this case the petitioner had reported back on his duties on the afternoon of 15th and yet shockingly without losing any time he was served with the suspension order just within a few hours despite the fact that the officer was conspicuous of the fact that the petitioner has been roped in a criminal case for which even the villagers of the locality were looking for him. The Assistant Commandant had also forgotten that it was our country's Independence Day, a most cherished and treasured day for all Indians. A day when the entire nation celebrates its freedom from foreign rule and remembers its freedom fighters and martyrs, it is a day that signifies liberty. Atleast the Assistant Commandant should not have snatched away the liberty of this petitioner and could have waited to ascertain the correct facts before initiating any precipitate action resulting in taking away the liberty, rights or livelihood of the petitioner. The respondents' action is unjustified and deserves to be quashed. Serendipitously, we are on the eve of another Independence Day when the nation is heady in the mood of celebration of freedom, we feel that there could be not better occasion to restore one's glory and honour which was unfairly snatched away about 15 years ago."

CHAPTER 10

CASES OF WRIT JURISDICTION

Caste – Equality and Exceptions

Delay in issuance of a caste certificate is quite a prevalent practise due to which the common man suffers in the longer run. The case of *Smt. Poonam* v. *Government, NCT of Delhi,* W.P. (C) No. 8508/2007 & *Ms. Pushpa* v. *Government, NCT of Delhi,* W.P. (C) No. 9112/2008 is yet another glaring example of the indifferent approach that is adopted by various government departments in discharging the functions they are entrusted with in a timely fashion. In the present case the department did not issue the caste certificate well within time irrespective of various representations made by the applicant herein which he was supposed to submit while applying for the post of Assistant Primary Teacher in the category of OBC. As a consequence, the applicant had to compense with his career.

The judgment herein below embodies that the caste certificate is only an affirmation of the fact which is already in existence and its late submission due to the fault of issuing authority should not prove detrimental to the rights of a candidates seeking employment under the reserved category.

Giving a background of how caste became the basis of identification, justice Gambhir held

> *"that caste is the only accepted criteria to identify underrepresented groups. The underlying theory is that the under-representation of the identifiable groups is a legacy of the Indian caste system. After India gained independence, the Constitution of India listed some erstwhile groups as Scheduled Castes (SC) and Scheduled Tribes (ST). The framers of the Constitution believed that, due to the caste system, SCs and the STs were historically oppressed and denied respect and equal opportunity in Indian society and were thus under-represented in nation-building activities. Later, reservations were introduced for other sections as well.*
>
> *No citizen may be discriminated against by the state only on any of these grounds. The exceptions to this principle are made in favour of women and children, the backward classes, the Scheduled Castes*

and the Scheduled Tribes, and the weaker sections. The principle of equality permeates the Constitution of India. All the citizens are entitled to be treated by the state equally, irrespective of their caste, race, religion, sex, descent, place of birth and residence, these are some of the lofty ideals which the supreme law of the lands envisaged."

Right to Health & Directions to Secretary, Telecommunication and Commissioner, MCD

The health concerns regarding the cellular towers erected in residential areas had come before the court much before they hit the headlines. The present case dealt with the onerous fees charged by the civic agency for erecting these towers and the resistance by the cellular operators. However, the court observed how mobile phones though may pose a health scare but have become indispensable.

Cellular Operators Association of India v. MCD, CM. 6546/2010 in W.P.(C) No. 3267/10 & Idea Cellular Ltd. v. MCD, CM. 6867/2010 in W.P.(C) No. 3423/2010

He advertently held that:

"It has culminated into a want, which is as natural as food and water. We cannot dispute our dependence on the mobile phone today when owning it has become proportional to personal empowerment. It is a silver bullet to the vagaries and vicissitudes of life. Earlier, the connectivity was scarce but now the service providers with their impeccable connectivity have lured the rickshaw wala and the millionaire alike to its consortium. This is one place where Marx's theory of class divide n social divides seems to fall flat in the face. From a pauper to a business tycoon own a mobile. It is as normal as the air they breathe."

"Political language ... is designed to make lies sound truthful & murder respectable & to give an appearance of solidarity to pure wind..."—George Orwell

The veracity of the impromptu promises made by persons in power has been rightly questioned on many occasions. In today's time, with a boom in the number of mishaps, it has become rather conspicuous that persons in power make hollow promises to the victims of such incidents and their families. It has become well known that such instantaneous promises are nothing more than a charade. The victims want the authorities to feel their pain and take up their cause instead of putting on mask of false pretense. What is the sanctity of on the spot announcements made by the Ministers and the others holding high positions whenever such kind of incidents, blasts and mishaps take place? This question has become very relevant in today's times as more and more incidents are taking place due to negligence or due to religious conflicts as a result of which innocent public has to bear the brunt and be at the suffering end. The victims of such incidents and their families do not need fake promises or consolations rather they want to see their grievances felt by those in authority and want the authorities to act and compensate for their loss.

The case of *Faryaz @ Fayaz* **v.** *Union of India,* W.P. (C) 1877/2015, is one such instance, wherein, the Railway minister raised the hopes of the victims of a blast and their families with one hand and crushed them with the other hand. The Minister also announced that the Ministry of Railways would give jobs in the Railway Department to one family member of each Indian killed in the blast along with compensation of 10 lakhs.

Hon'ble Justice Kailash Gambhir presiding over a Division Bench observed that, as public authorities or the powers that be, are morally, ethically and legally bound by the announcements that they make and that they should not make "hollow promises". He went onto slap a cost of Rs. 1,00,000 on the Railways for the prolonged delay in giving a job to the son of a victim of the 2007 Samjhauta Express bombings.

He opined as follows:

> *"a catastrophic event more often than not, is unforeseen and one cannot always be prepared to handle the consequences that ensue. The public functionaries holding high offices in order to provide solace and succour to those affected by such fateful events, make public announcements promising monetary compensation and employment to the family members of the deceased to tide over the difficult time. These promises are the silver lining for these family members and cannot remain unfulfilled, as otherwise people will lose faith in the authorities. The public office holders cannot use these promises in times of distress as a tool for salvaging public outcry and political turmoil. It no doubt goes to the credit of the public functionaries that as representatives of the government as a welfare State, they make these announcements on the spot which gives a ray of hope to the families affected, but at the same time, they being responsible for what assurances they give should be cautious about its feasibility and foresee any circumstances that would be an impediment to its potential practical implementation. It is a caveat for all those who occupy offices which are in a position to mitigate the pain and suffering of the family of the victims by way of promises,*

to be responsible and mindful while making them as they are not only bound by them morally, ethically but above all legally. The Indian Railways are the lifeline of our nation as they touch the lives of millions of people every day. Being the largest railway network in the world, it has and still continues to play a pivotal role in our vibrant economy. Unfortunate instances of train bombings and accidents are very distressing for those who lose their loved ones to such mishaps and such conduct of the people placed high up on the political ladder, as in the case at hand, who turn their back on such promises is agonizing and appalling, adding insult to injury. Such a somersault on promises gives an impression to the already distraught people that those were mere empty promises made at the spur of the moment and were never meant to be kept. In this regard, it is for the respondents to frame rules to meet such situations. Present is one such case where terrorist bombings on Delhi-Attari Express (link train of Samjhauta Express) killed the petitioner's mother and as promised by the respondents to give a job in the Railway Department to one family member of each Indian killed in the blast, was not adhered to, such should not be the conduct of a Government department like the Railways. High Public functionaries should not make hollow promises rather they should effectively monitor and ensure implementation of the announcements made by them and handle all such sensitive situations without any bias. As existing on this date, we find no reason to deny the relief to the petitioner who was given an assurance by none else than the highest functionary i.e. *the Railway Minister and to deny the said right to him would be a great injustice and also against our ethics and moralities."*

Teacher – Student Relationship: A Victim of Covetousness

In India, since ancient times, pupils were trained to idolize their Guru. Gurus were placed right after God in the hierarchy of worshipping. It is flabbergasting how; in the modern times, these Gurus *i.e.* Teachers have come to sexually abuse their own students. The instinct of lust overpowers morality and ethics resulting in such a heinous act, which shocks the conscience of the society.

Present was a case where the guide became the perpetrator of a crime. From ancient times we have placed gurus on the highest pedestal. second only to God. And we as a country are known for the fountain of compassion respect reverence that we have towards our gurus. We vouch for 'guru shishya parampara', and hold it in the highest esteem. A teacher has a profound impact on a child and like they say, a teacher sure affects eternity and his influence never ceases to exist.

While deciding one such case namely *Udai Singh* v. *Kendriya Vidayalaya Sangathan,* W.P. (C) 8440/2011 & C.M. Appl. No. 1370/2012, where the teacher harassed his female student on the pretext of providing tutorials, Justice Gambhir came down heavily on such act of the teacher while sitting in a Division Bench. He blatantly refused to set aside the termination of the KVS teacher, saying his "dissipated" conduct would set a bad precedent for the students, especially boys.

Taking a stern view having regard to the graveness of the matter, Hon'ble Mr. Justice Kailash Gambhir held that:

> *"Guru Govind Dou Khade, Kakke laagun paye..Balihari guru aapne, govind dio bataye." This immensely popular & often quoted couplet by Poet-Saint Kabir has a profound foothold. It says I face both God and my guru, who should I bow first? I first bow to my guru because he's the one who showed me the path to God. The importance given to a teacher or a guru in our society thus needs no special mention. Since times immemorial, the relationship between teachers and students has been venerated. It is considered to be a pious bond which is further strengthened by the knots of trust, respect and utmost devotion. Teachers play a pivotal role in shaping a child's life and to help decide the course which the child would eventually take in his life path. They are the torchbearers who lead from the front and mould a child like a potter moulds the clay to give it shape and being. Teachers have been known to influence their students by shaping their rational and moral values and hence, play an important role in moulding the society as a whole. But with the changing times, this pious and sacramental bond has also come under the scanner. Now-a-days even this revered relationship has become a victim of covetousness, lust and contemptible desires, because of which the students do not consider their teachers as their "gurus" in the true sense of the word. The teachers are also heard of exploiting students, going to the extent of sexually abusing them. This faith between them has been crushed with impunity with the protector turning into a beast. Similar are the facts of the case at hand wherein the fate of this girl was debauched at the hands of her teacher's unwanted desires who sexually harassed her on the pretext of tutoring. She was subjected to harassment at the hands of someone who instead should have been a concierge, a protector.*
>
> *Mahatma Gandhi, the Father of the Nation has stated that "a teacher cannot be without character." If he lacks it, he will be like salt without its savour. A teacher must touch the hearts of his students. These lines undoubtedly explain to us the importance of a teacher and a guru and how in our society we as humans rely on their*

conduct and character but to our utter surprise and shock, this very foundation is trembling in its roots. It is quite alarming to read about cases where for mere lust and pleasure, a teacher, a guru, whom we call a protector, has fallen below the standards expected of him. It is the responsibility and duty of the management of the school and colleges to protect young children, in particular the female child. Even the enquiry conducted in such like matters should always keep in mind the honour, self respect and dignity of the female child and how harrowing the experience could have been for her. One cannot lose sight of the fact that the petitioner was a teacher in a co-ed school and such dissipated conduct of a teacher would grub the entire atmosphere of the school setting a bad precedent for the students itself, specifically boys. This girl in an adolescent age was made to face such cantankerous situation, therefore, to not to believe that she was made to face such disgrace and ignominy in the entire set of circumstances would be inhuman. We fail to imbibe that the allegations were made with some personal objective or under the influence of other teachers and students; rather it is quite visible that it was the teacher who targeted Kumari Rekha for his own gratification on the pretext of making her secure good marks. On the contrary, we feel that such students who muster the courage to bring such terrible people out in the open should be lauded. The girl even told about the incident to her family and her father came forward to support her, all these facts do not seem to be concocted or constructed against the petitioner with any malicious purpose."

Police: The Custodian of Peace and Security

It is incumbent upon the police to deter people from breaking the law while maintaining peace and security. Therefore, the role of a police officer is very significant. He acts as a liberator of the society. The police have a professional and moral responsibility demanding from them the highest standards of conduct, particularly those of honesty, impartiality and integrity.

The case of *Neeraj Kumar* v. *Delhi Police,* W.P. (C) 2333/2015 embarks upon the issue of high standards of truthfulness expected from the police. A person making his way into the police force is expected to be a person of high moral rectitude, upright, and righteous. Deciding the appeal Hon'ble Mr. Justice Kailash Gambhir heading the Division Bench observed and held as follows:

"A candidate to be recruited to the police service must be worthy of confidence and should be a person of utmost rectitude, impeccable character and integrity. A person having criminal antecedents will

not fit in this category. Even if he is acquitted or discharged, it cannot be presumed that he was completely exonerated. Persons who are likely to erode the credibility of the police ought not to enter the police force (Ref: State of Madhya Pradesh *v.* Parvez Khan *(supra)). Character of a person is vital for adjudging his suitability for the job. Anne Frank has rightly summed up the "character" in these lines:*

> *"The final forming of a person's character lies in their own hands".*

It is pertinent for a country to have a morally upright, effective, righteous Police Force. Police are expected to provide security to people. It has to be made sure that right, ethical, upright, principled people find their way into the Police force. People repose a great deal of confidence and trust on Police, therefore, it is imperative that only those people who are worthy of that confidence are drawn into the Police Service. A starting point of cleansing the Police system is to weed out the possibility of infiltration by people with criminal antecedents and a chequered history. The disturbing levels of corruption and misdemeanour in the Police Force have compelled the Courts to prescribe high standards of rectitude and uprightness for people making their way into the Law Enforcement Agency."

W.P. (C) No. 3875/1996

The issues that involve public fore, are always close to the heart of Justice Gambhir. He always aims at recapitulating the existing issue and giving a social message to the masses to overcome the same, showing displeasure at the quandary of the innocent lives. He has been very vocal about any prevalent issue that is making a difference in the masses

Justice Gambhir happened to deal with Dengue virus in one of his cases *Courts on its own Motion Re: Dengue Fever* v. *MCD* where he reiterated the importance of human life. Dengue virus is a leading cause of illness and death of more than one-third of the world's population living in areas at risk for infection. When infected, early recognition and prompt supportive treatment can substantially lower the risk of medical complications and death.

Suo motu notice on account of thousands of cases of dengue fever and resultant deaths was taken. In spite of repeated pronouncements by the Delhi High Court issuing various directions, it cannot be comprehended as to why effective measures to prevent the spread and outbreak of dengue have not been taken. Initially the Court took *suo motu* action in 1996 when there was outbreak of dengue and hundreds of persons lost their lives.

Hon'ble Mr. Justice Kailash Gambhir remarked on this alarming and fragile matter that:

> *"Every human life is precious. The State cannot remain insensitive to the human miseries. If 3,000 cases and 40 odd or more deaths cannot wake up and cannot ring alarm, well, then we are in a sorry state. Whether on account of over-crowding, over population, the day is not far off when the whole city will be engulfed today with dengue fever, tomorrow with chickengunia and day after with any other unknown disease. Therefore, we have to act with promptitude and effectiveness"*

HIV: A Social Taboo

Societies being dynamic have evolved to become more sophisticated yet HIV has been perceived as a social taboo for a very long time. The inhumane treatment that is meted out to a person suffering with HIV is not morally acceptable and it is high time we as a society accept this ailment.

On Independence Day eve, Justice Gambhir while sitting in a Division Bench let an HIV-positive BSF constable breathe a sigh of relief, who, along with his wife and child, has been undergoing treatment in the capital by granting his plea to suspend his transfer from Delhi to West Bengal. In *Ct. Sunil Kumar* v. *Union of India,* W.P.(C) 5103/2014 the Court took up the cause of the constable and held that transfer at this crucial stage of his treatment would, not only lead to serious logistical problems associated with his shifting from Delhi, but also jeopardize their treatment and could even threaten their lives.

Hon'ble Mr. Justice Kailash Gambhir while expressing his serious concern about the way HIV positive people are treated in the society held as under:

> *"On the eve of India's Independence Day, when the entire nation is in the mood of celebration of freedom, we are confronted of a case which spells gloom but hopefully not doom of a Government servant, who has served the nation in defending its borders, as a Constable in the Border Security Force.*
>
> *This is indeed a most compelling and unfortunate case. The petitioner and his family comprising of his wife and a minor child are afflicted with HIV positive. The petitioner is a Government servant. He was transferred from Tripura to Delhi so that he could avail best available medical facilities. The affliction of HIV positive carries with it an unwarranted stigma and social ostracisation. Therefore, not only would it be incumbent upon the Government of the day to counter such unwarranted stigma and prejudice and to prevent instances*

of ostracisation of such patients, especially of children afflicted by the disease, but also to fund research for the better care of and enhancement and provision of medical care to the largest number of citizens suffering from AIDS. The need is immediate.

A human life is paramount. Case such as the instant one deserve to be considered with due care, compassion and an appreciation of all the facts relating to it. The State is expected not only to safeguard human life but also to provide best medical care to its countless citizens suffering from such afflictions, albeit within its financial means. The case of the petitioner is a prime example in which his and his family treatment should not be disturbed. This Court is of the view that the transfer of the petitioner at this crucial stage of his treatment would not only lead to serious logistical problems associated with his shifting from Delhi, it would also jeopardise his and his family's treatment and even threaten their lives.

Accordingly, it is directed that the treatment of the petitioner and his family shall continue in Delhi. The impugned order dated 28-7-2014 shall remain stayed."

SPEECHES AND ARTICLES

CHILD RIGHTS – PROTECTION FROM ABUSE – ROLE OF JUDICIARY

Good evening to all of you. If I correctly remember, it was on the evening of 10th October, 2014 when I received a phone call from Mr. Ramesh Gupta, Sr. Advocate, President of *Bachpan Bacho Andolan* and a close associate of Mr. Kailash Satyarthi informing me about Mr. Kailash Satyarthi being nominated for the Nobel Peace Prize., it was indeed great news about the first Indian born citizen being nominated for the highest international award. I instantly told Mr. Ramesh Gupta that we should invite Mr. Kailash Satyarthi to one of our lecture series to inspire young legal minds to use their professional skills in the noble cause of saving children from the menace of child labour and the evils afflicting the children.

Mr. Kailash Satyarthi, when invited to deliver his key note address on a topic concerning child rights he gladly accepted it.

Mr. Kailash Satyarthi is a Gandhian in a true sense. *"Be the change you want to see in the world"*, a famous quote by father of the nation Mahatma Gandhi, which Mr. Satyarthi has not only truly manifested, lived and personified, but has immortalized for times to come, this axiomatic but often unheeded mantra. Today we feel a matter of great pride and honour to felicitate Mr. Kailash Satyarthi the first Indian born Nobel Laureate and his biggest ever recognition for his selfless devotion to save the children of the world from the menace of child labour, infact is a matter of pride for each and every citizen of the country.

You may be aware that Mr. Kailash Satyarthi has been selected for this award from a list of 278 nominees, the highest number of candidates ever. Mr. Kailash Satyarthi's uphill journey started when he quit his job as an Engineer to pursue a mission, a mission to save the lives of children, to give them back their childhood, their innocence and what is rightfully theirs. The journey was not easy as he suffered various assaults, threats, endured political and bureaucratic resistance but nothing could deter him in his onward march to fight for the rights of the children and today he has become no less than a Messiah of the children.

It undoubtedly takes a great degree of altruism and selflessness to not want to be recognized, famous or lauded and to be invisible to the common man when on road towards achieving your goal, which he has demonstrated by choosing to invest in building a movement rather than building his image.

The judicial processes have crossed paths with Mr. Satyarthi's crusade many a times where he has approached the Courts, whether be it to seek directions or, to help in the rescue of children, bringing to the attention of the legal fraternity the perils of this problem the country is facing. The Courts in their wisdom, have done their bit as and when their doors are knocked to dispense justice, laying down the law to protect the vulnerable and today when Mr. Satyarthi has got the Nobel Peace Prize, we are proud to be, a contributor to the cause, a participator in his movement to globalize compassion.

A man, who is not deterred by the tears of his widow mother, cannot be deterred by any force, and this unflinching and resolute determination of Mr. Satyarthi is an example for all of us to emulate. We as lawyers, parents, and more so as aware citizens of this vibrant democracy have to make a concerted, collective and cohesive effort to lend support to this movement and make this country free of this malignancy.

Mr. Kailash Satyarthi, your consistent actions over the past three decades have suddenly garnered attention of somebody's and nobodies alike. Much has been spoken, written, tweeted in various forums nationally and internationally and my words by no means can begin to do justice to the appreciation that you deserve. Today we are here to felicitate not you, but your undying spirit, your courage, conviction and commitment towards eradicating this evil which is a crime against humanity.

Only a divine soul can see divinity in the smile of a child, and today we celebrate this divine soul amongst us who has dedicated his life to the cause of freedom of children. We are indeed privileged to have you share your thoughts with us today, a very warm welcome.

When we thought of inviting Mr. Kailash Satyarthi then there was no second thought for taking a decision to request Hon'ble Mr. Justice T.S. Thakur and Hon'ble Mr. Justice A.K. Sikri to participate in this session. Justice Thakur and Justice Sikri need no introduction to all of us. Justice Thakur as we all know in his short stint as Judge of this High Court endeared each and every one not only by his great sense of justice but also by his soft spoken and pleasing nature, humbleness and above all his nobility. We all keep reading his path breaking and landmark judgments. Yesterday itself the observation made by the Bench presided over by him shows his very strong views on the independence, fairness and integrity of the Judicial system. Giving a stern message that the Judiciary is not up for sale, the bench warned the people against trying to bribe judges and any such attempts made shall be dealt with iron hands. The Bench further observed that possession of tons of money must not prod people to try and bribe judges and highjack the justice delivery system.

For Hon'ble Mr. Justice Thakur I will only say

woh jo saamne baithe hain, unke kad ki nahi hai koi seema.
woh to aasma hai, per fir bhi sarjhukai bethe hain.

We are greatly honoured by your gracious presence and we welcome you Sir.

Mr. Justice Arjun Sikri for whom the Delhi High Court is his *karam bhoomi* started his professional career here, became a successful lawyer, a leader of the Bar and he is often referred to as a darling of the Bar. Because of his scholarly abilities he is also known as great academician Judge. Justice Sikri was recently speaking at the valedictory function of 3 days International Seminar on Human Trafficking where he said, various laws and judgments on human trafficking cannot regulate the problem as it is a social issue. He further emphasized that judiciary alone cannot monitor as implementation of various directions and guidelines are in the hands of enforcement agencies. Few lines will aptly describe him.

Work for cause and not for applause.
Live life to express not to impress.
Do not strive to make your presence noticed.
Justice make your absence felt.

We are greatly honoured by your gracious presence and we welcome you Sir.

We also welcome Hon'ble the Chief Justice Ms. G. Rohini under whose dynamic leadership we have been organizing these educative lecture series for the benefit of young lawyers and we are proud to say that she always !ended active support and cooperation and in fact an inspiring force in organizing these lecture series.

Today's topic of discussion "Child Rights - Protection from Abuse - Role of Judiciary" is a topic of great relevance. In the words of Mr. Kailash Satyarthi ″there is no greater violence then to deny the dreams of our children.″ Child labour is not unique to India. Worldwide about 217 million children work and many of them full time, African countries have the highest percentage of children who are deployed as child labour. 2011 national census of India found total number of child labour aged between 5-11 years to be at 4.35 million out of child population of 259.64 million. With the efforts of Mr. Kailash Satyarthi his organization succeeded in emancipation of 80000 children from various forms of servitude and helped in their rehabilitation. No doubt child labour is growing very fast, but it is not child labour alone but the children are facing chain of other problems destroying and ruining their childhood. Today only I was reading news that smugglers have devised a new method of ferrying illicit gold into the country using juveniles as the juveniles do not come under the purview of suspicious passengers and if caught only be tried under the Juvenile Justice Act. A 16-years old boy was caught carrying 3.5 kg gold on his person. I was also watching a short documentary film where it has been shown that in Taliban children are given training to become suicide bombers. From human trafficking, child labour abuse, child malnutrition, children being used for committing grave and serious offences, can we say that any one person or a few NGOs can bring the desired results? Essentially it is a socio-economic problem and it requires concerted efforts from all sections of society to create a dent in the problem to achieve the dream which Mr. Satyarthi has seen that is to restore the childhood of the children, free them from bondage of slavery and to rehabilitate them to place where they should be. *The world is a dangerous place not because of those who do evil but because of those who look and do nothing.*

Let us all join hands to accomplish to what Mr. Satyarthi cherished goal that child labour to go into the pages of history.

CORRUPTION: A TIME FOR SELF RETROSPECTION

"Power corrupts and absolute power corrupts absolutely"

Lord Acton

Who would have thought that these poignant yet powerful words written way back in the 19th century would more appropriately echo the state of affairs of the 21st century, more so of today?

Good morning to all present. It is indeed an honour and privilege for me to be addressing this august gathering constituting the people who give the not so pleasant news of the hard earned money to be parted from both the hard and the hardly working men towards the so called taxes which ultimately, today as we know, are a contribution to fatten the pocket of the man adorning the power yielding chair.

When I looked at the topic for the day for preparing this address, the first question that crossed my mind was *why now?* Why are we today discussing corruption when it has been always present? What is the need today for me or anyone of the esteemed guests sitting on the dais, to tell the intelligent audience here today about the menace of corruption. Is there something that is left unsaid, is there something I know and others don't, or is that they want me to say the unspeakable? The answer to all this came to be only one, that the malaise of corruption today has reached such mammoth proportions that it is the biggest roadblock or should I say has blocked the entire road to personal growth, freedom and achievement of every single common citizen of this country like never before.

Corruption has been present since times immemorial. To go back as far back in history I can, I am reminded of the legendary Kautilya who was once asked by his disciple if it is possible to find out whether the government servant was taking money, and the astute Kautilya answered that as it is not possible to find out how much water does the fish drink in which it swims, it is not possible that the government servant does not eat money of the King's revenue, thus illustrating the human nature's disposition to being corrupt. The coming of the Mughals led to the institutionalization of corruption in the form of the *nazrana* and *shukrana* paid to get favours done. Under the British, what is now known as corruption was a "commission" or "fee" to keep the officers and men happy to win their loyalty; it was referred to as the *outside income* and a harmless price to win the subservience of its subjects. The Britishers are to be blamed for most of the 'babudom' that exists today as they decentralized power centers and replaced it with the disdained *discretion* which provided leeway and alleys for corruption to percolate, and form its roots permanently, when everything depends on the whims and fancies of one man in the garb of discretion. The freedom struggle saw India fighting as a man fighting for his breath, but that did not stop the spread of this disease as well. The corruption in the ministries formed under the Government of India Act, 1935 was common knowledge when Mahatma Gandhi dubbed corruption as a moral failure and said that *"We seem to have weakened from within. I would go to the length of giving the whole Congress a decent burial, rather than put up with the corruption that is rampant"*. The independent India saw a hope in Nehru's agenda of development as he was the most honest of the politicians. One incident that comes to mind is when Nehru learnt that Anand Bhawan, his house in Allahabad, had been assessed to an unusually low rate of property tax, he protested and had the amount raised by 500%. But he was also let down when his close friend and aid V.K. Krishna Menon's jeep scandal hit the headlines tarnishing the image of the new vibrant democracy that would be India. The next decades saw the possibility for rejuvenation, a time when the country had dealt with the aftermath of the freedom struggle, but the introduction of the licence-permit-quota raj, where for doing everything and anything in this country, you needed a licence or permission, was nothing but the beginning of the nightmarish looting and diabolical amassing of wealth by the ones possessing even an iota of authority. The Bofors scandal saw the ushering of an era of a new kind of corruption, acclimatizing the public memory of what was to follow in the coming decades, which has only multiplied and reached gigantic scales today as back then the allegations were in thousands and crores sounded like fairyland. The numbers looted then look like a monk's cell if compared to the present ones.

It is a hard hitting reality, that today we are mired in the politics of corruption in the country. India is ranked 87th out of the 178 countries by the Transparency International on Corruption Perception Index (CPI), 2010. Wherever we look, there is spectre of scandals and scams staring at us. From the Radiagate, the 2G, to the Commonwealth, IPL and Adarsh land scam, there is no alphabet in the English language that's untouched by the felicitation to have a scam starting from it. We have seen it all, so much so that we can now make a lexicon on it. Not only politics, but corruption has infested all the limbs of the state machinery. Without the support of the Executive, the politicians cannot circumvent the procedure and hence the two act hand in glove to be able to help each other on the road to self enrichment. From Chief Ministers, Senior Politicians, to the top Bureaucrats, all have had a visit to the prison. Now even the judiciary is under attack. It started with allegations of corruption on V. Ramaswamy and now till the impeachment of Soumitra Sen, due to a few stray incidents, the portals of justice delivery are also looked upon with questionable eyes by the people; and all this due to the insatiable and unending greed of a few. This state of affairs which has made people to come on the road in protest is a betrayal of the democratic system.

It all starts and ends with one word *i.e.* power. The privilege, prestige, prerogatives, all come with power and it is in this race of having absolute power that one corrupts absolutely, himself and the one he meets on this road. On the political front, the elections see the money flow like water, every possible modus operandi is adopted to get the votes and the ones sponsoring this *tamasha* are the business tycoons. I often wondered how they could afford it. But the surety, that once in power they would recover it manifold gave them the heart to spend criminal amounts when the better half of the population still is devoid of basic needs. Today, the nexus of the industrialists with the moolah and no power with the politicians with power but no moolah has touched new heights as now it is not restricted to financing the elections to get favours when their candidate gets elected; which seemed to be somehow palatable and was regarded as natural phenomena, but has reached to the extent when the middlemen in the garb of sophisticated designations as that of PR managers on behalf of the capitalists are even deciding the portfolios of ministers, writing the fate of the economy of the country. Here it would also be not out of line to mention the role of the media in this whole outrage. It has been one of the most potent manifestations of the freedom of speech and expression guaranteed to us. No doubt with so much activism and investigative journalism by the media, the common man has become more watchful and vigilant about the acts and deeds of the people in power, but they have also not been taint free. The tape recording scandal is one such incident out in the open where the people we thought are walking with us to fight corruption are themselves involved in it. The damage which this watching and taking care of reciprocal interests in this deadly nexus is causing is nothing but alarming to say the least. It is also unfortunate to know that the amount of funds and aid released during the natural calamities is also viewed as an opportunity by the corrupt to fill their pockets. How insensitive can a person be to the misfortune and pain of the victims of a tragedy who sees it as a money making business. India, which is known for its rich cultural values, a land of the Vedas and the saints, which the whole world looks upto for its spiritual and moral values, is rotting in this vile malpractice.

But the question that arises is what has the common man got to do with all of this? It is because it has trickled down to affect the poorest man of this country. A man ploughing his fields in Haryana or a woman sitting in her kuccha house in Bihar does not even understand the story of spectrum allocation, but what they understand is how the simpler things like basic necessities are getting difficult for them to procure day by day. They feel the brunt when they have to run from pillar to post for getting a ration card made but ultimately grease the palm of the man sitting in that dilapidated office on the rickety chair, because there is no other alternative. However, the middle class has a bit better. The admission in schools have become so difficult that there are brokers which ensure the admission of your child to the topmost school in the city on payment, or if you are lucky then the little push from the right quarters and people with connections help. There is such a long queue for gas connections and a word from a high official can reduce the agony considerably. Even for booking a ticket for the train in this country you need a pull or at least for the confirmation of reservation. The mutation of your property, payment of house tax, getting your pension, everything can be had for a price thus making this nation a consideration state. I am reminded here of the popular TV serial *Office Office* which immortalized the labyrinthine journey of a file from cradle to grave. Nepotism, favouritism, discrimination; corruption in any form is omnipresent.

But the question that arises is why? Why are we so susceptible to it? It is because today it is the time of survival of the richest and the only way to survive is to be corrupt as the salaries through the chartered route are meagre as compared to the burgeoning inflation. The Marxian ideology seems a relevant proposition today. The theory of have and have-nots has regained importance as the rich are become richer and the poor poorer because of this endemic called corruption. The greed is so much that nothing satiates but money. But still after all how much land does a man need? The famous story by Leo Tolstoy in which a simple farmer is allured by greed of possessing land does not live to enjoy the fruits of his labour; is a message to everyone that there is no end to greed and one will not live to enjoy the fruits of his labour if he is busy collecting wealth. How much can you enjoy in your own lifetime when the coming generations will earn on their own, why should you indulge in immoral acts for the comfort of the unborn. There is no deterrent for the ones indulging shamelessly in it. There is no fear of the law, no moral guilt and is indulged into as if it is something legitimate. Unfortunately in India corruption leads to promotion, prosperity, popularity, publicity, profitability and not to prison, punishment or penance. There is no societal pressure as well, who looks at the corrupt as the out castes or socially boycotted, it is only a scornful look, a disparaging remark or expletive what they may attract which has no effect on the elephant skinned who have filled their coffers at the cost of others well being. But what they have not realized is the far reaching consequences of their misdemeanors. A corrupt minister giving away the tenders to the low quality arms and ammunition to accommodate his own share leads to the low quality weapons to the men guarding the border which is a threat to the security of the entire country. A minister giving tender for spurious drug supplies is causing the national health to deteriorate. But corruption is the quickest way to fulfill the needs and wants and is a high profit low risk business. But why to blame others when everyone has a stake in it? Why do we let them do it? It is because the standing in queue lowers the dignity whereas a word from a higher official is a feather in the cap, when the agony of going to the government offices time and again is mitigated by asking someone who knows someone who knows the son of the official who will do your work, then why not. Who wouldn't want that? But what we have not realized is that in the wake of us indulging in it in whatever way, we have eroded the social and moral fabric of the country. Starting from a one time indulgence one does not come to know when he crosses the line titling the entire balance of the society. Starting from the journey from knowing that honesty is the norm and dishonesty an exception it goes on to a reverse ideology which the generation next also looks on to, learns and implements. How many of us do not lure our children with rewards for performing well in exams? Almost all, it is the mentality of incentive that we are etching in their minds and hearts and telling them that this is how the world runs and this is something they should be accustomed to and not frown upon. The virtues, ideals and moral values we give our children while bringing them up are not implemented by our own selves then how will they and why will they want to learn it or believe it? In defense it is touted as the necessary evil and something that we have to live with and tolerate. Corruption; voluntary, compulsory or even pressurized has made a mincemeat of morality and distorted the truth and reality. The attitude and the mind-set has thus to be changed, more particularly of the middle class which is the most hypocrite of the lot. The upper middle class indulges in skullduggery in the day and in the night over a peg of premium scotch in the ambience of their manicured lawns bash the corrupt politicians, striking a moralist posture.

But again I come back to the same question, why all this ethical awakening and moral preaching now? Why are we today making such a hullabaloo about corruption when it was always present in the system? Are we as a country overreacting to what is shown to us flashing on the small screen day and night or are we really at the threshold of a breakdown? The answer to this is that the face of corruption has changed. Earlier, you had to satiate the greed to get the wrong things done but now you have to appease the authority holder to get the right things done. The breakdown has occurred because the common man is tired for fighting of what is legitimately his. Also, to mention that the recent movement against corruption which has yet again united this nation is because of the kaleidoscope of scams, frustration of the common man has reached the boiling point and they have put their foot down. The torture, torment and anguish of the people have made the high ups sit up and take notice and they have made it clear that the licence to govern does not mean the licence to be corrupt. The civil society, social activists, spiritual activists have all jumped into the bandwagon to pressurize the system to be more transparent. The judiciary is also doing its bit and assuring that the citizens do not lose faith in the justice dispensation of the country. When a man is dejected and demoralized from the system, he looks upon the judiciary for alleviation of his miseries and the last bastion of his rights. The courts have time and again denounced the practice of corruption and dealt it with a heavy hand. One of the landmark cases in this regard is *Swatantar Singh* v. *State of Haryana,* AIR 1997 SC 2105: 1997 AIR SCW 1941: (1997) 4 SCC 14 where the Apex Court held and I quote:

> *"It is sad but a bitter reality that corruption is corroding, like cancerous lymph nodes, the vital veins of the body politics, social fabric of efficiency in the public service and demoralising the honest officers. The efficiency in public service would improve only when the public servant devotes his sincere attention and does the duty diligently, truthfully, honestly and devotes himself assiduously to the performance of the duties of his post. The reputation of corrupt would gather thick and unshakable clouds around the conduct of the officer and gain notoriety much faster than the smoke."*

Even I had the occasion to deal with a case wherein a bus conductor had engaged into pocketing money by non issuance of tickets which had led to his removal from service. It was held and I quote:

> *"No doubt, it may look harsh and perhaps inequitable to uphold punishment of removal in cases where misappropriation of a small amount of money is concerned, more particularly when the big sharks are seen swimming comfortably without any fear of law and law enforcing agencies. Strangely, corruption is a paradoxical phenomenon as the highly placed corrupt officials, rich and influential, save themselves from*

the clutches of law by corrupting those whose primary job is to take action against the corrupt people. Henceforth, it is in this way how the evil of corruption is well-flourishing and has now, so to say, carved a comfortable niche for itself in the societal framework. It is not surprising that rather than becoming a hard hitting reality to which people should object and frown upon, looking with disdain upon those indulging in such unethical practice, it has gained acceptance as an indispensable virtue and is gradually becoming a way of life. Therefore, no leniency or sympathy can be shown even to a person who indulges himself in corruption even at a small level and by all means, corruption has to be checked and nipped in the bud. It is not the amount but the mind and intention of a corrupt person which has to be checked and the conductor on duty can only indulge in corruption at a small level and one cannot expect him to misappropriate amount of thousands and lacs of rupees as his job is to issue tickets and non issuance of the same can only result into pocketing small amounts on daily basis. However, nevertheless, by that process alone, his daily and monthly earnings sometimes may be more than his official income. Therefore, as a society this widespread malpractice has to be de-fenestrated."

It is also unfortunate that we as a nation have forgotten that how fortunate we are of having the most comprehensive Constitution in the world, granting almost all possible rights and freedoms imaginable in a civilized society. But what we have sadly forgotten is that rights and duties are two sides of the same coin and we cannot take the benefit of our rights and proudly exercise them without being alive to the duties of being the citizen of this country.

But the question is what has it all culminated into? In my opinion what India has lost in the midst of all this tumult is its soul as its national character and pride have been grievously hurt. Just because we have got used to grudgingly live with this clamour is no reason for us to accept unscrupulousness. The constant debate whether at a tea stall or in the Parliament is how to end this epidemic? And the only answer in my view is to change ourselves. The time has come for each one of us to rise up from our individualistic attitude and contribute to nation building. We should adopt an attitude of zero tolerance towards this vice of corruption. Scams hitting the headlines with sickening regularity should not make us flip the news channels but make us feel that it would no more be tolerated. Everyone does not have black money stashed away in safe havens abroad, but that does not mean that we should be taking things lightly. Today we as a nation cannot afford to be forgetful, forgetting the last scam and lamenting that this year ultimately belonged to the treasure hunters who looted public money which has zeroes that a common Indian citizen cannot even count and letting every year become the same by our inaction and feudal approach. The vicious circle has to be now changed to the virtuous circle. We need to strengthen the values and morals of the next generation to make them understand that merit should not be measured by money and success by acquisition. The approach should be that I should not do any act to indulge in it and not tolerate anyone else doing it instead of criticizing the ones doing it and indulging in it ourselves when our self interest needs to be served.

But the change is one's mind-set is one part but what is needed is the overhauling of the system. The democratic system needs shaking up for it to regain its essence where ideologies of political parties were the distinguishing factor and all worked towards the growth of the nation rather than today where the individuals are becoming the supreme factor and ideologies going down the drain. The second most important part is that the rules and procedures have to be de-mystified. Secrecy and delay in official dealings needs to done away with. Administrative procedures need to be made people friendly. The lurking fear that my file will get lost in the jungle of files out there so I should pay the price for keeping it afloat should be removed. Life is short and so the procedures cannot be long and none should be tempted to cut corners and queues to live in peace. The Apex Court is doing its bit in monitoring the various cases before it by way of continuing mandamus, and even taking action *suo moto* in various cases. The credibility of the emerging teeming profit making organizations in the garb of NGO's needs to be checked. The electoral reforms need to be in place, there should be put a limit to the audacious expenditure. The salaries of the government officials need to be realistic keeping in view the cost of living. Our effort now has to transform this beleaguered nation to a sustainable social order. We have to prove wrong the ones that say that corruption is in our DNA. It is a long road to changing the perception of the common man approaching a public servant that he will not be corrupt generally and only as an exception he might be corrupt to the existing notion where a man is considered corrupt until found otherwise. The iota of population which is not corrupt is also labeled as corrupt because it has become difficult to imagine anyone surviving without indulging in it. It might seem like a Herculean task today when materialism has achieved the status of being divine, but till the time we breathe we should not only dream to achieve the impossible but also attempt to achieve it.

There is hope and things are beginning to change. The Right to Information Act has done a great service to the common citizens and has brought about some transparency. The much debated Lokpal Bill is also likely to be passed in the winter session of the Parliament alongwith the

Citizens Right to Grievance Redressal Bill, the Public Interests Disclosure and Protection to Persons Making the Disclosure Bill, 2010 (The Protection of the Whistle Blowers Act), The Judicial Accountability Bill, 2010. These legislations are the great white hope of citizens to achieve a greater transparency and reinforce the trust and faith of the common man in the system. There are some developments which have already begun. The State of Uttarakhand has passed the Jan Lokpal Bill which is a big step. Also, the State of Punjab has developed an e-tendering process for any tender above Rs. 5 lakh, where the entire process being online is a sign of transparency. We might have to pay a price for this change as well and the only way is to do away with venality which may have its consequences. The recent deaths of the RTI activists are their sacrifice towards making the system more tolerable and we have to pave the way forward.

This or that incident of graft caused a furore, the impunity with which law is flouted by the corrupt is incredible and this breed is going to stay, only time will tell what would happen to this nation, India can never be a scandal free nation are some common lamenting that goes on in our living rooms which needs to stop. We are not sure of anything or anyone but what we can be sure of is that we should not forget the promise we make to ourselves and that is to do our bit in eliminating corruption. Our memory today is indeed shortened by the bright investments in petrol and vegetables, which will be overtaken by another din tomorrow, but now the time has come when we as an aware citizenry not only indulge in drawing room criticism but also take action. As the Father of our Nation said *"Be the change you want to see in the world"* Corruption destroys both faith and state and change cannot wait for some other time or for somebody else.

LEARNING TO SHARE – INAUGURAL ADDRESS

Learn to share what you have yourself learnt. Sharing your knowledge and a conscious zeal to share the consciousness always open much higher planes on which our mind can travel.

Sharing of knowledge brings the sub-line and the sub-conscious that continuously guides us throughout our life on our path to wisdom and to acknowledge and elevate our own conscious being. The process of sharing has to be developed, it does not come naturally. A child would always strive to keep everything unto self. It is only our realization with the progress in life that we attain this virtue of sharing and thus sharing has to be learnt by all.

We often lend up selecting a goal instead of selecting what is good and what is reasonably attainable, that can give us a foundation to develop a firm determination to reach that goal.

We often complain about lack of quality in our lives so also we complain the lack of quality as professionals and juristic in the visuals in professional endeavours as well as in juridical dispensation.

Swami Vivekanand said "do not find a fault, find a remedy".

Dissemination of knowledge ensures its growth amongst our own self. We do not even use a minimal percentage of our mind despite many of us being known for our achievements. This unexposed wealth of our knowledge becomes stagnant if we do not share it with others. In the gamut of life we only strive for or work on what is before us as a routine. We normally do not tend to explore. Exploration once again could only come when we wish to share what we have learnt or we ourselves strive for learning.

The entire edifice of administration of justice rests on two strong pillars *i.e.* the Bench and the Bar. We have taken various steps to train our Judges, specially lower Judiciary so that they are fully equipped and armoured with sufficient knowledge, skills, technical know how including e-learning etc. so as to face challenges thrown by the present era of globalization, modern technology, corporate and environmental laws with the setting up of Judicial Academy at the national level and at the State levels. However, while one pillar of the justice delivery system is being cemented and strengthened, the other *i.e.* a large portion of Bar that constitutes young lawyers and fresh entrants to the profession remain confine to the limited expanse of professional knowledge that they could get while working with some senior or with a little sharing with their own friends as we have not till so far created any institution or provided any forum for the training and development of these professionals. The gestation period for transformation from a young budding advocate to a experienced well accomplished lawyer is comparatively long, competitive and often economically constrained as well.

Recently, while addressing a congregation of lawyers at the District Court, Hon'ble Law Minister raised an issue of poor and mediocre lawyers, who remained just hand to mouth due to various inadequacies. They do not have funds to buy computers, create sufficient infrastructure for running their offices or maintain libraries or adequate study material which somehow is the basic necessity for development and growth of a legal professional.

I have often thought of establishing some such forum to provide a platform for these young lawyers who have an urge to learn and learn to progress. My idea is synonyms to the proposal of an academy for lawyers but it has yet to take a shape to put it to the reality.

While efforts are being made at various levels for developing the Court craft and advocacy skills for the lawyers by the Bar as well as the Bench, however, much more is required to be done in real sense.

I feel the primary task before us is to identify specific areas of litigation more so in a place like Delhi where multi level Government Agencies are a major litigant and majorities of the issues pending before the Court involves the said agencies in one way or the other. It has been generally noticed that knowledge of the Advocate specially, who is a first generation lawyer remained confined to what he has learnt from his senior confining to area of senior's practice. Resultantly if such an Advocate is confronted or approached for filing or contesting another stream of litigation either the Advocate would feel helpless or will redirect the said client to another lawyer known to him being well versed in such field. However, in the said process the Advocate either lend up losing the client or ill directing the course of litigation not only to the prejudice of the litigants interest but also to blemish the profession per se. Although the Bar has within its culture developed certain sharing of knowledge yet a lot is to be achieved.

We often feel the urge to share our knowledge but at times we fail to put it to practice as we are not apt at doing so. Never resist a generous impulse to share.

Life is the unfoldment and development of a being under circumstances tending to press it down. However, real education is that which enables us to stand on our own legs in such pressing circumstances.

Education is the manifestation of perfection already in man. However, this education can be supplemented by sharing the knowledge that we acquire during the process of our life and we should endeavour to let the light of knowledge kindle every heart.

We have to strive to bring light to the ignorant and more light to the educated for the vanities of education of our time are tremendous. There is no chance for the welfare of the world unless we share with others what we have learnt ourselves.

Learning to share is a process which has to emante from within ourselves. The High Court Bar Association has taken a lead in this regard which is a welcome step. A learning to share concept will provide the necessary foundation to lead a way to light the young lawyers path to professional excellence.

We may not, in the process, shirk from taking the help of leading lawyers having specialized knowledge in a particular field, our Judges and more particularly experts from various Departments, who shall be a great source for imparting this real education in practical and procedural concepts being adopted by the relevant Departments, Authorities in processing such cases. Obviously an good official from any particular Department would definitely be knowing much better rules and procedure then a layman or even a lawyer who may be practicing in that particular Department or matters relating to it. For example officials from MCD, NDMC, offices of Patents and Trademarks Attorneys, Labour Law experts, service experts can provide much better knowledge and professional guidance to these young members of the Bar who are willing to learn so that they can stand at their footing at an early stage of the practice and can withstand the competition with many others who might have been born with a silver spoon or take away the lion's share of litigation because of their legacy in profession.

The modalities of implementing the process may once again require participation of these experts, judicial officers, Judges and at times even academicians too and I hope and pray that this endeavour of the Bar shall bear the fruits soon.

I must compliment the Executive of the High Court Bar Association to have invoked the Almighty at the beginning of the proceedings today seeking a blessing for "enlightening the path of ignorance with the light of the knowledge and saving us from any ills. I am sure all efforts that are well begun are half done & I wish and pray all success to the efforts of the Bar in this regard. I would also request Hon'ble the Chief Justice to allow the infrastructure available at the Courts as well as at the Judicial Academy for such training to the lawyers till such time as the Hon'ble Law Minister and Hon'ble Chief Minister of Delhi shall in due course render their esteemed support in building up and establishing a full fledged Academy for lawyers for refining their professional skills. I am sure this would infuse strength to the other pillar of the justice delivery system *i.e.* the Bar, as, if the Bar is weakened then the entire edifice of the justice delivery system will crumble down, which will ultimately put the entire democracy in to peril and danger.

LEGAL PROFESSION

Today, the legal profession has become more lucrative than ever before with a number of colleges, including the national law schools being established, enticing the young generation to take this up as a career choice. But it is an open secret that this young talent is more inclined to be on the corporate front with big pay packages rather that choose to be a part of the active litigation circuit. The figures speak for themselves as in the year 2013, there were 6000-7000 fresh enrolments in the Bar Council of Delhi, but not more than 20% have joined active practice.

Undoubtedly, these law schools churn out best in the country, but when these fresh law graduates who show temerity to join litigation to satiate his/her thrill of appearing in a real courtroom, joins a lawyer, he is nothing but perplexed to find himself/herself between the devil and the deep sea as he/she is faced with the gap that exists in knowing the law and practicing the law.

In the wake of globalization and fast pace technological advancement, every now and then there are new legislations passed and it is not late when the squabble around their provisions enters the court room. Therefore, strategy so to say, behind learning to share is to organise a series of lectures to impart knowledge in the areas that pose the real challenge. The ultimate purpose is that when a client approaches a new lawyer, he himself should not be ignorant and feel handicapped so that not only can he convince his client but is also able to retain him and continue with him and then ultimately render effective assistance in the Court.

As you all know, our Bar is rich of great stalwarts. They must have also passed through the period of struggle during their initial days to achieve the present heights of success and I think now the time has come when these seniors should share their knowledge and experience with our young Bar, who are also passing through the same phase of struggle.

There is a famous Sanskrit shlok that says ***"Tamso Maa Jyotir Gamaya"*** which means to lead us from darkness to light and in my opinion it is only the light of knowledge that can lead a man from the darkness of ignorance.

It is indeed not a one way exercise, but an effort towards watering the tree whose fruit the whole fraternity would cherish. The Bar, undoubtedly is a reservoir of legal mavens and if we nurture the saplings today, only then can we enjoy the fruit in the future.

Hence, I hope that we responsibly fulfil our duty towards these new kids on the blocks that what they learn remains etched with them for life.

MEDIATION: A PANACEA FOR THE ANATHEMA OF DOCKET EXPLOSION*

Voltaire said "I was ruined but twice in life. Once when I lost a lawsuit and once when I won"

This statement echoes the emotions of the common man of this country chained in the shackles of the litigation system even today. The faith of the people in the adversarial system of justice delivery is fast eroding and hence a need to evolve an alternative to the anathema was felt which resulted in developing the systems of alternate dispute resolution, popularly called ADR.

In human society, the existence of different ideologies, thoughts and opinions is imperative for development of civilization but at the same time it often leads to conflicts. Disputes are thus part of the human existence and hence dispute resolution is also part of the peaceful societal co-existence. The system of resolution is not new to us, as since times immemorial we had the concept of elders and respectful people of the society acting as a third party to resolve disputes which led to the system of panchayats. These panchayats were effective in sorting out differences of people but soon the elders in this panchayat were replaced with influential people of some caste, religion or political allegiance, blemishing its efficiency. But now we see the resurrection of this concept in the form of alternative dispute resolution mechanisms like arbitration, conciliation, mediation and Lok Adalat.

This paper would focus on Mediation as the tool of an effective ADR mechanism in the context of India.

At the very outset, the question that needs to be answered is why should we resort to ADR mechanisms and not courts?

The foremost reason is the docket explosion that has paralyzed the justice delivery system. It is an open secret that once a person enters the alleys of the courts, there is no looking back. The litigative voyage in the country is not only long but grueling. The delay in handing out the decision in a case takes years, at a time when the fruit can no more be enjoyed by the person who put his heart and soul in achieving it. The arrears infesting the courts are an indication that the common man should

* Article published in ICADR.

try and resolve the disputes through settlement rather than resorting to court cases. Also the legal activity is often a mystery, where we lawyers and judges, as priests preside over rituals baffling to everyday citizens. Therefore the society today is on the verge of losing confidence in law courts threatening their dignified existence. Hence, there is a vacuum that needs to be filled addressing the pitfalls of the present justice dispensation system.

Mediation can be defined in a common parlance as a process where "dispute is resolved through the intervention of a neutral third party. It has been defined as a facilitative process in which disputing parties engage the assistance of an impartial third party, the mediator, who helps them try to arrive at an agreed resolution of their dispute. The mediator has no authority to make any decisions that are binding on them, but uses certain procedures, techniques and skills to help them to negotiate an agreed resolution of their dispute without adjudication."[1] It is also defined as negotiation carried out with the assistance of a third party. The mediator, in contrast to the arbitrator or a judge, has no power to impose an outcome on disputing parties.[2] Hence to put in simple terms, mediation is a process to resolve a dispute between two or more parties in presence of a mutually accepted third party who through confidential discussion attempts to help the parties in reaching a commonly agreed solution to their problems.

It is important to however understand the benefits of mediation vis-à-vis litigation to have a better idea of its potential.

- The first and foremost is that the mediator is a facilitator and not an adjudicator. The role of mediator is not to give a decision but to push the parties to arrive at a decision. Hence he is not adjudicating as to who is right and who is wrong but as to what is the workable solution to the problem that suits both the parties.
- Mediation is a participatory process as opposed to the court case where neither of the parties has their say but is only the judge who hands out the decision. The participatory role of the parties goes a long way in enforcing the decision in the long run.
- Mediation aims at finding a workable and a practical solution rather than a legal solution. The solutions are not restricted to

1. *ADR Principles and Practice,* by Henry J. Brown & Arthur L. Mariot (1997, 2nd Edn. Sweet & Maxwell, Lord on Chapter 7, p. 127).
2. *Dispute Resolution* (Negotiation, Mediation and other processes), Stephen B. Goldberg, Frank E.A. Sander and Nancy H. Rogers (1999, 3rd Ed. Aspine law & Business, Gaithesburg and New York) (Ch. 3 p. 123).

the confines of the statutes but what the parties find suitable to their interests.

- Mediation is an informal process where the parties repose faith and confidence in the mediator and feels free and open to present his case, documents and statements that may not be admissible in court as evidence. Hence it is a flexible process where there is no procedural rigidity like the formal court process.
- Mediation is a cost effective solution for resolving dispute as the expenses involved are nothing as compared to what the parties pay to lawyers over the years.
- In the adversarial process, the outcome of the case is uncertain and either a party loses the battle or wins it. In mediation, the solution arrived at is with the consent of both the parties which has the win-win situation as its solution.
- In mediation, the parties and lawyers work towards getting a relief rather than a decree. The process of enforcement of a decree is more arduous than the main litigation and hence the party cannot enjoy fruit of it despite long wait. Hence the decree remains a paper decree whereas in mediation the solution has the stamp of a legally enforceable decree and hence the parties are quick to enforce as they have their consent in the decision.
- The environment of a court room is very hostile and unfriendly and the parties pitted against each other have venom to spit. The process of mediation breaks the impasse and lets parties going home to a settlement be friends and not foes.

What has although to be kept in mind is that in search for a cost effective and quick procedure, the hallmarks of the justice delivery system, namely upholding the rule of law and impartiality are not compromised.

Mediation being a voluntary concept has now got the statutory mandate as embodied in section 89 of the Civil Procedure Code, 1908 which states as:

> **89. Settlement of disputes outside the Court.**—(1) Where it appears to the court that there exist elements of a settlement which may be acceptable to the parties, the court shall formulate the terms of settlement and give them to the parties for their observations and after receiving the observation of the parties, the court may reformulate the terms of a possible settlement and refer the same for—
>
> (a) arbitration;
>
> (b) conciliation;

(c) judicial settlement including settlement through Lok Adalat; or

(d) mediation.

(2) Where a dispute had been referred—

(a) for arbitration or conciliation, the provisions of the Arbitration and Conciliation Act, 1996 shall apply as if the proceedings for arbitration or conciliation were referred for settlement under the provisions of that Act;

(b) to Lok Adalat, the court shall refer the same to the Lok Adalat in accordance with the provisions of sub-section (1) of section 20 of the Legal Services Authority Act, 1987 and all other provisions of that Act shall apply in respect of the dispute so referred to the Lok Adalat;

(c) for judicial settlement, the court shall refer the same to a suitable institution or person and such institution or person shall be deemed to be a Lok Adalat and all the provisions of the Legal Services Authority Act, 1987 shall apply as if the dispute were referred to a Lok Adalat under the provisions of that Act;

(d) for mediation, the court shall effect a compromise between the parties and shall follow such procedure as may be prescribed.

Therefore, whenever the Court feels that there exists potential for a possible settlement then it refers the parties to resort to an ADR method to arrive at a settlement. The parties try and achieve a compromise which the court endorses and it thus becomes a decree. The statutory mandate accorded to the alternative dispute resolution mechanism is a giant leap in creating spaces to breathe in the litigation cycle. What kinds of cases are which the judge can refer for mediation? The following are a few illustrations:

(i) All cases arising from strained or soured personal relationships, including—
- Disputes relating to matrimonial causes maintenance, custody of children;
- Disputes relating to partition/division among family members/ coparceners/co-owners; and
- Disputes relating to partnership among partners.

(ii) Cases relating to commerce and contracts, which include—
- Disputes arising out of contracts (including money claims);
- Disputes relating to specific performance;

- Disputes between suppliers and customers;
- Disputes between bankers and customers;
- Disputes between developers/builders and customers;
- Disputes between landlords and tenants; and licensors and licencees.

(iii) Cases where there is a need to maintain the pre-existing relationship in spite of the disputes, which include—

- Disputes between neighbours (relating to easementary rights, encroachment, nuisance);
- Disputes between employers and employees;
- Disputes among members of societies/associations/apartment owners' associations.

(iv) Cases arising out of tortuous liability, which include claims for compensation in motor accidents/other accidents; and

(v) Consumer disputes where a trader or service provider is keen to maintain his business/professional reputation and credibility.

Of course, if the parties are willing, other categories of civil disputes may also be referred to mediation.

The phenomenon of mediation has engulfed all parts of the world in one way or the other. For example, Egypt requires mediation before a retired judge in each case brought by private parties' against the government. Throughout Europe, mediation is seen as a potentially promising mechanism for the resolution of both simple and complex disputes. Norway's Conciliation Boards (*Forliksradene*) provide a model of extensive comparative interest and international study. In 1995, France expanded the legislative basis for judicial conciliation and mediation. Diverse countries from Tanzania to the Ukraine are pursuing mediation reforms as a response to contemporary demands. In many of these jurisdictions, mediation is seen useful not only for small claims, auto accidents, family disputes and petty crimes in court systems clogged by a modern docket, but also as an alternative dispute resolution device for the most complex matters, including those involving environment and intellectual property law, previously considered to be irreconcilable. The speed of change is strong and national and emerging global markets puts increasing pressure on large business interests to resolve disputes quickly and inexpensively, as well as amicably, constructively and creatively, in order to maximize long-term interests and to maintain ongoing commercial relationships. In India, the courts have developed mediation centers attached with them for providing the facility of mediation. The Delhi High Court has the mediation centre known as *Samadhan* which is going from strength to strength. The greatest achievement of this centre has been its belief in indianising both the theory and practice of mediation, keeping in mind our Indian scenario and the need to adopt local analogues to resolve disputes in India. This year, the mediation centre has also initiated pre-litigation mediation services which are proving to be popular. Before a case is filed in court, or before any legal action is taken, parties are approaching the Mediation Centre for settlement of their disputes and succeeding. This has brought new strength to the movement. The mediators are trained persons suited for the job of acting as neutral third parties. It is their job to bring the parties to their senses and not to their knees. The mediators essentially have to be neutral, understanding, possessing persuasive skills with patience and the quality to maintain confidentiality of the party's information. He has to act as a man of integrity and skill.

The uncanny sense of insecurity among the legal fraternity can be no more seen and this feeling that mediation threatens their livelihood by reducing the number of matters they handle or fees that they can charge does not persist anymore. It is true that till the time the Bar does not recognize mediation as an effective part of the justice delivery system, no significant success can be achieved. There is hence an urgent need to impart training to more and more lawyers so that the advantages of this method of ADR can reach to numerous litigants.

Hence, mediation is a panacea to overcome the institutional challenges of national court systems. It is not there to supplant the need for public adjudication and normative judicial pronouncements on the critical issues of the day, but to compliment and preserve that core normative purpose of the judicial system. Hence it is only a way of easing out the surmounting pressure of burgeoning litigation. In short, mediation is an informal, collaborative, oral, facilitative, future-looking, interest based process that brings the parties to a calibrated, multi-dimensional, win-win remedy that is more durable because of the parties consent to the outcome. But however there needs to be a greater awareness for the benefits that mediation has on offer to the justice seeking citizens. Satisfaction of the persons resorting to the medium alongwith the Bar encouraging clients to resort to mediation would go a long way in proving it as a potent medium.

I would like to conclude in the words of Nelson Mandela which summarizes the theme of the concept of mediation; *"If you want to make peace with your enemy, you have to work with your enemy. Then he becomes your partner."*

RAGGING

It is indeed my proud privilege to be present here in the midst of such eminent academicians here today.

Writing a book is no mean task. In the era of technological revolution, writing a book takes courage and commitment and the status that books deserve cannot be undermined.

I congratulate the author for his unique choice of topic. It is the first time that such a subject has been taken up and dealt with comprehensively.

Ragging is a venomous practice prevalent in our society today. It no longer exists behind closed doors but is out in the open affecting the lives of many thus becoming an open secret.

In common parlance it was understood to be a healthy practice meant to be an ice breaker between the senior and junior students. A fun filled activity of interaction which would sow the seeds of future friendships. But the face of such an interaction has been distorted and destroyed by the ones aiming to get pleasure at the cost of others. It has gone beyond the imaginable forms including sexual abuse, violence, and torture.

Its history can be traced back to its mild form beginning at the Olympics in 8th century A.D. in Greece. Slowly it penetrated to the armed forces and underwent a major transformation during World War. I and reaching student organizations mainly in the west. It entered India with the advent of the British, starting in armed forces and English public schools and remaining and multiplying in its severity through various educational institutions. Earlier it was only the medical and engineering colleges in the country in its fold but now it has left no field untouched.

Started as a practice in the west as hazing or bullying or teasing it slowly converted to violence resulting in the first ragging related death in 1873 in Cornell University in the US and the universities in the West were quick to take note and devise alternative means of interaction. However it is now mainly confined to South Asian countries being India and Sri Lanka primarily. It is not teasing anymore but organized harassment having elements of regionalism, racism, financial disparity and casteism.

The supporters of ragging claim that it makes one bold and able to face hardships and difficult situations in life exposing them to the real world, but in reality it distorts the mental balance of an individual to an unimaginable extent. The so called confidence booster has become the confidence robber.

The psychological aspect of ragging is linked with the ragger having an inherent fear or weakness which he tries to conceal by humiliating the others. To establish the notion of his superiority, he resorts to autocratic behaviour feeling powerful. Even if one doesn't want to rag the junior he succumbs to peer pressure. It becomes a vicious circle with the oppressed become the oppressor the next time around making sure that if they were not spared by their seniors their juniors would also not be left untouched. It is important to realize that the ragger is also a victim of ragging: not only was he ragged in his first year, he was later co-opted in a system of abuse and exploitation, one that legitimizes violence and oppression, drug abuse and alcoholism, all as 'student life'. Hence my concern is not only the extent of ragging but the idea of ragging: the idea that you must abuse and exploit me just because you joined this college a year or two before I did, is so illogical.

As per expert opinions the seeds of such behaviour are sowed early in life. When a child sees discord and violence in the family, he becomes insensitive to feelings and emotions and does not bother when he inflicts others with violence. With the advancement of electronic media children are glued to the television or the internet watching nonsensical programmes, violent and aggressive games with bloodshed and the parents are so busy in their own affairs to give quality time to their children resulting in the influence of all sorts of violence and aggression on them. Hence the onus lies on the parents of today to give their children a secure environment and a value based upbringing to prevent them from becoming future raggers.

It is sad to know that ragging is prevalent in schools also especially the boarding schools. So preoccupied are we with academic excellence that we have ignored the emotional quotient of our young generation. Therefore, during the formative years of a child, he undergoes psychological trauma leaving an indelible mark in the mind of the children making them socially awkward and under confident. Hence from the top most institution in the country to the schools, ragging has showed its demonic face.

The book of Mr. Naveen deals with all the possible aspects of ragging like narrating incidents, giving guidance to institutions on imparting value based education and tackling the incidents, tips for freshers and discussing the various NGO's relating to the work.

The author's choice of topic was motivated by the sad demise of Aman Satya Kachroo. A promising young student aiming to be a doctor and serve humanity was sacrificed at the altar of ragging meting out unprecedented cruelty taking away his life. Such incidents bring tears to our eyes and warm our hearts to the grief of his family but it was about time that something was done and hence followed a series of discussions, with media playing a pivotal role in spreading awareness. The efforts of NGO's like CURE, SAVE, SPACE, SATHEE and the like are commendable.

In the year 1984 the Chief Justice of Himachal Pradesh High Court received a letter dated 4th April, 1984 from the guardian of a student of the medical college in Shimla, complaining about the ragging of freshers by senior students within the college campus and the hostels and treating such letter as a Public Interest Litigation, the Division Bench of Himachal Pradesh High Court had given certain directions to curb the menace of ragging in the said college including directions to the State Government to constitute a Committee consisting of Vice-Chancellor of Himachal Predesh University and the other State Functionaries to make recommendations and referred to the curative, preventive and punitive measures to be adopted by the college to control and curb the evil of ragging. The said committee was named as Anti Ragging Committee and one of the recommendations made by the said Committee was to bring the legislation by the State Government making ragging a cognizable offence. Acting on the said recommendations, the Division Bench of High Court gave directions to the Chief Secretary of the State Government to file an affidavit within a period of six weeks for bringing such a legislation, but unfortunately, the said recommendations of the Division Bench were challenged before the Apex Court and the Apex Court keeping in view the sanctity of separation of powers took a view that a direction would amount to usurping the powers of the executive and the legislature under the Constitution. It is unfortunate that the recommendations of the committee were on the verge of becoming a legislation and had the law been in place perhaps the precious life of Aman Kachroo could have been saved.

It is only in the year 2006, that the Apex court was seized with the Public interest litigation that it took note of this social evil and gave directions for the appointment of Dr. Raghavan committee to give recommendations which were then accepted by the Apex Court. The committee issued guidelines which were not swiftly implemented. But then the regulatory bodies like the UGC passed their guidelines to cancel the affiliation and aid to colleges where ragging would be prevalent and devised ways and means to stop the same. They have made mandatory filing of affidavits at the time of admissions that they will not resort to ragging, it has been giving the status of a crime making FIR mandatory in all cases of ragging attracting various provisions of the IPC. Various states like Tamil Nadu and Himachal Pradesh have enacted anti ragging legislations. Mr. Kapil Sibal inaugurated a ragging helpline for students available round the clock. The launching of the Aman Movement with the help of common people and the efforts of Aman's father is a feather in the cap for such initiatives.

However, we cannot shy away from the reality that ragging still continues but now is under shadows by the institutions to prevent their name and reputation. Some students have equated ragging to mental rape, by which we can imagine the harm it is causing the young minds today. In my opinion the problem has to be looked at with the point of view of human rights abuse as well together with the element of crime. However as per the recommendations of the Raghavan committee, 5.45 and 5.46 calls for a special law relating to ragging through amendments in the Indian Penal Code as in ragging are various elements of one or the other crimes. There has also to be a tough special central legislation in place in the wake of various state legislations to bring about uniformity in laws. On May 6, 2005, the Prevention of Ragging in Colleges and Institutions Bill was tabled in the Rajya Sabha, however, it is yet to see the light of the day. Ragging gives a sordid history of human rights violation. Article 21 of the Constitution of India with its ever widening scope gives everyone right to live with dignity. Under its umbrella the rights of every individual and his dignity is secured. One does not have to be a grown up to avail such rights, it is inherent in the constitution and is guaranteed by it to everyone. Ragging is violation of fundamental rights which are the heart of Indian constitution. Ragging is a blot on the democratic values enshrined in the constitution. Judiciary can dispense justice, but the real implementation has to come from the enforcement authorities at the state, district and institutional level. Those who have been tortured to the extent that they have taken their lives to save themselves from such an inescapable position are no more here to tell the others what it did to them, but we should become their voices and the author has become one of the first to lend his to the cause.

India is the land of Mahatma Gandhi, of virtue of non violence soaked in its soil. It has been talked about for decades because of its peace loving nature and values. It is now touted as the next big thing lauded all over the world for its young talent and academic brilliance. In the wake of such a heinous practice in place, the image of India is tarnished. It is unfortunate that for a country known for its spirituality is at the cross roads because of the great degeneration of moral values. Once the young generation suffers from such moral decay, it is reflected in their conduct when they grow up. Even when they settle down in their career it is shown when they humiliate their subordinates or female colleagues molesting them or outraging their modesty just because they are in a commanding position. This attitude of pulling down others by exuding power over them is drilled in the mind-set from the very childhood which results to devious acts by them later in life. It is like a cancer spreading in the society affecting everyone and resulting in grave consequences destroying the entire moral fabric of our society. Hence it has to be a concerted and cohesive effort on the part of the society to give the child of today a secure environment enriched in culture, traditions, ethos laid down by our great saints, philosophers and social reformers.

It is the time that everyone says no to accept such a practice as being OK and part of the routine environment in college. An atmosphere of zero tolerance towards ragging has to be cultivated for the prevention of any potential Amans. We should not wait for any other incidents to happen for us to wake up and take notice again of this social evil. A collective change in the societal mind-set may be the only answer, which has to begin with parental guidance. An overnight miracle is not possible because we are an amnesiac nation which forgets as easily as we are outraged. But for the sake of Aman and many like and before him let us hope that ragging becomes history.

Mr. Gulshan has taken the step to present his concern as an ordinary citizen bothered about the youth of the nation going waste. It is his effort to keep a burning issue still burning dispelling darkness and bringing light. The book is a hands on information manual about ragging. I appreciate and congratulate him for his endeavour and wish him luck with his book.

I thank all of you for being a patient audience and honouring me by having me here to do the responsible and auspicious task of launching this book.

SPEEDY JUSTICE: ROLE OF THE BENCH AND THE BAR

A very good evening to all present. It is indeed a proud privilege for me today to come back here to where I belong. My roots and my heart are still in the confines of this compound and I am forever indebted to the members of this Bar for having given unstinted support and love to me.

Innumerable conferences, seminars and lectures are taking place on the deteriorating of the system due to docket explosion. The problem is indeed grave as people are spending half of their lives in the alleys of the court rooms. Also, with the advent of new technology and globalization, new legislations are passed at very short intervals. This has led to an increase in the litigation, adding to the already existing insurmountable arrears.

In the face of such a dismal scenario, speedy justice seems like an oxymoron. The right to speedy justice is indeed a fundamental right guaranteed under Article 21 of the Constitution of India, but how much of it is reality. There are numerous studies that are conducted every now and then to estimate the pendency in different courts in the country but however what is not stressed is what are the solutions to it.

The topic for today in this context assumes insurmountable importance as we discuss the role of the Bench and the Bar in the dispensation of speedy justice. The Bench and the Bar are the two sides of the same coin and are complimentary to each other. Each one does not have any existence without the other and hence to achieve a goal that benefits the seeker of justice, we have to work together.

The prime reason for delay in the outcome of a case, in my opinion is adjournments. The lawyers take on so many briefs that before the hearing for a particular matter, the lawyer is not able to go through the file and takes an adjournment citing any reason. The judge in the effort not to be harsh and accommodating also gives a date and thus this vicious circle continues leading to the travesty of justice. It should be an endeavour of the members of the Bar to take on a limited number of matters and then to be thorough with the brief so that they can effectively assist the court. It is undoubtedly true that if the counsel is well versed with the case and is able to assist the court better then the quality of the judgment rendered by the court is also better and the chances of it being challenged and set aside are less. If the lawyers take upon themselves to seek lesser number of adjournments, it is my firm belief that there can be made a considerable difference.

Another effective role that the Bar and the Bench can resort to the Alternate Dispute resolution mechanisms like arbitration, mediation, conciliation and Lok Adalats. There was an uncanny sense of insecurity in the members of the Bar that adopting these means would imply less appearances and thus less remuneration. But now I see that there is a change in the attitude of the Bar and they are realizing that the end is to seek justice. I would also to appreciate the endeavour of the Delhi Mediation Centre in this regard. From the data available, it is evident that the subordinate courts of Delhi and especially Tees Hazari are doing a commendable job in settling disputes through mediation.

During the time of King Akbar a bell was hung in the palace for the people seeking justice and any person wanting justice had to simply go and ring the bell, which indicates the urgency with which dispensation of justice was treated. Such urgency is also the need of the hour. It has to be understood that the ultimate goal of both the Bench and the Bar should not only be to achieve justice but to achieve speedy justice. We cannot deny the fact that the faith of the common man in the justice delivery system is fast eroding. When the people do not get justice through the portals of law they resort to illegal and unethical means for settling their disputes which leads to chaos and anarchy in the society. The impression of the common man today is that if he approaches the courts for readressal, justice would be done to him when either he does not have the time or the will to enjoy the fruit of the years spent in achieving it. Hence, the very idea of speedy justice is illusive and elusive to him. The Bar and the Bench have to make a concerted, cooperative and corroborative effort to make sure that the right to speedy justice is not a mirage but a reality.

MEDIATION

First of all I extend my heartiest congratulations to all the members of Rohini Court Bar Association on the successful completion of their first year. Although being the first birthday, the Rohini Bar Association is at the infancy stage, but I am sure that it will not only grow faster, but grow achieving and dedicating its services to the cause and quest for justice. The function of today will go down in the history of our institution as on this day the Bar is celebrating its first anniversary and Delhi Legal Services Authority has established a Mediation Cell, which shows complete harmony between Bench and Bar. The efforts of Justice T.S. Thakur deserve a big applaud.

Judiciary as it is said is the last bastion of people's hope. Judiciary is the only temple worshipped by every citizen regardless of religion, caste, creed or place of birth. Bar and Bench together have to ensure that faith of common man is not eroded in the institution. The lawyers and Judges are the main pillars of the justice delivery system. The Bar and Bench are the two wheels of the chariot of justice and both the wheels have to be in proper alignment so as to reach to its destination. Bench and Bar must work in unison to achieve the ultimate goal of delivering justice to one and all. The Bar and Bench both cannot afford to talk in terms of I and you. Both will have to talk in terms of 'we'. Let me give another example to describe as to how important and inter dependent the relationship between Bench and Bar is. The Bench and Bar are the two wings of a bird, which symbolizes the administration of justice. The bird cannot even take off if the bird is without the wing of Bar or of the Bench. The bird also cannot properly fly and reach higher in the sky, if any, of the wing is infected or is wounded. The bird can rise higher and higher only when it's both the wings are strong and flap together. The Bench and Bar are, therefore, inseparable and it should be our constant endeavour to see that our relationship is strengthened day in and day out.

I once again express my deep gratitude to the Members of the Rohini Court Bar Association specially, Shri B.S. Rana and Shri Jatan Singh and all the Presidents of their respective Bar Associations, who came together to do the honours. I am really touched by their affection and warmth.

I am short of words to express my gratitude to all of you. In the last, I would say that let us all try to be good to each other and work together to strengthen our judicial system to provide justice to the common people may be through our traditional system or through the mechanism of ADR. The fragrance of flowers spreads only in the direction of wind, but the goodness of a person spreads in all directions.

My felicitation can be derived by every member of the bar specially, who are present at the District Court level. I have no hesitation in acknowledging that I am here as a Judge of Delhi High Court only because of the fact that Member of the Bar desired and wished it. It is only the prayers and best wishes of the Bar Members that led to my appointment as Judge of the High Court. As it is said that when prayers go up blessings of Almighty come down and the same came down to me in the shape of my elevation. I owe my appointment to all the Members of collegium of High Court and Supreme Court, who themselves have made it possible for me.

COURT CRAFTS & ADVOCACY SKILLS: LEARNING TO SHARE

Today's discussion is on advocacy skills, Court crafts and professional ethics. The presence of eminent speakers Justice Sikri and Mr. V.P. Singh itself shows the importance of the subjects to be addressed. Justice Sikri was a very successful, laborious and hard working advocate and with the same zeal he is adorning the seat of judgeship. Mr. V.P. Singh, Sr. Advocate is also not a new name to the Bar as well as the Bench. With his varied experience in diverse field of legal subjects he always presents his arguments with clarity, precision and legal acumen. When we talk of advocacy skills we must first understand what advocacy is.

As we all know that advocacy is a profession and not a business. When we say it is a profession simultaneously we also claim that it is the profession, which is known as a noble profession. Canadian Court on legal ethics is of the view that the Advocacy is a branch of administration of justice and not a money making occupation. In a business, any kind of conduct is allowed, which can increase your income, but in a profession a certain kind of conduct is not permitted, even if large fees is offered to them, because such conduct is considered as unprofessional. As we all know that advocates are not supposed to solicit work through advertisements or other such methods. This profession is considered to be of a great honour and dignity only because it is the only profession which is governed by rules of ethics and morality. In the absence of these rules the advocacy will regenerate itself into any trade or business. As we all know justice is the highest desire of mankind on the earth and it is the function of the advocates to espouse the cause of their clients.

So far the advocacy skills are concerned, their skills must match the dignity of their office. Today as the things are going, lawyers are more tempted to have fast results then putting hard work in their brief. I am not suggesting that lawyers are not hard working, certainly they are. The kind of inflow we are now getting from the best of the law colleges, there is no dearth of talent and caliber. One certainly feels disturbed when one comes to know that instead of working on the principles, the lawyers keep hunting for the Judge favoured faces. I am not denying that, there may be Judges who go by this but such kind of practice must be opposed with tooth and nail. I do not think that a lawyer who has put heart and soul in a brief and argues well before a Court will not get relief even though such a lawyer may be a new face or not a favoured face. It was startling to read the newspaper in "Indian Express", where it is mentioned that some lawyer from South Delhi had demanded an amount of Rs. 30 lakhs to appear before a Judge in Punjab and Haryana High Court and besides that Rs. 2 lakhs for conference charges were charged, charted plane from Delhi to Chandigarh so on and so forth. If these are called advocacy skills then even God cannot save our institution. Advocacy skills, as I understand, are those in pursuance of which one prepares his brief from all angles, factual and legal both. One should prepare the brief keeping in view that if an opposite client in such brief comes and engages him then how he would oppose such a brief and then prepare the same. So, the skills are primarily of putting hard work in the brief and then to present the same focusing on the important issues involved in the brief.

So far the Court crafts are concerned, as we all know that an advocate does not merely represent the interest of his client, but he is also an officer of the Court. His prime duty is to seek justice for his client. The lawyer has not to quarrel or fight with the Judge. He should do his best to convince the Judge with his persuasive and legal abilities. The advocate should also patiently hear the Judge whenever the Judge wants to convey something during the course of arguments. It is often seen that whenever a Judge speaks, the lawyer does not listen to him & starts bickering. Not only should the lawyers should have also patiently hear the arguments of the opposite counsel and some time from the arguments of the opposite counsel favourable solutions comes in. A lawyer should always be respectful to the Court. It is not a respect to an individual sitting on the seat of Judge but it is a respect to the Judge who is occupying the seat and to the Court. Justice B.N. Chaturvedi in his farewell speech, gave an example of an advocate leaving the Court room after addressing arguments without turning his back towards the Judge and Judge was so much impressed with the etiquette of such an advocate. It is set out that courts are nothing but temples of justice and, therefore, the advocates must keep the Courts in highest esteem. Even the Judges should give due respect to the lawyers as officers of the Court. I remember and hence its seen that before arguing a case, before a particular Judge, the lawyers in advance would come and sit in the Court to see the total demeanor of a Judge, that while hearing a matter what kind of questions he puts forth and how he reacts to certain situations, that how he feels pleased and how he gets furious or angry, in order to know the complete side of the Judge. It is even well known in the public domain, that Hon'ble

Mr. Justice Mahinder Narain, was one of the brilliant judges of his time and he had an in-depth knowledge of not only law but also numerous other subjects. In cases involving articles such as gem, jewellery, automobile, watches etc., he would get more inquisitive and put forth a number of product related questions than law based questions. The Court craft thus can be different for each and every Court, but to give respect and be humble and docile are the best crafts which can be used in any Court in general that is why it is said that lawyer should not merely possess good knowledge of law but also of various other subjects be it history, science, psychology, literature and so on and so forth. I need not say that not only the Judges but the lawyers also should be of a very high moral character. It is unfortunate that in the present time, success at the Bar is measured by the amount of money one earns and not by the degree of his ability and competence at the Bar. Members of the Bar are required to stick to the high moral standards even also when they are outside the sphere of the professional activities.

MILES TO GO BEFORE YOU SLEEP*

Good evening to all present

Today we have gathered here to bid adieu to the graduating class of 2009. And I know that all of the students sitting here feel what is ever so good about goodbye? You are leaving your friends, your most cherished memories, entering into a new brutal and competitive world which would intimidate you. Some of you may have big paychecks waiting for you, but they still don't lure you enough to feel good about the goodbye. I could not agree with you more. What I find ironical about graduation is that it is an event where the commencement speaker tells hundreds of students dressed in identical caps and gowns that "individuality" is the key to success.

Nevertheless, today we cannot change the fact that change is the only constant in life and is inevitable. It is inevitable that structures and processes and relationships will change in your day-to-day lives. It is inevitable that you will face new challenges and it is inevitable that things may seem a little different in the year ahead. Yes, life is definitely going to become a little "shaken up and stirred".

But as you look back this evening on a journey – a journey that started out with hesitant, tentative steps, you would see just how far you have progressed and today I feel honored and privileged to be a part of your journey because I belong to this institution which has been imbued with wonderful memories, where they strive not only for academic excellence but all round development. Everyone has memories and allow me to share two such memories with you – memories that serve to illustrate that while some things will change and rightly so – the core fundamentals in our lives will remain the same.

Today, I think is the right time that I would like to take the opportunity to thank each and every one present here. You have all left and will continue to leave an indelible legacy of excellence, achievement and a fine ethos and tradition for generations to come in this institution.

Some things come into our lives and quickly go but some like our college life stay for a while, leave footprints on our hearts, and we are never, ever the same. I would also like to pay tribute to the wonderful

* Address to the graduating Batch of 2009 at Law Faculty.

teachers, the parents, past pupils – you have all guided, molded and shaped me and these fine young ladies and gentlemen standing here tonight. Your role has been hugely instrumental in moulding us.

So Ladies and Gentlemen, as you face and tackle the inevitable changes, hold true to yourself. Put your future in safe hands, that is your own. The fireworks begin from now on. Each degree is a lighted match. Each one of you is a fuse. A man who has never gone to school may steal from a freight car; but if he has a university education, he may steal the whole railroad. Keep in mind that neither failure nor success is ever final and there is no shortcut to any place worth going. The only thing between you and the top of the ladder is the ladder and that ladder you can climb with hard work.

I would like to quote what I read somewhere:

"The future lies before you
Like a field of driven snow,
Be careful how you tread it,
For every step will show."

But remember, that today's achievements may fade or even be forgotten. The applause may become a distant memory and your certificates and medals may gather dust on a shelf or in a drawer. But, you will always be remembered for caring enough, for helping someone and the values that this institution has instilled in you.

I in my journey, when faced with obstacles, I always remembered what Robert Frost said and would like you to keep it with you too:

The woods are lovely, dark, and deep,
But I have promises to keep,
And miles to go before I sleep,
And miles to go before I sleep.

Your life is a remarkable occasion – I have no doubt that you will rise to it.

So now if you ask me what is good about the goodbye? I would say that the return makes one love the farewell.

COLLEGIUM SYSTEM: FAILED STEP TOWARDS AN INDEPENDENT JUDICIARY

I feel honoured and privileged to be invited to give my inaugural address on the most debatable topic regarding the appointment of the Judges of the Supreme Court and High Courts through collegium system or through the process of National Judicial Commission.

To this august gathering of very enlighten people I need not refer *S.P. Gupta* v. *President of India,* AIR 1982 SC 149: 1982 Rajdhani LR 389: 1981 Supp SCC 87 where the majority view led by the most eminent Judge Justice P.N. Bhagwati took a view that the opinion of Chief Justice of India does not have primacy in the matter of appointments of Judges of Supreme Court and High Courts and in case of difference of opinion the Government view would prevail over the view of the Chief Justice of India on appointments and transfers of the Judges. That was post 1982 till the evolution of the collegium mechanism the executive played a dominant role in the appointment of the Judges of High Courts and Supreme Courts and many of the names recommended by the Chief Justice of India were not cleared by the Executive till the names desired by the Executive are also included in the list. The famous saying during those days was "better to know Law Minister then the law".

The judiciary had a consultative role in the appointment of Judges of higher judiciary till the 9 Judges Bench of the Supreme Court overruled the majority view of the *S.P. Gupta's* case in the *Advocates-on-Record* v. *Union of India* case in the year 1993. The majority view in this case was led by Hon'ble Mr. Justice J.S. Verma, who later rose to the position of Hon'ble Chief Justice of India and unfortunately died recently after submitting a well documented report after Nirbhaya murder case. The said judgment gave clear supremacy to the judiciary over the executive in the appointment and transfer of Judges. It was perceived as a welcome step in securing the independence of the judiciary, in fact by the said judgment the Supreme Court became the only Court in the world which could select and appoint its own Judges.

The term "collegium" nowhere has been used in the Constitution of India by the framers of the Constitution. However, the judiciary through the power of interpretation of the Constitution under Article 149 had expanded the term "Chief Justice of India occurring in Article 124(2), 217(1) and 222(1) to mean the collegium of select Judges, which was three in two Judges case (1993) and further extended to five in three Judges case (1998).

The Executive made a Presidential reference under Article 143(1) of the Constitution of India in 1998 and in the said reference the 9 Judges Bench again confirmed primacy of the collegium of Judges in appointment and transfer of Judges in the higher judiciary. The appointment of Judges through the process of collegium system came under serious attack not only from the executive of this country but even from eminent legal luminaries including those who are even part of judgment in Advocate-on-Record Association case. In fact the Government began thinking about scraping the collegium system of appointment of Judges by bringing a Constitution amendment bill as early as in 2010 when Mr. M. Veerappa Moily was Law Minister. The Chief Justice of India P. Sathasivam after taking over the reins of top seat in the judiciary in his interview to the media felt complete satisfaction with the existing collegium system and what he said I quote:—

> "The appointment of Judges to the Supreme Court and the High Courts is made by the President and is, therefore, ultimately an executive act. The judiciary's role is limited to making recommendations. The power to make recommendations is not absolute. It is always open to the Government to seek reconsideration of the recommendation made by the collegium, for strong reasons or adverse material in their possession. In fact, in the recent past, the Government has exercised its power to keep a check and prevent the appointment of persons considered to be unsuitable."

In view of this, it cannot be claimed that the Government has no role in the appointment of Judges and the setting up of a National Commission will not solve the problem. On the other hand, if the time schedule is strictly followed by all the authorities, according to me, the present system will solve the problem. Hon'ble Mr. Justice J.S. Verma himself admitted that the collegium system had not worked properly, though he did not say it had failed. He had suggested its replacement in the form of an independent National Commission.

We are all aware that the Constitution (120th Amendment) Bill 2013 seeking to create a National Judicial Commission has already been passed by the upper House of the Parliament. The suggested composition of the National Judicial Commission, as we all know is the Chief Justice of India, two senior most Judges of the Supreme Court, the Law Minister and two eminent persons to be selected by a panel comprising of the Prime Minister, CJI and leader of the opposition in the Lok Sabha. We also know this configuration of 6 members is not a part of the Constitution and is not constitutionally entrenched. This composition of Judicial Commission can be modified or altered by the Parliament through an ordinary law (Article 124A).

The Bar Council of India has already opposed the constitution of such a National Judicial Commission, which as per the BCI would affect the independence of judiciary and the basic structure of the Constitution. The Bar Council further said that the existing collegium system has been functioning well and constitution of NJC only would weaken the judiciary. However, Bar Council of India also felt that the system needed to be more transparent and the mechanism of the appointments should be strengthened.

Another eminent jurist Mr. Fali Nariman also took a view that the present collegium system is not working well as there has been no sense of accountability or of transparency. He, however, also said that he may not agree with many of the provisions forming part of the Judicial Appointment Commission Bill.

Why there has been so much criticism of the existing collegium system and why the legal stalwarts started feeling that this system has failed? In my view no system can be fool proof as every system with whatever good intention is made will have some drawbacks and shortcomings. The main drawback confronting the present collegium system is that this system has not been able to ensure timely appointment of Judges in various High Courts and at every point in time one can find around 1/3 of the Judges of the High Court not in strength. Secondly, there are few instances where the names for the appointment of the Judges were recommended brazenly out of favoritism due to multiple factors, which you all know and I may not spell out and thirdly no proper mechanism is in place to take any action against the tainted Judges or those became liability on the system due to their misconduct and deviant behavior. From Justice V. Ramaswami to Justice Soumitra Sen, we have noticed that the system has totally failed because of the cumbersome procedure provided for impeachment of such Judges being the only solution.

Undeniably the said shortcomings have to be addressed but not to be addressed in a manner which can threaten the independence of the judiciary. Independence of the judiciary is sacrosanct and it is for everyone to see including the Parliament that the same is not compromised. Mr. Anil Divan another eminent jurist in one of his articles has raised an apprehension that if the said Constitutional bill is adopted the same will emasculate an independent judiciary and will pose a great threat to the rule of law. He further quoted the Supreme Court and said that "the rule of law is a basic feature of the Constitution, which permeates the whole of the Constitutional fabric and is an integral part of the constructional structure. The independence of the judiciary is an essential attribute of the rule of law." He also said that the doctrine of separation of powers cannot be stretched so as to set up a mechanism which is capable of being abused by making judicial appointments completely subservient to the will of the executive.

Another most eminent legal luminary former Chief Justice of India Justice M.N. Venkatachaliah who headed the National Commission to review the working of the Constitution held the view that, it would be dangerous if the primacy of the CJI in the appointment process was done away with. It would against the basic structure of the Constitution.

The Judicial Appointments Commission Bill, 2013 has many pernicious features and the same as have been taken out from the article by Mr. Anil Divan, Senior Advocate are:—

> "The composition of JAC can be modified or altered by Parliament by ordinary law (Article 124A). This configuration of six members is not part of the Constitution and is not constitutionally entrenched. The JAC can be 'packed' by pliant elements in future by the executive even by an Ordinance and the JAC can recommend non-meritorious persons even on the basis of caste, religion or loyalty to the government.
>
> The appointment of the CJI, the CJ of High Courts, and judges of the Supreme Court and the High Courts and transfer of High Court judges are to take place on the recommendation of the JAC. Thus, a JAC can, even by a majority, recommend a junior judge of the Supreme Court to be a CJI—or even a Chief Justice or Judge of the High Court can be recommended to be the CJI. Further, with six members as contemplated in the JAC, a casting vote for the CJI is essential.
>
> *Secondly*, there is no provision recognising the convention that the seniormost Supreme Court judge will be appointed as the CJI (unless physically impaired)—a constitutional convention adhered to from 1950 except for the two supersessions concerning Justice A.N. Ray and Justice M.H. Beg. Such a provision will prevent lobbying and will preserve collegiality in the apex court.
>
> *Thirdly*, the JAC Bill provides that the Central Government will appoint the officers and employees of the Commission, making its secretariat a government department. This is the most dangerous provision. The officials and personnel of the Commission should

be appointed in the same manner as those of the Supreme Court (Article 146), *viz*, by the CJI or such other Judge or officer of the court as he may direct. If the secretariat or officers and servants of the JAC are treated as government departments, there are a hundred ways of making the JAC dysfunctional. In addition, the confidentiality and secrecy of the JAC deliberations cannot be maintained. The importance of an independent secretariat is a *sine qua non* for an independent and politically neutral JAC.

Fourthly, all expenses including salaries allowances and pensions should be charged upon the Consolidated Fund of India as provided for the Supreme Court and the High Courts (Article 146 and 229). The JAC must be financially independent of executive budgetary control.

Finally and, most importantly, the criticism against the collegium system was lack of transparency, no consultations with the Bar, favouritism, the lack of a level playing field for meritorious members of the Bar, no list of potential candidates prepared after advertisements and nominations to be put up in the public domain and lack of guidelines and criteria in the selection process. These core concepts must be incorporated in the Constitution Amendment and not left to be addressed by the Central government or the JAC. One opaque collegium need not be substituted by another, raising the apprehension that future vacancies may be shared by internal accommodations within the JAC."

The above short comings are so pernicious and if the same remain on the Judicial Appointments Commission Bill, 2013 the same will pose a serious threat to the independence of the judiciary. The Parliament is supreme in framing laws and we hope that when the said Bill is introduced in the Lok Sabha proper and effective debate takes place on each and every clause of the Bill so that finally the bill can pass the test of the spirit and mandate of the Constitution of not interfering with its basic structure of upholding the rule of law and not undermining the independence of the judiciary.

ADR: THE PATH TO TREAD ON

Good evening to all present. As the last speaker I have a heavy burden on me not to put you all to sleep. As the responsibility of the last batsman at the crease is to score the maximum in whatever time is left, I fortunately have no such onus as the ones before me have already scored very well.

A peaceful societal co-existence of all is a dream we no doubt aspire for, but the human nature begets conflicts and thus resolution of disputes is an essential characteristic for societal peace, harmony and easy access to justice. It is evident from the history that the function of resolving disputes has fallen upon the shoulders of the powerful and experienced ones. With the evolution of modern States and sophisticated legal mechanisms, the courts run on very formal processes and are presided over by trained adjudicators entrusted with the responsibility of resolution of disputes on the part of the State. The adversarial mode of resolution of disputes is time consuming and leads to docket explosion. Need for alternatives to the formal legal system are the need of the hour and has become the cynosure of the legal fraternity.

This Indian-institutionalized, indigenized and now, legalized concept for settlement of dispute promotes the goals of our Constitution. It is rightly said that Law and system of justice are not like antiques to be taken down, dusted, admired and put back on the shelf, but they are rather like a vigorous tree which has its roots in history and takes on new graft, puts out new sprouts and occasionally drops dead wood. It is a dynamic instrument fashioned for the purpose of achieving ameliorative and harmonious adjustment, and settlement of disputes arising out of human relations by eliminating social tensions and conflicts and it must, therefore, change with changing socio-economic conditions. The winds of change are blowing through the Indian legal system and propelling India to embrace the alternative modes of dispute resolution again alongside the formal litigation system.

We are fighting the two dastardly venomous demons *firstly*, the pendency of cases in courts and *secondly*, the cost that the common man has to bear for accessing justice. It is common knowledge that many a times cases often end up as dead cycles of litigative voyage in the courts and resultant lengthening of the life of dispute resolution process.

@ The figures reflect a dismal picture. At present, there are 2.7 crore (27 million) cases pending with the trial courts, the lowest rung of judiciary. The High Courts are grappling to deal with a pendency of ·4 million cases and the Apex Court has around 53,000 cases pending. The improving and increasing number of disposal of cases does not bear fruit because of the increasing number of institution of suits. The root cause for this is as the CJI puts it the "chronic shortage of judicial officers". Justice Department figures a few months ago showed India's 21 High Courts as having 234 of 886 High Court judgeships vacant and Subordinate Courts with a sanctioned strength of 16,946 as having 2,783 vacancies. Hence, the judge to population ratio is a far cry from what is needed today.

In my view, today ADR is not only an alternative method but also an appropriate method of resolving differences and these vital ADR mechanisms will go a long way in resolving the disputes at comparatively no cost to the litigants and with minimum delay. At the same time, they are not meant to replace and supplant the Court system. They are an attempt to decongest the Courts from heavy burden of cases. There is an incumbent need for decentralization of justice. But what I want to emphasise here is that it should not be treated as just another mechanical process of dispute resolution. It might look like an activist legal aid philosophy, but it is something more potent than that. It will promote the rule of law in the society, promote peoples participation and self reliant development and create legal awareness and respect for the rights of others. If we could find alternatives like the metro or the monorail for the burgeoning population so we can also find alternatives in the justice dispensing system and hence both the concepts are a "revolutionary evolution of resolution of disputes".

Efforts have been made by institutes like the ICADR which are commendable and worth applauding. Every High Court has also now set up mediation and conciliation centers to facilitate settlement of disputes. Like the Delhi High Court Mediation Centre ***"Samadhan"*** established in 2006 has been successful in its endeavour. Out of 1348 cases referred to it from January 2009 until now, 374 have already been settled. It covers in its ambit vast variety of disputes ranging from commercial to family and custody and hence gives an open level playing field to the parties to mutually reach a solution. Also the pre-litigative mediation initiated by the banks like the ICICI has been successful and this trend should be followed by others. Western countries were no doubt quick to resort to this method, but now also nothing is lost.

We have all noticed that there has been a lot of hullabaloo around the concept of Alternative Dispute Resolution (ADR). A number of conferences, meetings, publications and courses have come up in recent time, but today we need to ask the question as not why we should adopt ADR but how to strengthen it, so that it does not crumble under its own expectations.

Almost every dimension and aspect of ADR has been addressed in this conference, but I would like to speak on some of the issues that need to be addressed in the present scenario.

- *Firstly* and fore mostly, the awareness of these alternative mechanisms should be spread to the common people. The common man has started looking upon legal system as a foe and not as a friend. For him, law is always taking something away. If we do not educate them about its advantages than they will not be able to reap the benefits of the infrastructure that has been developed. The *aam aadmi,* who seeks justice with the courts, slowly realizes that the system itself is his toughest opponent; therefore, it is necessary to spread awareness of these alternative methods and to facilitate the rights of common people to speedy and inexpensive justice. The suggestion of the Malimath Committee and the 129th Report of the Law Commission to establish Gram Nyalayas are still in the pipeline. In my view it is a potent tool of ADR at the grass-root level from where the people can get justice at their doorstep.
- *Secondly,* mediation as a form of ADR has to be brought under a statutory mandate. No doubt the field has been left open to devise its own procedure to wriggle out of the vicious circle of the procedural laws, but at the same time this leads to mediators taking leeway and there has to be a legislation in place for the same.
- Also the quality of justice dispensed in ADR is a cause of worry for a lot of people. The mediators, arbitrators and the third neutral parties no doubt receive training from institutions like the ICADR and the like but the faith of the common man in it would come only if it has the sanctity of a decision as that of the court, and hence there have to be devised some Code of ethics and rules for them. They should be subjected to a continuous evaluation procedure. We cannot shy away that becoming a mediator has become a lucrative option for many, but it should not be treated by lawyers as an additional means of income to be restored over the weekend or after court hours. Hence we have to be on our toes to watch that this system of dispensing justice is not diluted.
- We should not forget that we are resorting to ADR because of pendency of litigation, but if the same bleeds into this system then the whole effort would go futile. *Justice hurried should not become justice buried.*

- It has been observed that matters of commercial nature are opting for arbitration. We have to accept that it is an expensive option but what is worrying is that after one round of settling the matter in arbitration there is another round in the court challenging the same award on one pretext or the other, resulting in waste of money, time and effort. This aspect needs to be looked into and a legislative action needs to be there in place to curb such cases coming to the court.
- In case of the Legal Services Authority Act, it provides for setting-up of permanent Lok Adalats for settling of disputes relating to public utility services. But the intent of the Act has been misconstrued as it provides by virtue of section 22C for the Lok Adalat to decide the dispute whereas what we were aiming at by them was settlement through mutual consent.
- To begin with mediations started with judges being the mediators and then it was handed down to the trained lawyers. But still at the level of the subordinate courts judges are acting as mediators, which in my view is a waste of judicial time and money. If they are gaining on one end by resolving a dispute they are losing on the other hand as they are spending their judicial time out of courts. This needs to be changed and the judges should only supervise these mechanisms and not act themselves as the mediators.
- It is common knowledge that Government is one of the largest litigants in the country today. In my view to cut down the influx of cases every Government department should have a redrressal forum in place backed by not Government Officers but people with legal acumen so that grievance of the citizens are solved at that level and they are not compelled to approach the court.

The inflow of cases can be curtailed but the solution is not to stop people from approaching the court as the doors of justice should never be closed. It is no doubt an oft repeated saying that it is the spirit and not the form of law that keeps justice alive, which holds true in the case of alternative dispute resolution mechanism, but we cannot afford to overlook its shortcomings and should be prepared to tackle them.

It will only be apt to say that we hope that like other attempts this is also successful and does not become a bubble that bursts.

Let me conclude with a sound but an imperative that we must be ever mindful that *"Yesterday is not ours to recover, but tomorrow is ours to win or lose"*, and, therefore, let us get together, stand united, and strengthen our Bench and Bar in an irrevocable unique partnership and make collaborative endeavour in popularising, proliferating and pioneering, concept and philosophy of important institution – alternative dispute resolution mechanism – so as to strengthen our pluralistic democratic values, rule of law and thereby invigorate the commandment, *"Justice shall never be rationed"*. Let us therefore make all efforts to advance and strengthen "equal, inexpensive and speedy access to justice", the heart of the Constitution of India, a reality.

BREAKING THE IMPASSE: *ALTERNATIVE DISPUTE RESOLUTION*, AN ANTIDOTE TO LITIGATIVE VOYAGE

George Washington, the first President of the United States, borrowing from his experience as an arbitrator of private disputes in the 1770s, crafted it into his last will and testament:

> *"I hope and trust, that no disputes will arise concerning them; but if, contrary to expectations, of the usual technical terms, or because too much or too little has been said on any of the devices to be consonant with law, my will and direction expressly is, that all disputes (if unhappily any should arise) shall be decided by three impartial and intelligent men, known for their probity and understanding; two to be chosen by the disputants – each having a choice of one – and the third by those two. Which three men thus chosen, shall, unfettered by law, or legal constructions, declare their sense of the testators' intention; and such decision is, to all intents and purposes to be as binding on the parties as if it had been given in the Supreme Court of the United States."*

A peaceful societal co-existence of all is a dream we no doubt aspire for, but the human nature begets conflicts and thus resolution of disputes is an essential characteristic for societal peace, amity, comity, harmony and easy access to justice. It is evident from the history that the function of resolving disputes has fallen upon the shoulders of the powerful and experienced ones. With the evolution of modern States and sophisticated legal mechanisms, the courts run on very formal processes and are presided over by trained adjudicators entrusted with the responsibility of resolution of disputes on the part of the State. The adversarial mode of resolution of disputes is time consuming and leads to docket explosion. Need for alternatives to the formal legal system are the need of the hour and has become the cynosure of the legal fraternity.

Historical Backdrop

The concept and philosophy of Alternative Dispute Resolution (ADR) is an innovative Indian contribution to the world jurisprudence. ADR methods are not new to India and have been in existence in some form or the other in the days before the modern justice delivery system was introduced by colonial British rulers.

There is considerable evidence that ADR was widely used in ancient India, Rome and Egypt for the settlement of varied disputes. Even the sacred texts of the major religions and also reflections of words of great philosophers and thinkers are pertinent and evident. In ***Bhadranayaka Upanishad***, Sage ***Yajnavalkya*** has referred to various types of arbitral bodies, commonly known as Panchyatdars and its members as Panchas. Proceedings before these bodies were of an informal nature, free from cumbersome technicalities of domestic laws.

Aristotle in ***Rhetoric and on Poetics*** said, "Arbitration was introduced to give equity its due weight". ***Cicero*** has also said that for a larger assessment of fairness processual justice many times would march over the substantive justice. He has also advocated the process of arbitration. ***Blackstone*** in his famous ***Commentaries on the Law of English*** has observed about the strict justice and formal rules on process and the requirement of adopting principles of process to deal with equities which matter in the controversy.

Modes of Alternative Dispute Resolution

Alternative Dispute Resolution (ADR) should not be treated as just another mechanical process of dispute resolution. It might look like an activist legal aid philosophy, but it is something more potent than that. It will promote the rule of law in the society, promote peoples participation and self reliant development and create legal awareness and respect for the rights of others.

Following are the common modes of ADR:

- ***Arbitration***: It is basically a private determination of dispute by a third party; it is adjudicatory in nature and is governed by the statute.
- ***Conciliation***: Again governed by the statute, it is a mediation that is governed under the agencies of law. In many regards this is method is being increasingly used by the Family Courts.
- ***Mediation***: It is called a structured negotiation process wherein the third neutral party by its ability and tact resolves the dispute. It is a customized procedure conducted as per the will of the parties.
- ***Negotiation:*** This is when the parties are at it on their own and try to resolve the dispute on their own. There is also what is known as assisted negotiation.

The mixture of these methods gives rise to variety of resolution processes which can be chosen depending upon the nature of the problem and attitude of the opposite party. Hence it gives a customized procedure benefiting the parties. These blended forms of resolution are, Expert Appraisal, Early Neutral Evaluation (ENE), mini-trial, summary jury trial, med-arb and court annexed ADR.

They are useful because of their creative ability at dispute resolution. ADR in fact is dispute management with resolution potential. These are a kind of self controlled processes where the parties have a decisive role in initiating, continuing, concluding and enforcing the settlement.

Statutory Mandate

Now the proven vital mechanism of ADR is covered by the statutory umbrella. The Arbitration and Conciliation Act, 1996 which replaced the Act of 1940 is based on the UNCITRAL model law which has brought uniformity in the law for conducting Arbitration all over the world. Conciliation is also covered in this Act in detail and provides for the duties of the conciliator and the method of conducting the procedure.

The most important in this mechanism is the Amendment of 2002 to the Code of Civil Procedure, 1908 by virtue of Section 89 which directs the court to see if there exists an element of settlement, to refer the parties to any of the four modes of settlement; arbitration, judicial settlement, conciliation and mediation.

The old system of the banyan tree justice has now got the statutory mandate of the Legal Services Authority Act, 1987 by providing for conducting Lok Adalat for people to have justice at their doorstep. This been a success where there is a provision for Permanent Lok Adalat for matters concerning Public Utility services. The provisions of the Act based on indigenous concept are meant to supplement the Court system.

In India, till lately tribunals were alternatives to formal courts. However, tribunalisation of justice has not, successfully, clicked to prove its true mettle. Many a times, experience has shown that the tribunals often end up as dead cycles of litigative voyage in the courts and resultant lengthening of the life of dispute resolution process. However these statues providing for ADR will go a long way in resolving the disputes at comparatively no cost to the litigants and with minimum delay. At the same time, they are not meant to replace and supplant the Court system. They are a legislative attempt to decongest the Courts from heavy burden of cases. There is an incumbent need for decentralization of justice. Its process is voluntary and works on the principle that both parties to the disputes are willing to sort out their differences by amicable solutions. Through this mechanism, disputes can be settled in a simpler, quicker and cost-effective way at all the three stages *i.e.* pre-litigation, pending-litigation and post-litigation.

The Benefits

According to an estimate there are three crore cases pending across the country at different levels of courts, which may take a minimum of 354 years to resolve each and every case pending now. Hence it is the need of the hour and a wise step to resort to ADR. The principal benefits of ADR are that it saves time; saves legal expenses; provides the parties an opportunity for greater control over the dispute resolution process; allows parties to resolve their conflict in a more creative way than might be possible if it were left to a decision by a judge or jury; gives the parties greater privacy in resolving their dispute than is afforded in a public courtroom; reduces the emotional toll a lawsuit can take on everyone concerned and can permit valued relationships among the parties to be preserved. Disposal through ADR today is the only panacea for controlling the arrears of cases. It is a participative, promising and potential method. It revolves around the principle of creating awareness amongst the disputants to the effect that their welfare and interest, lies in arriving, at amicable, immediate, consensual and peaceful settlement of the disputes.

Globalization is not a phenomenon as commonly perceived but a fact to be responded to. Business has achieved as pivotal a role as politics in international relations. As rightly said the world is flat. With India being a forerunner in the business league, many developed economies are keen on business relations with India. Hence in commercial world, when economic activity sustains development and keeps the nations to go on, previous enmity hampers the progress and demands collaboration and co-operation. Lengthy and cumbersome court trials, however, act as a disincentive for such business ventures which we do not want the reason to turn the investors away. Therefore, the international business community is increasingly using arbitration to resolve commercial disputes arising. International commercial arbitration awards are recognized by national courts in most parts of the world. India cannot afford to lag behind in the race and therefore resorting to ADR is a prudent choice. We have to accept that ADR comprises the attributes of a successful resolution of dispute and help the business to effectively manage them. It is therefore, necessary that the foreign investor is assured of early resolution to disputes.

The Philosophy Behind

The concept has been gathered from system of Panchayats, which has roots in the history and culture of this Country. It has a native flavor known to the people. There is no doubt that the justice delivery system today needs "healers of conflicts" for a viable alternative to the adjudication process. It is also necessary to spread awareness of these alternative methods and to facilitate the rights of common people to speedy and inexpensive justice. The common man has started looking upon legal system as a foe and not as a friend. For him, law is always taking something away. When they go to court, they think that we are going to win all or lose all. Whereas, when if they go to any method of ADR or for informal settlement, they go with different expectations, they may not get all that they want, but they will not lose everything. The bottom-line is the resurrection of faith of the common man in the justice system. We might have thought that ADR was a fad, that ultimately the pendulum will swing back towards the traditional litigation and hence hesitant to resort to it. But it is undoubtedly here to stay.

Conclusion

The threat is looming large that the catastrophe of justice derailed might become a reality. India cannot by any means grapple with problems of delays unless Indian courts and members of the Bar as well as the litigants realize that the problem is their own and each one of them has a commitment to prepare an efficient and fast track justice system with a holistic approach.

It has to be realized that participation, accommodation, fairness, expectation, voluntariness, neighbourliness, transparency, efficiency and lack of animosity are undoubtedly, all important characteristics of this unique Indian institution rooted in India's history and culture and environment.

It has provided an important juristic technology and vital tool for easy and early settlement of disputes. It has again been proved to be a successful and viable national imperative and incumbency, best suited for all sections of the society and getting justice to the *aam aadmi*. The concept is a "revolutionary evolution of resolution of disputes". The finest hour of justice is the hour of compromise when parties after burying their hatchet reunite by a reasonable and just compromise. This Indian-institutionalized, indigenized and now, legalized concept for settlement of dispute promotes the goals of our Constitution. Law and system of justice are not like antiques to be taken down, dusted, admired and put back on the shelf, but they are rather like a vigorous tree which has its roots in history and takes on new graft, puts out new sprouts and occasionally drops dead wood. It is a dynamic instrument fashioned for the purpose of achieving ameliorative and harmonious adjustment, and settlement of disputes arising out of human relations by eliminating social tensions and conflicts and it must, therefore, change with changing socio-economic conditions. The winds of change are blowing through the Indian legal system and propelling India to embrace the alternative modes of dispute resolution again alongside the formal litigation system.

Let me conclude with a sound but an imperative that we must be ever mindful that *"Yesterday is not ours to recover, but tomorrow is ours to win or lose"*, and, therefore, let us get together, stand united, and strengthen our Bench and Bar in an irrevocable unique partnership and make collaborative, concerted, cooperative, creative, collective and cohesive endeavours in popularising, proliferating and pioneering, concept and philosophy of important institution – alternative dispute resolution mechanism – so as to strengthen our pluralistic democratic values, rule of law and thereby invigorate the commandment, *"Justice shall never be rationed"*. Let us therefore make all efforts to advance and strengthen "equal access to justice", the heart of the Constitution of India, a reality.

CELEBRATING CHILDREN— EVERY CHILD IS SPECIAL*

I am greatly impressed by the boldness of the motto of your school "ALWAYS MORE AND ALWAYS BETTER" and also your school anthem that says "Oh life is a test where we must do our best. Whether in work or play, Strengthen your efforts, Maintain your zeal. Play up, play the game, always". These are indeed great ideals. I sincerely hope each one of you imbibes these values as you pass out from this revered institute of learning.

I consider this my privilege to be addressing such an august gathering, with the majority of you being children, dear children; you are the foundation on which a strong dynamic India shall be built. And we adults are the ones bestowed with the responsibility of inculcating the sense of values, dedication and commitment in their young impressionable minds.

One of the greatest achievements of developing economies in the last century is to have rightly understood the role of the "child" in the societal milieu.

"the child of today cannot develop to be a responsible and productive member of tomorrow's society unless an environment which is conducive to his social and physical health is assured to him. Every nation, developed or developing links its future with the status of the child. Neglecting the children means loss to the society as a whole. If children are deprived of their childhood-socially, economically, physically and mentally, the nation gets deprived of the potential of human resources for social progress, economic empowerment and peace and order, the social stability and good citizenry. The founding fathers of the Constitution of India, therefore, have emphasised the importance of the role of the child and the need of it best development". (Reference: *Bandhua Mukti Morcha* v. *Union of India*).

Like Dr. APJ Abdul Kalam had once said and I quote "every child has tremendous potential to become unique and they should fight hardest against till they achieve it, the young and ignited minds should dream big and not be dictated by failures".

---

* Address on the occasion of golden jubilee celebration of Holy Child School, Sonepat.

THE SECRET BEHIND SUCCESS

A burning desire is the starting point of all accomplishments. Just like a small fire cannot give much heat, a weak desire cannot produce great results. There has to be a burning urge in you to do well and succeed in life, that desire is essential, without which no success can be achieved.

It is said that politics and weather are the two most talked about topics in any part of the world, but if you ask parents anywhere in the world, especially in India, then obviously their children's career would be the oft-discussed topic. Parents start planning even the minutest details of a child's life even before the child is barely able to walk. The prime concern and the cause of grief among most parents is whether their children will grow up to be the next Einstein on earth, for heavens sake, somebody please tell these parents that even Einstein for that matter was not academically gifted, he was quite slow even in learning how to speak. He received private education in order to get prepared for school. In order to make his living he gave private lessons in mathematics and physics. He had to struggle a lot to become a teacher.

Albert Einstein had said and I quote "I think I used about 25% of my intellectual capacities during my life." But he went on to become the most reckoned figures in the field of science and the rest as they say is history.

Each one of you is special and has immense potential within yourself, who knows some of you present here may go on to become the next Sania Mirza or Sachin Tendulkar or Lionel Messi in the making, or you might just give Lata Mangeshkar a run for her money.

Children need not only focus on getting academic distinctions and sideline everything else, sports and other extra curricular activities are equally important. But dear children, this nowhere means that you shun all your books and start crooning the lyrics of the song from three idiots "concentrated H_2SO_4 ne pura pura bachpan jala dala, bachpan to gaya jawani bhi gayi ik pal to ab hame jine do".

These lines stress upon the need to maintain a work life-balance and enjoy what you do and do what you enjoy, because all work and no play makes jack a dull boy.

Even parents have a huge role in shaping their child's future, but this nowhere means that they should act like an albatross around their child's neck. There are two sets of parents, the ones who decide every move their child takes and even go on to decide their child's careers and there is another set of parents who want to make a robot out of their child and expect them to be super achievers and with the excess/overflow of reality TV shows, you can often spot tiger moms pushing their children to excel so that they can bask in their reflected glory.

Well this nowhere means that I am professing that parents should show a clear lack of interest in their child's life, but the best way is to allow children to explore all available options and to choose for themselves the best, be it dance, music, science etc. Just because your neighbour's son plays cricket, you can't expect your son to suddenly start playing it and excel in it, when his interest lies in some other domain. It is all about the right interest and skills coming together.

J.F. Kennedy had once aptly remarked and I quote "children are the world's most valuable resources and its best hope for the future".

Children are like clay, it requires the most ablest of potters, to mould them in the right way, they are innocent and pure human beings. They have a childlike and naive approach to intricate things. Although they get into fights but are the first people to make amends and hardly do you see them hold any grudge against the other.

Every kid is different and special, it is for parents and teachers to realize their true potential, home and school are the two most important grooming-grounds for any child. It prepares them to face the world with courage and hold their chin up. The Movie Taare Zameen Pe-revolves around the same concept and its tag line "every child is special" is something all parents and teachers should keep in mind while dealing with children. The movie beautifully captures the life of young Ishaan, who is dyslexic and struggles to do simple things of life, like tying a shoe lace. There are some parts of the movie that we should never follow, parents should never shout at their children, like how Ishaan's father does in the movie, and never inflict harsh punishments on them because of some mistakes they had done, because it may affect the mind of the children.

Children are like wet cement, everything that falls on it creates an impression.

It is my request to the parents that don't cut arts, sports, music, excursions, debating etc. in order to push children to get academic accolades. Nothing is more core than a child's passion and interest. A well balanced curriculum is what your child needs. And don't judge your child's potential by looking at his test marks. Every child is gifted and talented, they just unwrap their packages at different times. By this I do not mean that parents and teachers should impose their thoughts and beliefs on children, but rather should be their "go-to-person" and act like mentors, however children should also understand that parents and teachers play an imperative part in their life, and the foremost requirement is that they are able to gauge their importance and know how to value their efforts and dedications. Give your teachers and parents the respect that they deserve because they are the ones who can help you get where you need to go and make the path of life easier if not perfect.

When you are a child you have very few responsibilities, you do not have to worry about paying Bills, do household chores or go to work. You can enjoy life free of obligations and you have ample free time to do what you like. In a way you get everything on a platter and you must learn acknowledge those people who make it possible for you.

Respect you parents, the most important thing in the world is to see your parents smile and to know that you are the reason behind it.

And I can't end this speech without mentioning about the importance that teachers hold in our lives, they are the ones who believe in us, push us to reach great heights, and like the great American Historian, Henry Adams had aptly remarked, teachers affect eternity and they can never tell where their influence stops.

Ours is a budding and sprightly nation, but an ancient civilization. The world has knocked at our doors for centuries in search of wisdom, knowledge and prosperity. Today, as a young nation we must delve into our cultural and social legacy and draw on our insight in responding to the challenges of the future.

The major problem in the education field today is that a majority of students still opt for Engineering or Medical courses. Are we seriously limited to these two options as career choices in India? There have been numerous instances of students opting for medicine and dropping out in the long run, simply because of their aversion to blood. Students and parents must look at the bigger picture; they need to look beyond these two courses. Today, the job market demands skill and not just a degree. Going after a course just for the sake of getting a degree will take you nowhere. You need to broaden you horizon and look beyond orthodox profession, these days courses in Mass-Comm, Journalism, Hotel Managements, Photography, Diet & Nutrition are flourishing and brimming with a plethora of opportunities.

Hard work is not a sure shot guarantee to achieve success, but no success is achieved without hard work for sure. And don't be afraid of failures, as failures are the pillars of success.

I sincerely hope the education you have received in this great institution will help you in your journey of life. I hope it will make you better, more creative and more productive citizens. I hope it will make you better human beings. I wish each one of you a life-time of creativity and a life of exploration and enterprise. I hope you will all live your lives as happy children of our great country. Your school has served the country with great distinction for the past 50 years. But as they say, the best is yet to come.

To End—I may recite an often quoted beautiful Ancient Poem.

I WILL FLY.

"I am born with potential.
I am born with goodness and trust.
I am born with ideas and dreams.
I am born with greatness.
I am born with confidence.
I am born with wings.
So, I am not meant for crawling,
I have wings, I will fly.
I will fly and fly."

With these words, I greet the Students, Teachers and all members of Holy Child Sr. Secondary School and wish all of you to achieve more success with higher goals in this endless journey through knowledge and enlightenment. So that wherever you go you should feel proud of this great School. May your path be blessed.

ENVIRONMENT: JURISDICTION, STRUCTURE AND CIVIL PRACTICE IN INDIA

Salutations

Good afternoon to all dignitaries present on and off the Dias here today. It would be unbecoming of me to cut short my greetings because of the strict time frame. Therefore first and foremost I would like to express my heartfelt gratitude to the Land and Environment Court of New South Wales and the entire team behind this conference for giving me the opportunity to be amongst such an august gathering here.

"Human destiny is bound to remain a gamble, because at some unpredictable time and in some unforeseeable manner nature will strike back."

Industrialization

Industrialization and economic growth have become the buzzwords of this era of globalization and we have forgotten in this mad rush of becoming developed that we are becoming over developed to the extent that the human race might just become the cancer of this planet. Unlike pre modern human beings, who lived lives mostly determined by the elements, like a farmer praying for the monsoon to arrive, modern human beings expect the world to obey their dictates. Finding a solution to this we might just want to reset the dial, which sounds lucrative at the first blush, but might not be a solution possible today as once the genie of industralisation is let out of the bottle it is difficult to put it back. Hence today an ecological approach to development is not a luxury, but is a necessity.

Timeline of Development

My speech is a timeline that captures the growth and development of the green consciousness in India. It is a primer of the institutional structure, the governance and the practice of the legal wing of the country.

Vedas

India is the most diverse and the fastest growing nation of the world in every way. Being still a developing nation, it is not that now we have woken upto the responsibility of caring for our environment. We, as a country, derive our sensibilities and roots from our ancient texts and scriptures the *VEDAS*, which are called the first texts in the library of mankind. In recent days, environmental science and ecology are disciplines of modern science under which study of environment and its constituents is done with minute details. As science, they are established in 20th century, but their origin can be seen long back in the Vedic and ancient Sanskrit literature. Being thousands of years old, these scriptures present a picturesque, spectacular and diversified range of fauna and flora. They urge the human beings to protect, preserve, nurture and nourish the environment and natural habitation in its pristine glorious form. They attach great importance to environmental protection and purity. They insist on safeguarding the habitation, proper afforestation and non-pollution.

Pancha Bhutas: Five Elements

The Vedas specify the cosmic *Pancha bhutas* (five elements) which are *Akasah* (space), *Vayuh* (air), *Agnih* (fire), *Apah* (water) and *Prithivi* (earth). The nature has maintained a status of balance between and among these constituents or elements and living creatures. A disturbance in percentage of any constituent of the environment beyond certain limits disturbs the natural balance and any change in the *natural balance* causes lots of problems to the living creatures in the universe. The Vedas glorify the earth as one's mother and advise one not to cause injury to the earth. They proclaim that earth is the bestower of happiness, sustainer and supporter of all forms of life. The glorious brightness of the sun, the blaze of the sacrificial fire, the sweep of the rain-storm across the skies, the recurrence of the dawn, the steady currents of the winds, the violence of the tropical storm and other such natural energies, fundamental activities or aspects are glorified and personified as divinities. One of the most beautiful verse of the Rig Veda says, ***'Heaven is my father, brother atmosphere is my navel, and the great earth is my mother.'***

Mother Earth

Considered as Gods

As God's Mascots: Ganesh, Durga

A glance at the idols worshipped in India would also show that God is in one way or the other connected with nature and wild life. One of the goddess **Maa Durga** is seated on a tiger and **Lord Ganesha**, considered the harbinger of good luck has a mouse as his lucky mascot. Thus India's history and culture are replete with such examples of our early approach towards environment protection.

Mahatma Gandhi

"Earth provides for every man's need, but not for every man's greed" are the powerful yet poignant words of our Father of the Nation, Mahatma Gandhi who is synonymous the world over with peace and non violence. But little does the world know of the environmentalist in him. Almost a century ago in 1909, Gandhi had already envisioned the insatiable and unending pursuit of material pleasure and prosperity in the society as a threat to the planet and its resources. He opposed industralisation in the garb of development at the cost of our nature. He said:

> *"Nature works unceasingly according to her own laws, but man violates them constantly. In different ways and at different times, Nature tells man that there is nothing in the world which is not subject to change... And yet extraordinary occurrence startles us and sets us thinking. There has been one such in Paris. This river in Paris rose in such a heavy flood that huge buildings were washed off. A picture gathering was in imminent danger. Strongly built roads, on which millions of pound has been spent sagged at places. Men were drowned. Some who escaped drowning were buried alive. Rats, deprived of their food, attacked children. How did this happen? The people of Paris had built the city to last for ever. Nature has given a warning that even whole of Paris may be destroyed. It certainly would have been had the floods subsided a day later."*

Stockholm Conference: Magna Carta

Now coming to the heart of the topic in question, what is that triggered India to enact various legislations relating to environment. The precursor was the *Stockholm Conference* of 1972, considered the *Magna Carta* of environmental law that had a far reaching impact on India. It is generally forgotten in today's world where every head of the nation state is talking about climate change that in 1972 the only head of state to attend the UN conference on environment other than Mr. Oalf

Palme (who attended as the host), was Mrs. Indira Gandhi. This is a very significant detail as I see that India had the environmental sensitivity at the highest levels even in the 1970's. Fulfilling its responsibility towards the goals and principles stipulated therein, India enacted a host of statutes with regard to environment, which are very comprehensive in detailing and second to no other nation.

Statutes

They are:

- ***The Environment (Protection) Act*** was enacted in 1986 with the objective of providing for the protection and improvement of the environment. It empowers the Central Government to establish authorities [under section 3(3)] charged with the mandate of preventing environmental pollution in all its forms and to tackle specific environmental problems that are peculiar to different parts of the country. The Act was last amended in 1991.
- The ***Forest Conservation Act, 1980***; enacted to help conserve the country's forests. It strictly restricts and regulates the de-reservation of forests or use of forest land for non-forest purposes without the prior approval of Central Government. To this end the Act lays down the pre-requisites for the diversion of forest land for non-forest purposes.
- The ***Indian Forest Act, 1927*** consolidates the law relating to forests, the transit of forest-produce and the duty leviable on timber and other forest-produce.
- ***The Air (Prevention and Control of Pollution) Act;*** enacted in 1981 and amended in 1987 to provide for the prevention, control and abatement of air pollution in India.
- ***The Water (Prevention and Control of Pollution) Act*** was enacted in 1974 to provide for the prevention and control of water pollution, and for the maintaining or restoring of wholesomeness of water in the country. The Act was amended in 1988.
- ***The Water (Prevention and Control of Pollution) Cess Act*** was enacted in 1977, to provide for the

levy and collection of a cess on water consumed by persons operating and carrying on certain types of industrial activities. This cess is collected with a view to augment the resources of the Central Board and the State Boards for the prevention and control of water pollution constituted under the Water (Prevention and Control of Pollution) Act, 1974.

- The ***Prevention of Cruelty to Animals Act***; enacted in 1960 to prevent the infliction of unnecessary pain or suffering on animals and to amend the laws relating to the prevention of cruelty to animals. After the enactment of this Act, the Animal Board of India was formed for the promotion of animal welfare.
- The Government of India enacted ***Wild Life (Protection) Act, 1972*** with the objective of effectively protecting the wild life of this country and to control poaching, smuggling and illegal trade in wildlife and its derivatives. The Act was amended in January 2003 and punishment and penalty for offences under the Act have been made more stringent. The Ministry has proposed further amendments in the law by introducing more rigid measures to strengthen the Act. The objective is to provide protection to the listed endangered flora and fauna and ecologically important protected areas.
- The ***Biological Diversity Act, 2002*** was born out of India's attempt to realise the objectives enshrined in the United Nations Convention on Biological Diversity (CBD) 1992 which recognizes the sovereign rights of states to use their own Biological Resources. The Act aims at the conservation of biological resources and associated knowledge as well as facilitating access to them in a sustainable manner and through a just process. For purposes of implementing the objects of the Act it establishes the National Biodiversity Authority in Chennai.
- The main objective of the ***Public Liability Insurance Act, 1991*** is to provide for damages to victims of

an accident which occurs as a result of handling any hazardous substance. The Act applies to all owners associated with the production or handling of any hazardous chemicals.

- It is also worthwhile to mention that a ***Forest Rights Act, 2006*** which recognizes the rights of forest-dwelling Scheduled Tribes and other traditional forest dwellers over the forest areas inhabited by them and provides a framework for according the same is one of the most potent legislations of recent time.

Constitutional Provision

With these statutory mandates it was the safe sounding board provided in the most lengthy and exhaustive Constitutions of the world, that of India and hence, the most landmark development with regard to India's environmental consciousness was when it inculcated in its Constitution the most potent of weapons, Article 48A and Article 51A(g) being one of the first nations to make it a part of its Constitution.

The State's responsibility with regard to environmental protection has been laid down under Article 48A of our Constitution, which are called the **Directive Principles of State Policy**, which reads as follows:

Article 48A.

> ***"The State shall endeavour to protect and improve the environment and to safeguard the forests and wildlife of the country".***

Environmental protection is a fundamental duty of every citizen of this country under Article 51-A(g) of our Constitution which reads as follows:

Article 51A(g)

> ***"It shall be the duty of every citizen of India to protect and improve the natural environment including forests, lakes, rivers and wildlife and to have compassion for living creatures."***

It would be befitting to mention here that Professor Michael von Hauff of the Institute for Economics and Economic Policy, University of Kaiserlantern, Germany, in his article "The Contribution of Environmental Management Systems to Sustainable Development: Relevance of the Environmental Management and

Audit Scheme" aptly observed that, ***"it is remarkable that India was the first country in the world to enshrine environmental protection as a state goal in its Constitution".***

Enshrining these in the Constitution of India as a fundamental duty and Directive Principle of State Policy, a goal to be achieved by the nation collectively coupled with the enactment of the statutes, the judiciary had the opportunity to develop its green jurisprudence.

PIL, Article 32, 226

The most significant development which was instrumental in making the judiciary adjudicate on the environmental aspects was the advent of the phenomena of ***Public Interest Litigation*** in the country. The courts relaxed the rule of ***Locus Standi*** and entertained writ petitions under Article 32 and 226 of the Constitution of India filed by public spirited individuals, Non-Governmental Organizations who espouse the cause of environment.

Article 21

The most powerful ammunition of the constitution that paved the path for the most iconic of decisions by the Judiciary and development of much of the green jurisprudence was under Article 21 of the Constitution of India.

Article 21 states:

> ***"No person shall be deprived of his life or personal liberty except according to procedure established by law."***

Widening the scope and ambit of this Article, the Supreme Court and the High Courts have developed an enviable jurisprudence on key issues in relation to protection and preservation of Environment. A quick glance of the lexicon of the cases and issues addressed here would give you an overall idea of the role of the judiciary has tackled the most vital issues.

SC Judgments

- *M.C. Mehta* v. *Union of India,* AIR 1987 SC 1086: (1987) 1 SCC 395: 1987 (1) Supreme 65; *Oleum Gas Leak* case. The court said that the concept of *"absolute and non-delegable duty"* to the community.

  "We are of the view that an enterprise which is engaged in a hazardous or inherently dangerous industry which poses a potential threat to the health and safety

of the persons working in the factory and residing in the surrounding areas owes an absolute and non-delegable duty to the community to ensure that no harm results to anyone on account of hazardous or inherently dangerous nature of the activity which it has undertaken."

- *Municipal Council, Ratlam* v. *Vardhichand,* (1980) 4 SCC 162: AIR 1980 SC 1622: (1981) 1 SCR 97; an important case under the section 133 Crpc to compel municipality to make drains and sewerage affecting the health and convenience of the residents. One of the first cases to realize the importance of the insufficiency of legal mechanism to deal with environment related problems.
- T.N. Godavarman cases are a high water mark in the field of forest conservation.
- *Narmada Bachao Andolan* v. *Union of India,* AIR 2000 SC 3751: 2000 AIR SCW 4809: (2000) 10 SCC 664, held that right to water is a fundamental right under Article 21 of the Constitution of India.
- *Intellectuals Forum, Tirupathi* v. *State of Andhra Pradesh,* AIR 2006 SC 1350: 2006 AIR SCW 1309: (2006) 3 SCC 549; explained the public trust doctrine,
- *Subhash Kumar* v. *State of Bihar,* AIR 1991 SC 420: 1991 AIR SCW 121: (1991) 1 SCC 598; held that right to pollution free water and air for full enjoyment of life is covered by Article 21 of the Constitution of India.
- *M.C. Mehta* v. *Union of India,* 1991 AIR SCW 2989: (1992) 1 SCC 358: AIR 1992 SC 382; directions to issue to all cinema halls messages relating to environment and pollution.
- *M.C Mehta* v. *Union of India,* AIR 1997 SC 734: 1997 AIR SCW 552: (1997) 2 SCC 353; Taj Mahal Trapezium Case; ordered the shifting of the 292 industries from near Taj Mahal.
- *Noise Pollution (V), In re,* AIR 2005 SC 3136: 2005 AIR SCW 3525: (2005) 5 SCC 733; held that freedom from noise pollution is a fundamental right.

- *M.C Mehta* v. *Kamal Nath,* AIR 2000 SC 1997: 2000 AIR SCW 1854: (2000) 6 SCC 213, held that pollution is a civil wrong.
- *Chhetriya Pardushan Mukti Sangharsh Samiti* v. *State of Uttar Pradesh,* AIR 1990 SC 2060: (1990) 4 SCC 449: JT 1990 (3) SC 685 held that right to quality of life and living is guaranteed under Article 21 of the Constitution of India.
- *Rural Litigation and Entitlement Kendra* v. *State of Uttar Pradesh;* closure of lime stone quarries in Doon valley.
- *M.C. Mehta (II)* v. *Union of India,* AIR 1988 SC 1115: JT 1988 (1) SC 69: (1988) 1 SCC 471; Ganga river pollution case. Held the holding of classes relating to environment protection in the elementary classes mandatory in educational institutions, distribution of text books in relation to environment free of cost. Organizing of cleanliness week in each city in the country throughout the year on rotational basis.
- *Vellore Citizens Welfare Forum* v. *Union of India,* (1996) 5 SCC 647: AIR 1996 SC 2715: 1996 AIR SCW 3399; polluter pays and precautionary principle became part of the environmental law of the country. It would be apt to quote from the above said judgment here:

  "The traditional concept that development and ecology are opposed to each other, is no longer acceptable. "Sustainable Development" is the answer. In the International sphere "Sustainable Development" as a concept came to be known for the first time in the Stockholm Declaration of 1972. Thereafter, in 1987 the concept was given a definite shape by the World Commission on Environment and Development in its report called "Our Common Future". The Commission was chaired by the then Prime Minister of Norway Ms. G.N. Brundtland and as such the report is popularly known as "Brundtland Report". In 1991 the World Conservation Union, United Nations Environment Programme and World Wide Fund for Nature, jointly came out with a document called "Caring for the

Earth" which is a strategy for sustainable living. Finally, came the Earth Summit held in June, 1992 at Rio which saw the largest gathering of world leaders ever in the history – deliberating and chalking out a blue ring for the survival of the planet. Among the tangible achievements of the Rio Conference was the signing of two conventions, one on biological diversity and another on climate change. These conventions were signed by 153 nations. The delegates also approved by consensus three non binding documents namely, a Statement on Forestry Principles, a declaration of principles on environmental policy and development initiatives and Agenda 21, a programme of action into the next century in areas like poverty, population and pollution. During the two decades from Stockholm to Rio "Sustainable Development" has come to be accepted as a viable concept to eradicate poverty and improve the quality of human life while living within the carrying capacity of the supporting eco-systems. "Sustainable Development" as defined by the Brundtland Report means "development that meets the needs of the present without compromising the ability of the future generations to meet their won needs". We have no hesitation in holding that "Sustainable Development' as a balancing concept between ecology and development has been accepted as a part of the Customary International Law though its salient features have yet to be finalised by the International Law jurists.

11. Some of the salient principles of "Sustainable Development", as culled-out from Brundtland Report and other international documents, are Inter-Generational Equity, Use and Conservation of Natural Resources, Environmental Protection, the Precautionary Principle, Polluter Pays principle, Obligation to assist and cooperate, Eradication of Poverty and Financial Assistance to the developing countries. We are, however, of the view that "The Precautionary Principle" and "The Polluter Pays" principle are essential features of "Sustainable Development". The "Precautionary Principle" – in the context of the municipal law – means:

(i) *Environmental measures – by the State Government and the statutory authorities – must anticipate, prevent and attack the causes of environmental degradation.*

(ii) *Where there are threats of serious and irreversible damage, lack of scientific certainty should not be used as a reason for postponing measures to prevent environmental degradation.*

(iii) *The onus of proof is on the actor or the developer/industrialist to show that his action is environmentally benign.*

- *M.C. Mehta* v. *Union of India,* AIR 1988 SC 1037: JT 1987 (4) SC 630: (1987) 4 SCC 463; called the *Ganga Tanneries* case. The Supreme Court ordered the shifting of the tanneries near the Ganga River.

  "The financial capacity of the tanneries should be considered as irrelevant while requiring them to establish primary treatment plants. Just like an industry which cannot pay minimum wages to its workers cannot be allowed to exist a tannery which cannot set up a primary treatment plant cannot be permitted to continue to be in existence for the adverse effect on the public at large which is likely to ensue by the discharging of the trade effluents from the tannery to the river Ganga would be immense and it will outweigh any inconvenience that may be caused to the management and the labour employed by it on account of its closure"

  "We are conscious that closure of tanneries may bring unemployment, loss of revenue, but life, health and ecology have greater importance to the people."

One of the most interesting innovations introduced in recent years, entirely because of the Supreme Court of India, is what is often referred to as the CAMPA innovation. **CAMPA**, which stands for **Compensatory Afforestation Management and Planning Authority**, is an innovation of the Supreme Court ordered in 2002 according to which every party, whether the Government or a private party, that diverts forest area for non-forest purposes, has to deposit a certain amount equivalent to the total value of benefits lost per hectare

CAMPA

diverted for such purpose. The value of benefits lost is arrived at by taking into account the Net Present Value (NPV) accrued the stipulated compensatory afforestation amount, and the funds accrued under the catchment area treatment plans submitted. Today, we have almost, Rs. 11,000 crores that have been deposited by private and public companies who have diverted forest areas for non forest purposes. This is the money available to the State Governments for reforestation and regeneration of natural forest cover.

India following international norms

India has imbibed all the norms of the International environmental law used to save the green cover. The concept of polluter pays, public trust doctrine, inter-generational equity, etc have all been adopted by the country. A tool of international significance used by India is the ***Environmental Impact Assessment (EIA).***

Environment Impact Assessment (EIA)

Environmental Impact Assessment (EIA) is an important management tool for ensuring optimal use of natural resources for sustainable development, and was introduced in India initially for River Valley Projects in 1978-79. The scope of the EIA has been enhanced to cover other developmental sectors such as industries, mining schemes, energy, etc. To facilitate project proponents in collection of environmental data and formulation of environmental management plans, it is now mandatory under the Environment (Protection) Act, 1986, for different categories of developmental activities involving investment beyond certain thresholds.

Another statute that is worth mentioning here is the **Right to Information Act**, has critically transformed the way citizens can seek transparency in decision making and implementation of policies, programmes, legislations in any given sector or particular project. At the same time the Act allows one to demand for disclosure of information which an authority or department has failed to *suo motu* put in the public domain. When it comes to environmental governance, RTI undoubtedly is a key advocacy tool. Groups all across the country have been using it to seek information related to clearances of development projects, government expenditure on programmes as well as development of legislations.

Measures undertaken: Present and future

Measures

- As every country in the world has its own climate and geography and the challenges that come along with it, India to has its own share of tasks to deal with. Keeping the environment related litigation as a top priority, the Supreme Court and the various High Courts of India have set-up the a ***Green Bench*** dedicated to hearing of cases only related to environment. This Green Bench deals with the most important and emergent problems relating to the environment protection, a cause that the Indian Judiciary has decided to deal on priority basis. (***Supreme Court, Madhya Pradesh, Punjab and Haryana, West Bengal***).

Green Bench

- India has also set-up a Green Tribunal recently dedicated to the cause of environment. This is a very important initiative taken to address the demand for having specialized environmental courts, because environment now is increasingly a matter of science. The idea to have a ***National Green Tribunal*** is to have a specialized environmental court that will deal with all the civil cases when it comes to laws relating to the environment and the forests. This would also have the regional benches and this would be a specialized mechanism for providing relief to individuals, to civil society organizations, and to State Pollution Control Boards who are aggrieved by the non-implementation of laws relating to the protection of environment and forests. And I firmly believe that this will go a long way to supplement and complement the already in place legal infrastructure of the country.

National Green Tribunal

- Another new initiative to address the challenge of institutions to take up the task of effective implementation of the statutes in place is the establishment of the ***National Environment Protection Authority (NEPA)*** whose job would be to ensure that the laws of the land are implemented, that the compliance of the standards under which projects are cleared both from an environmental and forestry point of view

National Environment Protection Authority (NEPA)

would actually be implemented. Therefore the establishment of NEPA, an independent, science based and professional national authority would prove to be address the lacuna in infrastructures as far as the institutions are concerned.

Green Federalism

- India is also in the wake to introduce ***Green Federalism,*** an idea whose time has come. It is a system of incentives given to the state to build a certain amount of forest cover. This is because when they are told not to cut forests, they complain that they need jobs, employment and investment and hence in a way forests are becoming a hurdle in the development of the states. Therefore green federalism would create a system of incentives for states and local governments which are instrumental in driving the movements of environmental protection.

Act for Animal Welfare

- A legislation for ***Animal Welfare*** is soon to be introduced in the Parliament of India. Therefore, it is evident that India is alive to its responsibility of environment protection and devises ways and means to protect them with the change in time and technology.

Green Domestic Product

- India also aims to redefine the concept of GDP, which is known as the Gross Domestic Product as ***Green Domestic Product*** which should work towards a system of natural resource accounting. The percentage then would have taken into account the ecological costs of the growth of the country. It would be conveying to the people what is the economic growth net of the damage that it has caused to the environment.

Active Citizenry, NGO's

The world today is undergoing a metamorphosis with environmental concerns and mishaps staring blatantly in the face. India in its aware and active citizenry has an asset which cares for the air we breath in, the earth we tread on, the animals that are our responsibility. The judiciary cannot sit behind closed doors and gauge every action of every individual that harms the environment. It is only when it is brought to the forefront by sensitive people and organizations working towards the cause of environment that the courts take action. Hence, the hard work of these bodies and people cannot but be applauded.

Silent Valley Project

India has many a times witnessed the might of such individuals. The government in 1973 scrapped a project called the Silent Valley Project, a hydro project to be built in Kerala, due to public pressure and thereafter there was opening of the Silent Valley National park in 1985. Another famous movement was the ***"Chipko Movement"*** of the early 1970's where the women took to hugging trees when they had to be cut for setting up a project. Not only did the movement, spear headed by village women start a local movement to save the Himalayan forests, it compelled attention of the idea of people owning local resources and their inclusion in policy making.

Chipko Movement

We often talk about economic growth versus environment protection. But in my view the economic growth that weakens the foundations of ecological security, which pollute our rivers, that destroys our forests and threatens our bio-diversity can neither be equitable nor sustainable. Modern technology thus owes an apology to our ecology.

Sustainable development

A recent glaring example in India is when the country is being eyed by corporate giants for investment and recently it was the Vedanta Group that wanted to undertake bauxite mining in the eco-fragile area of Niyamgiri Hills in the State of Orissa. Rejecting a proposal of $ 1.7 billion for a developing nation is not an easy decision, an investment that would have led to a great deal of development in that state. But to protect the rights of the tribals of that region and the forest cover, as estimated about 1.21 lakh trees would have been cut, India has shown that environmentalism is not only for the developed but is possible also by the developing countries standing by its principle of protection of environment even if it at the cost of economic growth. It has shown that left or right green is right.

Vedanta Mining Issue

Hence, it would be to state the obvious that environment and development must go hand in hand and that we must build safeguards so that environmental concerns are embedded fully in the framework of economic growth.

Active Judiciary

International treaties and obligations do bind a nation but the real force comes from the enforcement of the laws and the active legal mechanism of a nation. Even where the countries that have appropriate policy, legal, and regulatory frameworks, effective implementation, enforcement, and compliance continue to pose challenges and the judiciary plays an important role in meeting these environmental enforcement and compliance challenges. India has in place the structure and most importantly a willing judiciary to uphold the law of environment as we understand that this nature we have not inherited from our ancestors but is a loan borrowed from our progeny, so we have to at least hand over to them at least what was handed over to us.

Loan from Progency

Motive of Conference

Discussions like the present one, and this conference generate the most animated headlines in the media and the civil society, but I truly believe that we collectively can imbibe from each other what ideas and innovations each one of us have been instrumental in introducing in our own country which would address major concerns and would reduce the confrontationist atmosphere that we have in discussions on the environment, as positions get taken on environmental debates which are really not conducive to decision making. Moreover, the essence of a conference is not to just debate but to constructively view what can be done to solve the issues facing each one of us in our country today.

Conclusion

At the end I would like to say that the earth we abuse and the living things we kill, will, in the end, take their revenge; for in exploiting their presence we are diminishing our future. Because we have modified our environment so radically that now we have to modify ourselves to live in this environment. We have to understand that when we heal the earth, we heal ourselves. Nature provides a free lunch, but only if we control our appetites. Therefore we should pledge to celebrate every day as earth day.

Heal Earth, Heal ourselves

Every day, Earth Day

Soil disappears Soul disappears

In times of crises, we remember the Almighty, but in this case we might just have to think that why should man expect his prayer for mercy to be heard by who is above him when he shows no mercy to what is under him? When the soil disappears is when the soul disappears.

Thank You

HATING POLITICS IS A CRIME AGAINST DEMOCRACY

When I was intimated about the choice of topic for discussion today, I was not only amazed but discomforted that today the need has arisen for such an issue to be deliberated upon. Hating politics is a crime against democracy, but the vital question is why do we hate politics? Do we hate the politics or the politicians?

Today, it is an unsaid reality that the morning *chai* is not savoured without the milk of the newspaper headlines and the salt in the dinner is replaced by the breaking news flashing across the small screen. We cannot deny that we eat, breathe and drink politics. Nothing around us is untouched by it, be it the IPL, the commonwealth, the price rise or the fate of the common man. Politics has engulfed all of us in one way or the other and we cannot shut ourselves away from it.

But why does the common man think talking about politics is an assault upon his integrity. Where from has so much of anger emanated? It is not that politics has become dirty word all of a sudden. Politics has been present from times immemorial. It was at the time of the Mahabharata and Ramayana with Lord Krishna being the most astute politician. Then it came to be a study of the polity, a study of ideas of thinkers like Marx and Rousseau. We saw its accentuated avatars at the time of the British Raj but now it has undergone a metamorphosis not resulting in a pretty picture.

The days of the British rule gave us reasons to unite as a nation and put our faith in the leaders of freedom struggle. After we gained independence, we expected the nation to develop as a vibrant democracy. We saw our leaders as the messiahs of hope, of prosperity and freedom. But as time passed, perhaps we were disappointed. Time and again our faith shattered and what it resulted in was an ugly head rising waiting to rip apart the thread that held the country together. Demonic forces like regionalism, casteism, communalism came to be the weapons of the pseudo-intellectual politician which led to a turmoil in the mind of the common man, who to believe and who not to believe?

As citizens of the largest democracy, we all engage in the decision making process. We all elect our leaders and cast our votes and then criticize them. I am not vouching for their cause here but strongly feel that more than being an institutional or a constitutional problem, hating politics has become an attitudinal problem. We very commonly hear the term "hate politics". Hate politics has emerged out of the political vendetta but hating politics has emerged out of our frustration. It is a hard hitting truth that no one would like to face that we hate politics the way we hate terrorism.

But the question is, what are we doing about it? Let us face it, what all of us indulge in is sitting at the fence and watch the drama unfold. With the advent of blogging and social networking, and media playing a pro active role, we no doubt have an aware country but at the same time we cannot shy away from the fact that we are a highly individualized and not a politically naïve citizenry who should not be disappointed with the kind of muck politicians throw at each other and when the discourse of the so called collective decision making, which is the hallmark of our democracy, is affixed on us, because all we do is gather that muck and throw it back at them.

Please do not mistake me for some political leader trying to lure people in this lucrative profession, as that would be well taken care of by others on the dais. I am a common man realizing from my past mistakes that all this drawing room activism gives us the tag of a successful democracy but all this activism is not productive and is certainly not progressive. We create a hullabaloo about a politician unmasked and corruption decoded, but no one chooses to raise a voice against it. It could not be more apt than now what Mahatma Gandhi said, not ask what the country can do for you but what you can do for the country. The shadow boxing of hating politics would do us no good.

Our forefathers gave to us the Constitution, which is the best constitution in the entire world. The preamble also says "we the people of India give to ourselves this constitution". Thus, it is we, as a collective nation that has to clean up as it is not the system that is faulty but the people manning it.

The nation has become a rainbow of chaos and is crippled and disabled, and it is we who can, with our mind, body and soul in whatever way we can and however we can save it from our own hatred. Let politics not become a foe but a friend because we all breathe in its air.

HUMAN RIGHTS OF TERROR VICTIMS AND RESPONSIBILITY OF GLOBAL COMMUNITY TOWARDS THEM

To celebrate the International Human Rights Day, to focus on the victims of terror in my opinion is the most suited topic for discussion when the vision of the world is farewell to terrorism.

To define human rights in this age would be defining our very existence. We live in times where the survival of mankind without the basic human rights is unthinkable, leave apart being impossible. Awareness to protect human rights has grown to such an extent that today it is being used as a yardstick to measure the civilization of societies, states, regimes and positive law. There was a time when we fought for recognizing human rights, then when we fought for achieving them, and again when we struggled when there was a threat of them being snatched away. But why did we not graduate beyond struggling? Why is that we have stagnated on the stage where the threat that human rights would be stripped away from us still looms large.

The answer to these questions is one word; terrorism. I would not like to define terrorism as it has been over defined by various academicians, conventions, treaties. I think the apt way to put it would be how an ancient Chinese philosopher said; kill one, frighten 10,000. Terrorism is not a novel concept that all governments are up in arms with 'war against terror' and 'zero tolerance against terrorism' policies. To put it in the analogy of Karl Marx to revolutions that said that they are like water on the stove, until the water reaches the boiling point it only changes in terms of degree, but once it hits 212 degrees and becomes steam it changes its very nature. Terrorism is also the simmering discontent of various factions that has today achieved dangerous magnitudes threatening the entire humanity. It would not be overstating that no part of the globe has been saved from the scourge of terrorism in one way or the other.

Standing here I am reminded of Mahatma Gandhi, who pitted force of soul against force of sword by satyagraha, who called a bomber as a froth of an agitated liquid. In another time when Madan Lal Dhingra in 1909 pulled out a gun and killed Sir Curzon-Wyllie, Gandhi referred him as a drunkard; a man in grip of a mad idea. Therefore, terrorism can be a political, religious or an ideological mad idea. But the use of mindless violence, killing innocent people, spreading panic and creating an acute sense of insecurity is the common thread that runs through its veins. Terrorists can be Maoists, Naxalites, LTTE, ULFA depending on their agenda but what is paradoxical is that they more often victimize the people whose very cause they are espousing.

That brings us to the question of the nexus that human rights has with terrorism. We heard a lot of human rights organizations create a hullabaloo when Ajmal Kasab, the lone surviving terrorist of the Mumbai attacks was adjudged guilty by the public and media. We heard the theory of human rights of suspected terrorists and their right to free and fair trial and their right of being represented by a lawyer. But what about the human rights of the victims of that terror? We saw the horrific images of the victims of that ghastly attack, bombard our living rooms on small screens for days together turning them into a nightmare. But what happened after that. Admittedly the public memory is short and once out of sight then it is out of mind. Nobody knows, of what happened to the ones left behind, neither you nor me.

Whenever humans clash, human rights are the first causality. The aim of terrorism is to make the innocent live in fear. What are the rights of the people who are killed with no fault on their part? What about the rights of those widows, orphaned, homeless and dying who are left behind? Time and again when an attack takes place, the State and the Central governments announce compensations to the victims and their families. What kind of compensation can be adequate for someone who has lost his only child? What kind of compensation can be adequate for the child who has been orphaned and what is the compensation for a woman who lost her husband. There cannot be a monetary estimation of the pain and suffering of these people and neither we should as a democracy venture into such an inhuman exercise. But the answer to all these questions in my opinion is the formulation of an emphatic national policy for dealing with the victims of terror.

Besides death, torture and cruelty, victimization of the people take place in different forms and is manifested in other ways.

Displacement

Mass exodus takes place and people are displaced from their natural habitation and livelihood and face enormous challenges from the new situations. They face constant hostility and harassment from the local communities, administration and police. Their attempt to cope with the new socio-economic situation often becomes futile because no development schemes as such are available to them. In this regard it would be pertinent to mention a recent ruling of the Delhi High Court where the Kashmiri Migrants occupying government accommodation in the capital were being evicted and the High Court held that the migrants are victims of terror attacks and cannot be expected to go back to their native place till the time the State does not take measures to rehabilitate them.

High Drop Out Rates

The most suffering lot of the population due to terrorism is the children. They suffer from stigma and are not able to make peace with what happened to the extent that some are even carried away to join terrorist groups.

Rapes and Assaults

The burnt of hatred and violence are borne by the women in every place and where violence due to terrorism exists for a long period. In this regard the police and the armed forces are often taken into the dock for being responsible either as perpetrators of crime or failing in their duty to stop such heinous acts.

Identity Crisis

Muslims from Jammu and Kashmir, individuals from the North Eastern States and for a while Sikhs experienced similar identity crisis where people would treat them as enemies or suspicious people. These people face serious problem to get shelter, employment, education and social recognition.

Terrorism aims at destabilization of the state and society and it is thus important that it is fought and defeated in all its forms and manifestations. Punishing the terrorists for their nefarious activities is also a part of the Rule of Law that does justice to the victims of terror.

Thus what is to be seen is that not only the victims are compensated monetarily but also that they are rehabilitated in terms of the above mentioned problems. They cannot be treated as mere victims of some tortuous action and given *ex post facto* benefits evolved by legal regimes as psychological effects and trauma of terrorism cannot be exaggerated. Providing roof is also not enough, what has to be seen is that they are not living under the stigma of the atrocities committed upon them. An overall development and constant mechanism for monitoring of such victims has to be in place. They lost their home, hearth and loved ones. Human rights of such people should be the focus of policy makers of our country, which has been long committed to ensure human rights of its citizens. Right to development in the developing country itself is a human right and to protect this right is the solemn duty of the Nation State.

The criminal justice systems of most of the countries of the world like the UK, US, Canada, Australia have policies in place for dealing with victims of terror. The 1985 General Assembly Declaration of Basic Principles of Justice for Victims of Crime and Abuse of Power (General Assembly resolution 40/34 of 29 November, 1985) also talks about the measures that should be adopted for victims of terror, alongwith the four Geneva Conventions and Two Additional Protocols, but they do not have a binding effect. Unfortunately in India, there is no legislation that is forthcoming in this regard. The Delhi High Court in the case of *Kamala Devi* v. *Govt. of NCT of Delhi* in deciding compensation for the family of the deceased victim of the Delhi Blasts highlighted this void. The courts however in exercise of their plenary powers when confronted with such issues have granted compensation and relief to the families of victims. But I would not shy away from stating the open truth that the litigative voyage in our country is grueling and thus for the family of the victim to knock the doors of the court of law for relief would take years and till then they live in destitution and anguish. Hence, there has to be formulated a policy that deals with this issue in detail. Therefore, desperate times call for desperate measures. Krishna was born to wipe out evil, Rama was incarnated to kill Ravana and so we also now need a policy to wipe out the miseries and suffering of the victims whose souls have been scarred by the blade of terrorism. I would like to put in the words of Abraham Lincoln, whose moral stature is a marvel to the modern world when he said:

> *"The dogmas of the quiet past are inadequate to the stormy present. The occasion is piled high with difficulty, and we must rise with the occasion. As our case is new, so we must think anew and act anew. We must disenthrall ourselves."*

I hope the Law Minister present here today would pay heed in this regard.

Today we live in a world that is flat. Everything is technology driven and happens at a fast pace. Similarly terrorism also knows no boundaries and is not confined to any specific geographical area. A person sitting in one part of the world plans to attack another part of the world. In these terms, terrorism has become truly global and consequently the responsibility of ensuring rights of terror victims has also become global. The very right to be human is possible only if essentials of existence, material and moral, are preserved and provided to every human being thereby creating a tension free and violence free society. We cannot deny that today terrorism poses the greatest threat to human rights and dignity. The free man, in the fullness of his infinite potential, is the answer to a tense world overcast by macabre episodes, sombre threats and terrorist tantrums. It is the effort of the global community at large that would show results that we are able to preserve only one religion that is known to us, called humanity. We as a global world now should not need dramatic descriptions and statistical profusion on T.V. and newspapers to make us realize the ubiquitous presence of terror but the wailings of our bereaved neighbours who lost their kith and kin when a bomb suddenly went off in a public place should have been enough to act. Hence when humanity is besieged by revolutionaries and counter-revolutionaries, even when man holds in his mortal hands power to abolish either all poverty or all life, the desideratum of the hour is not a flight on the moon but MAN, not missiles but morals, not 'terrorist' punishment but rehabilitation of terror victims. I would like to conclude in the words of great Hon'ble Justice V.R. Krishna Iyer who said that: *I conclude with the entreaty that we turn the hopeful, healing focus on MAN and turn away from murky obsession with crime if our goal is not breakdown but breakthrough.*

THANK YOU

EFFICACY OF UN CHARTER

The dawn of the present century has brought into focus various international legal problems which need urgent combined efforts of jurists and statesmen to ponder over them with a view to regulate them for a just and equitable world order keeping in view the diverse interests of heterogeneous character of the members of the world community. Therefore, it is necessary that international law should be cohesive, progressive and must have wider acceptance. This would mean, in common parlance, a systematic, thoughtful codification and progressive development of international law relating to various problems which are staring and troubling the international community.

There is a need to make the UN more meaningful and effective in the context of the changing realities of the global politics. The UN as at present has grown into a complex organization with a wide mandate in global reach and a governing body of 191 member states where diverse political and economic interests in the egocentric environment have to be recognized and reconciled. Nevertheless the fact remains, that the international society cannot do without the UN whatever changes may be made in its structure, powers and functions-because it has come to play an important role among the community nations. It is the visible bastion of hope and expectation of co-existence, peace and security and provides ready forum for discussion of all issues. Inspite of many achievements to its credit, some of the political issues have drawn adverse criticism because of the extreme unilateralism practiced by powerful states blocking consensus and preventing a democratic process. The unfortunate part is that instead of criticizing such members for their actions, it is the organization which is blamed.

Some of the important issues which need to be addressed relate to the composition, powers, functions and voting in the Security Council, maintenance of international peace and security and the peace keeping measures, budget/financing of the UN, role of the UN in economic development of its members particularly the developing and the least developed countries. One of the questions for urgent consideration is the use of 'unilateral armed force' by a state against another, without the mandate of the UN.

International terrorism, which is threatening the very foundations of international legal order, poses a great challenge to the community of nations. The present day terrorism knows no boundaries. Even the most powerful nations are its victims. It is practiced widespread through uncommon and most heinous acts as exemplified by various means without any regard for its consequences resulting in mass killing of innocent civilians including women and children. The recent terrorist attacks in the United States on 11 September, 2001 is an example of their challenge to the might of a powerful state and so were the attacks on Indian Parliament on 13 December, 2001 and the places of worship in Turkey on 15 November, 2003. The destruction of innocent lives and property was so much that the conscience of humanity was shaken by these dastardly acts.

Security Council Resolution, 1373 clearly states that all states shall ensure that any person who participates in financing, planning, preparation or perpetration of terrorist acts or in supporting terrorist acts is brought to justice. It reiterates that national legislation should prosecute those who are responsible for act of terrorism and its perpetrators. Security Council in general, may have reason to feel satisfied and happy with the above thinking but the public at large remains enraged with the acts of terrorism taking place all over the globe causing immense sufferings and destruction and with no end in sight. And, hence, the animated debate casting doubt about the efficacy of international law as a guardian of world over continues.

The widespread recognition, development and implementation of human rights by the community of nations remain, undoubtedly, one of the greatest achievements of the U.N. The provisions of the UN Charter provides a dynamic basis for the development of human rights. The ideas were concertized by the adoption of the Universal Declaration of Human Rights by the General Assembly in 1948. Further, it is encouraging to see that human rights are implemented through regional judicial mechanisms like European Court of Human Rights and other national judicial bodies. International Criminal Court of Human Rights will have jurisdiction to try and punish those who are responsible for committing heinous crimes such as genocide, crimes against humanity and war crimes.

An impressive regime of international humanitarian law has been put in place comprising Geneva Conventions of 1949 and the 1977 Additional Protocols for the protection of victims of armed conflicts. However, formulation of a comprehensive code prohibiting the development and use of weapons of mass destruction would go a long way to prevent the scourge of war and the consequent suffering.

The discussion during the conference was intense and vigorous and generated new ideas. There was a strong desire among the participants that a separate volume of select articles may be published which should be available for the benefit of everyone concerned with international law. The selection of the articles, however, remains our responsibility. These articles are not intended to provide final answer to the various questions discussed therein, but they definitely raise issues which generate ideas of concern and fulfill in great measure the object of research.

In the morning of 11 September, four American passenger aircraft' that took off from the US east coast airports between 7.58 a.m. to 8.43 a.m. (EST) were hijacked by reportedly nineteen unknown militants, some of them had got their training as pilots in US itself and turned into airborne bombs carrying the full load of aviation fuels and manoeuvrably crashed into the twin towers of the World Trade Centre in New York City and the Pentagon in Washington, D.C. the heart of the US financial and military might. The fourth hijacked place, which as subsequently learnt was attempting to attack the White House or the capital building housing of the US Congress, crashed on its way, in Pennsylvania.

The horrendous terrorist attack was watched live on TV the world over, for the first time ever. The twin towers of the World Trade Center holding more than 150 top businesses and around 25,000 people of 60 different nationalities erupting into huge fire balls, in desperation people jumping from the various floors out of a 110 floor building.

When smoke and several million ton debris of glass, steel and concrete settled down, some 7,000 innocent people were dead or missing, thousands were injured and several billion dollar worth property was destroyed. For days, normal life was severely disrupted.

When President, George W. Bush returned to the national capital, he referred to the terrorist attacks as an act of war and vouched that US was firmly resolved to retaliate and to make no distinction between terrorists who committed the crime and those harboured them.

From then on, President Bush and his senior cabinet members repeatedly used the word "war". Bush asserted that the hidden enemy would not be allowed to hide.

Two days later, the US Congress, both the House of Representatives and the Senate, authorized the President to wage war against global terrorism and the countries harbouring and encouraging terrorism.

Pakistan which has common border with Afghanistan is also one of the three states having diplomatic relations with the Taliban Government; indeed, its pivotal supporter was put on notice, to quote President Bush, that "US would give it (Pakistan) a chance to cooperate and participate in tracking down those who did this unbelievable and despicable act."

President of Pakistan caught between the devil and the deep sea opted for the devil and promptly promised "unstinted cooperation" to the US fight against terrorism.

As noted earlier, the US President treated this heinous terrorist attack a declaration of war. He named Osama Bin Laden and Taliban Government of Afghanistan as the culprit. Then in a manner characteristic of a cowboy of the Wild West, he shooted from the 'lip': "we will find those who did it.... we will smoke them out of their holes.... we want Osama bin Laden dead or alive."

Indeed, on 24 September, such news agencies as AFP and Reuters quoted US administration to the effect that "US did not need UN approval to strike back at the terrorists."

However, the UN itself has not just been sitting on the fence and watching. It has taken due cognizance of the growing menace to international peace and security and also engaged in preliminary talks to meet the challenging task.

On 11 September, the UN, as UN Centres all over the world, were observing "International Day of Peace." The opening of the General Assembly Session, which was scheduled on the same day, was postponed.

The UN Secretary General, Kofi Annan issued yet another statement, once again condemning the attack and supporting and welcoming the world-wide response that has emerged to fight this scourge for as long as is needed. Then he went on to add:

> The UN uniquely is positioned to advance this effort. It provides the forum necessary for building a universal coalition, and can ensure global legitimacy for the long-term response to terrorism. The UN conventions and Security Council resolutions, he noted, already provide a legal framework for many of the steps that may be taken to eradicate terrorism. Terrorism today threatens every society, every people, and as the world takes action against its perpetrators, we have to be reminded of the necessity of addressing the full range of conditions which permit the growth of this kind of hatred and depravity. We must continue to address the ills of conflict, ignorance, poverty and disease. (Emphasis added)

Despite this preparatory work to bring the on-going crisis situation within the purview of the UN, no member-state made a formal request in that regard. Obviously, all of them were looking at the attitude of USA in this regard and since no US official or any representative of the western countries did initiate UN involvement, no other country dare to take the initiative.

The UN Secretary General, once again took the initiative of addressing the UN General Assembly on 24 September and asserted that "in no way do these tragic events make the broader mission of the UN less relevant."

Throughout its history, the US has interpreted international law in its own unilateral way, as served its national interest which in turn is not defined narrowly but covers the entire globe. The disintegration of the Soviet Union and the emergence of the US as the unchallenged superpower have further emboldened it to pursue unilateralism. When George Bush (senior) took over as President (1985-92), he repeatedly talked about the "New World Order" and advent of unipolar moment. His National Security Adviser, Brenat Scowcraft talked of US leadership, attended by its Western allies and Soviet compliance policing the world and penalizing the wrongdoers. This was evident in the Gulf War which killed half a million Iraqis including women and children – and through carpet bombing, destroyed the industrial and communication structure of the country, pushing it back to pre-industrial age.

There are several other instances of US penalizing, through of less magnitude, in terms of death and destruction, those it found as "wrong doers", in recent years, let us not go back as far as twenty years of death and destruction unleashed on Vietnam.

Thus, it seems that US would not seek UN endorsement of its projected armed attack against Taliban in Afghanistan. Indeed, as noted earlier, US administration has stated that UN nod is not necessary to strike back at the terrorists. It is not just sheer "arrogance of power" but also calculated strategy inasmuch as US does not want at this stage to specify its target or targets.

In the absence of a resolution specifically authorizing force against regime by any country, Taliban's refusal to hand over Bin Laden cannot legally be construed as justification for US attack on Afghanistan. It is intriguing to note that a resolution No. 1368 (2001) adopted on 12 September, 2001, makes a passing mention in the Preamble of "the inherent right of individual or collective self-defense" and calls upon international community to redouble their efforts to prevent and suppress terrorist attacks and to bring to justice the perpetrators, organizers and sponsors of these terrorist attacks (of 11 September, 2001). However, no specific mention has been made of Taliban or Osama bin Laden as responsible for that dastardly act.

The attacks in New York and Washington, D.C. eventually constitute an act of armed force committed by armbands. Nevertheless, in order to justify attacking Afghanistan, the US would at the, very least have to prove that Osama Bin Laden was responsible and that he acted on or behalf of the Taliban Government of Afghanistan. Besides the ICJ judgment learned scholars have held the view that Article 51 gives a right to defend against a visible armed attack cutting across national boundary. This right does not allow retaliation for armed attacks or (force) to deter future attacks. That is why the US has held it would be illegal for India to attack terrorist camps in Pakistan or for Milosevic's Yugoslavia to have gone after Kosovo Liberation Army (KLA) bases in Northern Albania.

Whether President George Bush or Senator Jesse Helms like it or not the reality is that over the decades, the UN has evolved itself as the most single purveyor of international endorsement or otherwise of the policies, claims and acts of States. Its recommendations and decisions, not precisely authoritative but carry the weight of international legitimacy and more ready acceptability than any writ or directives by such mighty States as the US.

Since 1973, and more intensively during the last one decade, UN has remained seized with issues concerning international terrorism. Over the period, it has adopted a dozen international conventions, more significant are: (a) International Convention for the Suppression of Terrorist Bombings (adopted by the UN General Assembly on 15 December, 1997), to date, 59 Member-States have signed it and 24 have ratified it (b) International Convention for the Suppression of the Financing of Terrorism (adopted by the UN General Assembly on 9 December, 1999), to date: signature 43, ratification : 3.

The current situation is likely to speed up the process of accession and ratification.

The Terrorism Prevention Branch of the Centre for International Crime Prevention of the UN has been, over the years, involved in Global Terrorism Survey and studies on (de) escalation of violence of terrorist with links to drug production or trafficking.

The Legal Committee (Sixth) of the UN General Assembly and its Sub-committee have been working for the last three years on a draft treaty for the suppression of acts of terrorism and also a comprehensive convention on the elimination of terrorism; the draft will be taken up for consideration and adoption during the current session of the General Assembly.

Thus, as of now, the General Assembly is fully involved with the overall problem of international terrorism. The Security Council is seized with the situation resulting from 11 September terrorist attack.

To what extent and effectiveness the UN can play a role to meet this unprecedented threat to international peace and security, remains a moot point.

Let us turn to an overall question; how well-equipped the UN is today to meet its objectives enshrined in the UN Charter, especially in terms of collective measure to ensure peace and security and to build-up constructive global cooperation meeting humanity's social and economic needs?

The UN tender become an anti-Communist alliance.

It was indeed the conflicting interests of haves and have nots which eventually led to an altogether different kind of crisis situation.

The most unfortunate part is that Five Permanent Members have established a coterie and as a situation demands they get-together in an informal meeting and reach a decision which is then imposed on larger membership of the Council.

The UN, over the decades, has become an integral part of international politics. Its proceedings were influenced by forces of power politics and in turn, it also had its impact on forces of international politics at a given time, although to a lesser degree.

In a limited space and time, it is not possible here to go into details (which could be taken up for discussion at the Conference) but one point need be emphasized. Short of World Government, which is not feasible in near future, the UN provides a ready forum, a vast apparatus, political processes and institutions – meet any exigency or challenge, as also the present one posited by international terrorism. Ofcourse, there is scope for improvement in its apparatus and political processes especially relating to decision making. However, the vital need is attitudinal change among the Member-States and more so the major powers especially the US.

The four page Resolution mandates 189 Member-States to deny support and sanctuary to terrorists and obligates them to make "willful" financing of terrorism a criminal offense. It calls for immediate freezing of terrorist funds and preventing movements of individuals and groups of terrorist suspected or having terrorist connections within their territories and by effective border control as well.

There is a long list of do's and don'ts obligatory to all Member-States and a Committee composed of all members of the Security Council has been appointed to oversee its compliance; the US has assumed the responsibility to work hard to ensure its implementation.

It is significant to note that while the Preamble of the Resolution reiterates "right to self-defense" and determines terrorist attack of 11 September as threat to international peace, it has not named any country or Government or even a group of people as responsible for that terrorist attack. It has not defined who a "terrorist" is. Further, it has not authorized use of armed forces across national borders to combat terrorism. But who can stop the US to interpret the Resolution as suits its strategy.

Where a clear need manifested itself, the international community succeeded in overcoming its inherent divisions in order to achieve agreement. Today, the number of multilateral treaties deposited with the Secretary-General amount to over 500 and they cover the spectrum of human interaction, including on human rights, humanitarian affairs, terrorism, international criminal law, refugees and stateless persons, the environment, disarmament, commodities organized crime, the oceans, transport, communications, space etc. While these treaties are essentially designed to govern the behavior of States and establish through meticulous negotiations enforceable rights and obligations among themselves, increasingly, they also reflect the concerns and dreams of ordinary people and civil society.

The attention that breaches of the rules of international law attracted is itself an indication of the importance that the international community had begun to place on the need to comply with them. Even when a State chose not to comply with a particular rule of international law, such non-compliance was almost always justified on the basis of some other rule or an interpretation of the rules. The need to be legal appears to have been almost always acknowledged.

The contribution made by the UN to consolidating and advancing the international rule of law has been significant. Although the UN's role in this regard has not been dramatic and has not been the subject of many flattering headlines, it has been a quiet and effective achievement. In one respect it has been clearly successful. The culture of compliance with the internal rules of conduct which largely pervades the international community today, may be attributed to a significant extent to the work and the influence of the Organization over the years. However, much remains to be done before it could be claimed that the Organization has realized its Charter mandated responsibility.

•••